Praise for The Somatic Workbook for Nervous System Regulation and Anxiety Management

"*The Somatic Workbook for Nervous System Regulation and Anxiety Management* offers an accessible, compassionate, and evidence-informed guide to understanding and regulating physiological state through body-based practices. Kaitlin Harkess integrates foundational principles of polyvagal theory with psychological flexibility and practical tools for healing, making this a valuable resource for those navigating anxiety and striving to reconnect with safety and self. This book will empower readers to explore the wisdom of their nervous system with clarity, kindness, and scientific grounding."

—**Stephen W. Porges, PhD,** Distinguished University Scientist, University of Indiana, creator of polyvagal theory

"This workbook helps readers build a compassionate relationship with their own body and emotions. Through simple, creative practices, it teaches people how to feel, reflect, and act with purpose—even when things get tough. Grounded in experiential wisdom and aligned with the processes of psychological flexibility, it's a powerful tool for growth and resilience."

—**Steven C. Hayes, PhD,** Foundation Professor of Psychology Emeritus, University of Nevada, Reno, originator of acceptance and commitment therapy

"*The Somatic Workbook* is a compassionate and empowering guide for anyone navigating stress and anxiety. Drawing from both her professional expertise and her lived experience, Dr. Kaitlin Harkess offers deeply validating insights and actionable exercises for reconnecting with the body in a safe and supportive way. This workbook helps readers move from fear of their symptoms to a grounded understanding of the body's signals, teaching practical tools for regulation and healing. I'll be sharing this with my clients!"

—**Jessica Borushok, PhD,** author of *The Complete Guide to Acceptance and Commitment Therapy* and creator of *The ACT Therapist* YouTube channel

"*The Somatic Workbook* is a delight to read. This comprehensive yet practical guide will help you connect with your body and senses, soothe anxiety, and foster a sense of safeness and calm. Dr. Harkess gently and skillfully guides her readers on a journey to self-compassion, weaving together personal stories with simple exercises and providing options to suit any reader. Wrap yourself up in this book. Your body and mind will thank you!"

—**Jennifer Kemp, MPsych (Clinical),** author of *The ACT Workbook for Perfectionism* and coauthor of *The Neurodivergence Skills Workbook for Autism and ADHD*

"Dr. Kaitlin Harkess has created the ultimate guide to caring for both body and mind in the chaos of modern life. Whether you're burnt out, anxious, or just in need of a reset, this book belongs in your self-care toolkit. It's packed with practical, evidence-based tools for managing stress, regulating intense emotions, and staying grounded. I can't think of anyone who wouldn't benefit from reading it."

—**Rachel Samson, MPsych (Clinical),** coauthor of *Beyond Difficult: An Attachment Based Guide to Dealing with Challenging People*

"*The Somatic Workbook* is not just a set of exercises—it's a guided return to embodied presence. Dr. Kaitlin Harkess offers clear, research-informed tools for emotional regulation, trauma recovery, and nervous system attunement, while also inviting readers to connect with themselves in a meaningful and empowering way. She brings the rigor of psychological science together with the wisdom of the body in a way that is accessible, compassionate, and deeply respectful of each person's unique healing journey. Whether you are a clinician looking to support your clients with somatic skills or an individual on your own path of self-discovery, this workbook is a powerful resource. Kaitlin's voice is warm, wise, and skillful—exactly what's needed in a time when so many are seeking to come home to themselves."

—**Dr. Diana Hill,** clinical psychologist and author of *Wise Effort*

"This is so much more than a workbook—it's a powerful toolkit that provides both immediate and long-term relief from anxiety. It's an instant classic, a must-read for anyone who suffers with anxiety and trauma. Every page was vital—page after page of unique stories and personal examples, enlightening explanations based on medical science, actionable exercises that I truly wanted to do, and even visual aids that helped immediately clarify and simplify a very complex issue into a clear path forward. By the time I finished the workbook, I knew I was holding a resource that I would recommend again and again to every patient who suffers with anxiety. Thank you, Dr. Harkess, for the best book on anxiety I have ever read."

—**Laura Koniver, MD,** physician and author of *The Earth Prescription*

"A powerful, practical resource—this somatic workbook is a game-changer for nervous system understanding and embodied, real-life integration. It offers the missing link in clinical work: concrete, body-based tools that support clients to shift from knowing to truly feeling regulated."

—**Renee Cachia, PhD,** author of *Parenting Freedom*

"For anyone who has struggled with anxiety, this workbook is a game-changer! Dr. Kaitlin Harkess has created a beautiful book that brings it all together: body, mind, and spirit. Like a wise, kind friend, she provides clear explanations and practical, powerful exercises to help you live your fullest, most rewarding life."

—**Tom Nehmy, PhD,** author of *Apples for the Mind* and *Inspired Life, Beautiful Death*, and founder and director of the Healthy Minds Program

"This workbook is a treasure trove of embodied wisdom. Dr. Kaitlin Harkess offers readers practical tools for grounding, healing, and growing resilience from the inside out. It's an essential guide for anyone seeking to navigate emotions with clarity and compassion."

—**Jennie Rosier, PhD,** author and associate professor of interpersonal communication at James Madison University with an expertise in attachment and neurobiology

"As a psychiatrist, I see this workbook as an invaluable resource for clients navigating mental health challenges. It provides an excellent out-of-session tool that encourages meaningful homework, enhancing the therapeutic experience. The workbook is easy to follow and seamlessly integrates psychoeducation with a diverse range of strategies from various therapeutic techniques, all in one place. It will empower clients to apply what they learn beyond sessions, making it a fantastic companion on their journey toward growth and resilience."

—**Dr. Lisa Myers, BMedSc, MBCHB, FRANZCP, Cert. of Advanced Training Child Adol. Psych.,** psychiatrist and author of *When the Light Goes Out*

"In a world where anxiety and overwhelm are at an all-time high, *The Somatic Workbook for Nervous System Regulation and Anxiety Management* offers precisely what many of us are searching for—a grounded, compassionate guide back to the body and a transformative resource for our overstimulated times. These 85 powerful practices will help readers move beyond coping and toward true healing and resilience by reconnecting with their inner wisdom."

—**Dr. Heather Moday, Integrative MD,** author of *The Immunotype Breakthrough: Your Personalized Plan to Balance Your Immune System, Optimize Health, and Build Lifelong Resilience*

"*The Somatic Workbook* is a much-needed and valuable book for the field of mind-body science and practice. Dr. Harkess brings together a vast amount of knowledge from neurophysiology, psychology, and mindfulness while providing an opportunity for the reader to engage in deep self-reflection as they interact with the exercises. The book provides inspiration, creativity, and actionable ways to communicate these ideas and to integrate this work into clinical practice to benefit others. I highly recommend this book, as it truly provides a foundation for knowledge to move from the cognitive to the lived experience."

—**Marlysa Sullivan, DPT, CIAYT, ERYT 500,** author of *Understanding Yoga Therapy: Applied Philosophy and Science for Health and Well-Being*

"*The Somatic Workbook* is a rich and engaging resource for anyone wanting to better manage anxiety or mood, whether as a stand-alone self-help book or as an adjunct to therapy. More broadly, it is a great resource for anyone wanting to develop better awareness of mind-body connections. It is full of helpful exercises and insights, beautifully integrating clinical wisdom with practical science. Highly recommended."

—**Dr. Greg Smith,** psychologist and author of *Purposeful Breathing*

"*The Somatic Workbook* is a beautifully accessible and compassionate resource that bridges science and embodied practice in a way that's both practical and deeply human. Dr. Kaitlin Harkess has crafted a guide that empowers readers to understand their emotional responses as meaningful nervous system adaptations, not flaws. With warmth, clarity, and grounded clinical wisdom, this workbook invites readers to reconnect with their bodies, regulate their emotions with kindness, and support well-being from the inside out."

—**Dr. Andrew McGonigle, MD,** author of *The Physiology of Yoga* and *Supporting Yoga Students with Common Injuries and Conditions*

"*The Somatic Workbook* beautifully embraces what we've forgotten: We're embodied beings, and what we feel and do with our bodies impacts our experience of the world and whether we thrive under the pressures of modern life—or the opposite. The author shares her deep understanding of using self-compassion constructively to ask probing questions and think critically about what we value. The practical, action-oriented exercises are simple to use and offer immediate insights and relief. I highly recommend this book, both to therapists who need effective somatic-based solutions for their clients' nervous system challenges and to individuals who are tired of only talking about such challenges, who want to use the wisdom of their bodies to heal and step into calm and well-being."

—**Delia McCabe, PhD,** nutritional neuroscientist, author of *Feed Your Brain* and *Feed Your Brain: The Cookbook*

"*The Somatic Workbook* is a compassionate and skillfully structured guide that empowers readers to reconnect with the wisdom of their bodies. Dr. Kaitlin Harkess offers a rare blend of clinical insight, personal authenticity, and psychological depth, grounding each exercise in both scientific evidence and embodied experience. This is a well-founded approach to integrating practices such as mindfulness and yoga into the everyday lives of those seeking a thoughtful path to emotional resilience and healing."

—**Holger Cramer, PhD,** professor and chair for the Study of Complementary Medicine Methods, University of Tübingen; director of research, Robert Bosch Center for Integrative Medicine and Health, Bosch Health Campus; chairperson, German Society for Naturopathy (DGNHK)

"With her signature warmth, Dr. Kaitlin Harkess offers a rigorous, grounded path to lasting nervous system healing. This is not just another book of coping skills. It's a rare integration of science and intervention specifically for those already well-versed in personal growth who are seeking depth, not just direction. Dr. Harkess translates complex psychological theory into actionable tools without watering down concepts, guides readers through poignant self-inquiry, and teaches strategies that truly work. This is a profound resource for anyone ready to stop managing anxiety and start transforming it. I'll be recommending it to many of my clients!"

—**Hayden Finch, PhD,** author of *The Psychology of Procrastination* and *The Easy Habits Journal*

"Dr. Kaitlin Harkess delivers what we all need right now: a way back to ourselves."

—**Rebecca Ray, PhD,** author of *Setting Boundaries*; *The Art of Self-Kindness*; *Small Habits for a Big Life*; *Good, Great, Perfect*; *Believe*; and *Difficult People*

"*The Somatic Workbook* is an incredible resource for therapists and for anyone looking for evidence-based and heartfelt ways to regulate their nervous system, reduce anxiety, and come home to themself. Dr. Kaitlin Harkess shares over 85 body-based practices grounded in polyvagal theory, acceptance and commitment therapy (ACT), internal family systems (IFS), yoga, and mindfulness to guide readers gently toward nervous system regulation and resilience. I highly recommend this workbook—it's the perfect companion for anyone exploring embodied well-being and healing."

—**Dr. Lauren Tober, DPsyc (Clinical),** clinical psychologist, yoga teacher, author of *Mental Health Aware Yoga: A Guide for Yoga Teachers*, and founder of the Yoga Psychology Institute

"While most books talk about the *why* and *what* of resilience, Kaitlin N. Harkess has given us the *how-to*. She teaches us how to manage our nervous systems for our success. *The Somatic Workbook* will help anyone struggling to calm their own emotions or helping others to do so. It is full of practical ways to challenge the discomfort of anxiety and pressure. I cannot recommend it highly enough for anyone who is looking for a manual on emotional excellence."

—**Dr. Amy Silver, ClinPsyD, MPhil, MA, BSc (Hons),** author of *The Loudest Guest* and *Conversations Create Growth*

The SOMATIC WORKBOOK

85+ Body-Based Practices for Deepening Awareness, Navigating Emotions, and Building Resilience

KAITLIN N. HARKESS, PHD

The Somatic Workbook for Nervous System Regulation and Anxiety Management

Published by
PESI Publishing, Inc.
3839 White Ave
Eau Claire, WI 54703

Cover and interior design by Emily Dyer
Editing by Chelsea Thompson

ISBN 9781683737162 (print)
ISBN 9781683737179 (ePUB)
ISBN 9781683737186 (ePDF)

Printed in the United States of America.

To Rob, for believing in me, your unwavering support, and making my writing possible in ways both seen and unseen.

For my daughters. May you always trust in the wisdom of your bodies, stay connected to the love of those who came before you, and keep your hearts open to joy—you've certainly taught me how to do so.

With all my love, forever and always.

Table of Contents

Introduction

"When we honor the body with our attention, we begin to reclaim our feelings, our instincts, our life."

—Jack Kornfield, *A Path with Heart*

"Is it all in my head?"

No, the emotional pain you're experiencing is not all in your head.

At least, it's not all in your brain.

Your mind quite literally extends through your body. You are an embodied being, and your body holds your history. This means that your issues are in your tissues, as the saying goes. This is why the journey to anxiety relief is focused on getting out of your head through body-based healing.

No, You're Not Alone

Sarah is a successful lawyer in her early forties with a beautiful home, a loving partner, and two busy children. On the surface, Sarah seems to have it all together. But underneath the facade, she's struggling. She feels a constant sense of loneliness and unease. She's deeply insecure, and no matter how many accomplishments she has to her name, she's terrified she'll be found out as the ultimate failure. So she pushes herself to keep working harder and for longer hours, berating herself whenever she feels like she isn't on top of things. Sarah is getting frequent headaches, feels a heavy weight on her chest, and has a racing heart she can't explain. She's started drinking more than she used to, just to take the edge off in the evenings.

Cole is in his late twenties and feeling stuck. While he hasn't had great luck with romantic relationships, he has plenty of friends. He is focused on building a healthy lifestyle and honors his body as a vessel for wisdom. He knows that chronic anxiety is bad for one's health, so he is determined to eradicate all anxiety from his life. Yet despite his positive affirmation ritual and ever-growing library of self-improvement books, he just can't find the feeling of peace and stability he desperately craves. Cole is exhausted all the time, despite getting plenty of sleep, and his stomach is always in painful knots, regardless of the juice cleanses and elimination diets he has tried.

Do either of these scenarios sound familiar? If so, you're not alone. Psychological suffering is commonly accompanied by stomach pains, headaches, exhaustion, and even cold and flu symptoms. These physical experiences are not just a coincidence; they are your body's natural response to stress, overwhelm, and disconnection.

Your Nervous System

Imagine it's about two million years ago, and you're out on the savanna foraging for berries. You hear a rustle in the bush and, without even thinking about it, you turn your increasingly dilating pupils toward the noise. Your skin prickles, your breath stops, and you listen intently for the source of that sound. Your shoulders jump slightly as a little yellow-headed bird flaps out of the bush. With a soothing sigh, your shoulders drop, and your attention returns to the berries.

Had your gaze met the yellow eyes of a crouched tiger instead of the bird, you would not have had to even think about what to do next. Your blood pressure, heart rate, and breathing rate would automatically increase, while blood in your body would be redirected from your digestive system and your brain's prefrontal cortex (the part that does complex problem-solving) to your energy-demanding arms and legs, fueling you to run for your life. If those eyes belonged not to a tiger but to an animal you could have fought off, or perhaps a member of a warring clan, you would have had the same physiological response in a different form: the strikes and blows of physical combat. This lifesaving reaction, known as the *fight-or-flight response*, is controlled by your autonomic nervous system (ANS). Whenever you perceive a stressor, this response is activated to help you achieve your main evolutionary goal: survival.

Any individuals on the savanna who failed to anticipate the worst-case scenario or who hesitated, even for a moment, would not have lasted long enough to pass on their genes. This means you are a descendant of the most anxious of the anxious . . . or, as I like to think of it, those with the most sophisticated nervous systems.

Flight and fight aren't the only options in our arsenal of survival reactions. The ANS can also trigger us to freeze. Should your system decide that you won't safely get away from that tiger or overpower that dangerous enemy, you will experience momentary paralysis. Stillness and silence allow you to blend into the environment, effectively hiding from the danger. This response may also trigger a dissociative mechanism to give you a sense of being disconnected from your mind and body, a last-resort defense against the trauma and pain of such an attack.

Fawn: The Fourth Survival Response

When it comes to relationships with other people, we have another, slightly more complex survival reaction in our arsenal: the *fawn response*, which integrates the freeze response with social engagement. In threatening situations where fighting, fleeing, or freezing are unlikely to be successful, the fawn response guides you toward nonthreatening, appeasing behavior intended to make you seem valuable to the dangerous person.

Ideally, you don't end up as lunch or a battle casualty. When you realize that you've successfully survived, you can shake the stressful experience off . . . literally! As you wake up from the daze of dissociation, your body starts trembling as a way of releasing the tension of containing the fight-or-flight energy that was redirected into a freeze response. We see this with animals when they are doomed to be captured. For example, a popular YouTube video shows an impala captured by a leopard. At first, the impala, entirely immobile, appears dead. But when the leopard darts off for a moment, the impala starts to tremble. Moments later, the trembling stops, and the impala runs away.

While animals will shake off a stressor and then carry on, we modern humans have developed the unfortunate habit of trying to bypass this release by increasingly living from the neck up. We tune in less and less to what our bodies are feeling and what they need to release. Consequently, we may not even realize how much tension and stress we're holding until we're totally exhausted and our mental health is impacted.

Why You're Struggling Now

I know what it's like to get home from a day feeling totally exhausted yet unable to wind down. It's a feeling I describe as "brimming"—this sense that your cup is filled up to the edge with stress, about to overflow and drown you. It is nearly impossible for your mind to settle when you physically feel so wired. This is a painful side effect of how your ancient nervous system has evolved to navigate the modern world: every stressful event leaves you scanning for another. It makes sense—a tiger sighting should prime you to look for another, and staying on edge makes you quicker to respond the next time. But while the threats we face today might be less deadly than the tiger, they are about a billion times more frequent: the buzz of your phone, the ding of your email, the to-do list that is constantly updating in your mind.

Our brains effectively evolved to time travel. We can mentally navigate out of the present to reflect on the past and anticipate the future. You might better know these processes as *rumination* and *worry*. The tigers aren't just hiding in the bushes as you go about your day—they can pounce on you even after you've entered your bedroom, closed the door, and crawled under your cozy duvet. Because your mind is always "on," your body needs to discharge the physiological stress that accumulates before you can truly relax.

This sense of being always "on" is intensified by our constant connection to our devices, which, among other things, keep us passively engaged with mass media, wherein body image, social status, and achievement are presented as though they determine our worth. Our habit of constant social comparison is another form of automatic threat identification. You see, as humans, we don't really deserve to be at the top of the food chain—that's where the tiger belongs, with its fangs and claws, its speed and stealth. While our unique ability to work together with our "clan" of fellow humans has given us an evolutionary edge over other species, the downside is that surviving this way has wired us to fear social rejection like we fear death.

Along with technology leaving us more vulnerable to low self-worth and social anxiety, our boundaries have been blurred by constant access to (and from) our work environments. Our nervous systems are under increasing pressure to withstand the stress and anxiety that accompany extended working hours, increasingly sedentary lifestyles, and ongoing physical isolation.

But it doesn't stop there. Every time we turn on our computers or slide open our phones, our attention is pulled to images of political extremism, billionaires blasting off into outer space, and our planet burning. Without effective release strategies, this mental load is far too much to process. Instead, the brain resorts to greater disconnection and disembodiment. It's not surprising that over 300 million people around the globe report feeling depressed, with nearly as many reporting clinical levels of anxiety. These stress-related illnesses are the leading cause of global disability, and depression is a significant contributor to suicide, which results in the loss of 800,000 lives every year (World Health Organization, 2018).

The rise in diagnoses has brought an increase in anxiolytic and antidepressant prescriptions, in spite of ongoing controversy about their effectiveness and the established evidence that such medication is not a long-term solution (Moncrieff et al., 2023; Le Noury et al., 2015, p. 329). Where some turn to medication as a treatment for emotional pain, others turn to "positive thinking," vague spiritual approaches, or therapeutic modalities that focus excessively on changing internal experiences. Such solutions carry a subtle message: that you shouldn't experience emotional pain or negative thoughts.

All this attempted avoidance requires a lot of effort. What if it doesn't make things better?

What if the key to healing your emotional pain and achieving psychological well-being lies not just in talking about your problems, or avoiding and challenging difficult thoughts, but in exploring and processing your nervous system responses?

What if ancient wisdom traditions and Indigenous cultures have been correct in their belief that your mind, body, and spirit are one?

What if healing isn't about "feeling better" but about learning to *feel* better?

You've Got to Feel It to Heal It

Somatic therapy, named for the Greek word for "body" (*soma*), takes you on a journey beyond traditional talk therapy and into your body's wisdom. Grounded in cutting-edge research showing that our bodies hold essential information about our emotional and mental states, somatic practices are increasingly recognized as effective treatment for stress and anxiety, as well as supportive of general well-being. Physical symptoms can be alleviated as we assist the body in releasing old psychological patterns and accumulated tensions, while long-term healing happens through improved body awareness, tolerance for physical sensation, and the release of trapped emotional energy. Techniques such as grounding, breathing, movement, and touch form the basis of these practices, underpinned by acceptance and compassion.

This workbook draws on the wisdom of neuroscience, evolutionary psychology, attachment and systems theory, psychoneuroimmunology, and mindfulness-based psychotherapy. In particular, we'll be using a framework called acceptance and commitment therapy (ACT), which affirms your health as interconnected with the physical, emotional, and spiritual aspects of your being. ACT emphasizes a concept called *psychological flexibility*—your ability to adapt and adjust to difficult experiences and circumstances. Psychological flexibility ensures that you can attune to your somatic sensations rather than become overwhelmed by them. This capacity to release and process the overwhelm stored in your nervous system is complemented by psychological strategies that foster a felt sense of inner harmony and balance.

The Journey Ahead

In the chapters ahead, I'll teach you the somatic psychology practices needed for your healing. You'll come to understand (and actually feel) how formative experiences impact your current emotional and physical well-being. You'll learn basic grounding skills to help you stay present and connected with your body, even in the face of stress and anxiety. You'll be introduced to somatic principles and techniques, while learning how to apply them to both calm and revitalize. You'll be guided through mindfulness practices like yoga and meditation, movement practices to release energy stores, breathing practices, intuitive imagery, bilateral tapping, and strategies to integrate lifestyle medicine into your purposeful living.

Ultimately, remember that this book is a tool rather than treatment. Treatment involves sitting in a shared space with a regulated nervous system (a.k.a. a therapist). However, this book can provide you with a therapeutic adjunct. Use it wisely. Make sure you take breaks and pauses where needed. Go ahead and skip any material or practices that you feel cannot be safely explored at this point in time. And remember that your brain and nervous system do have healing power—just because something isn't accessible to you right now, that does not mean that it will not be available in times to come.

Purpose Comes from Pain

I practice as a clinical psychologist, and my primary area of research has been exploring the impacts of somatic practice on symptoms of chronic stress, anxiety, and depression. Cultivating the conditions for those "aha" moments of connection and transformation is my passion.

My own healing journey took me from the experience of being with myself on the yoga mat and meditation cushion to seeking therapy, where I was guided to unpack my sense of self. While my focused pursuit of higher meaning provided an alternative to unhelpful ways of trying to avoid distress, it eventually became another way that I was abandoning my wounded parts and trying to control what I was experiencing. Therapy helped me recognize this pattern. The guidance I received to reflect on my conditioning and cultivate psychological flexibility allowed me to access the transformation I sought; I could finally open enough to process the somatic experiences that arose through my body-based practices. Through the integration of psychology and somatics, I found deep healing and have built a life that feels joyful, meaningful, and authentic. While I still experience pain, as we all do from time to time, the knowledge and practices I've learned empowered me to process pain in a way that enhances the quality of my life and guides me toward my purpose.

This is what I want for you—the freedom to step into your skin, make peace with your mind, connect with your deep wisdom, experience vitality, and live intentionally.

How to Engage with This Workbook

Whether you are struggling with overwhelming stress and anxiety or are simply seeking to deepen your connection with your body and emotions, this workbook will offer you step-by-step guidance for feeling, healing, and returning to wholeness. Each chapter builds on the previous one to ensure you have established the capacities you need for later practices.

Part 1 is all about building your awareness and nervous system nurturance. You'll learn the science behind somatics and be supported in creating a toolkit of emotional regulation resources. You'll learn practices to ground, resource, and center yourself in moments of distress. This focus on the present is balanced by traveling back to explore your history, providing you with a framework to make sense of your felt experience.

In part 2, you'll focus on cultivating your capacity for acceptance (rather than resistance). You'll bolster your emotional awareness and learn practices to disentangle your body and mind from difficult experiences while activating an attitude of openness. You'll also start cultivating a repertoire of experiential practices that allow you to access your body's wisdom, release energy stores, and expand your sense of connection beyond yourself.

Finally, part 3 is all about integration and engagement. Having laid the foundations of building a safe connection with your body and mind, you'll focus on direct processing of patterns of tension and anxiety you're holding. You'll be introduced to dynamic somatic practices that support the final stages of release and transformation. From this healing space, you'll take empowered and purposeful action to create a vital and embodied life.

PART 1

Somatic Awareness

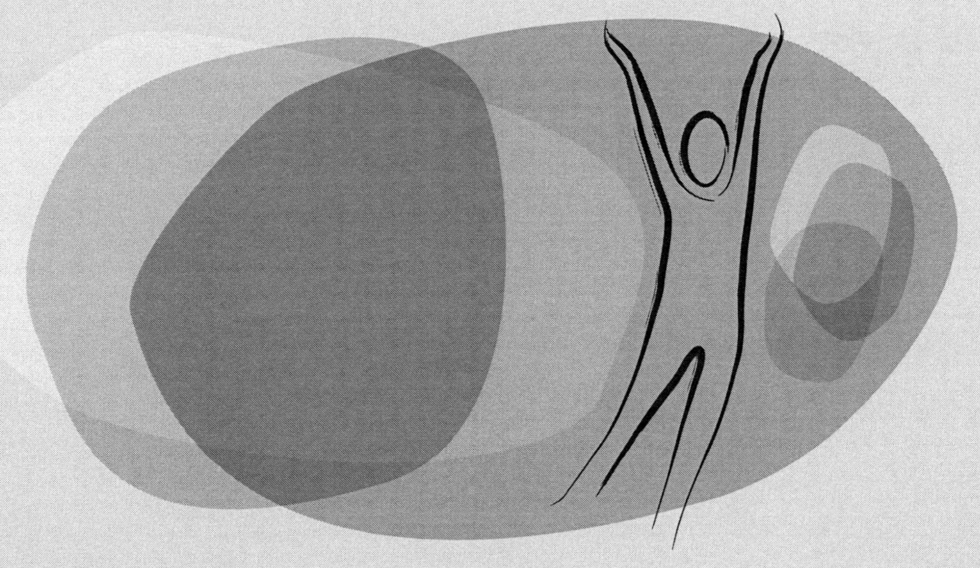

CHAPTER 1

What You're Doing Isn't Working: The Causes (and Treatment) of Anxiety

"Inviting our thoughts and feelings into awareness allows us to learn from them rather than be driven by them."

—Daniel J. Siegel, *Mindsight*

Life Is Full of Suffering

No doubt you've experienced setbacks in your life, from stubbed toes to shed tears to sleepless nights. I have, too. Suffering is an unavoidable part of living a meaningful life.

I first encountered this Buddhist truth during a Philosophy 101 lecture. At the time, I was grappling with a relentless need for control, a shield from the chaos and battles that raged inside me. I craved a semblance of order and predictability in life. I yearned to feel connected, to be beloved and admired. I believed this yearning could be satisfied if only I were pretty enough, skinny enough, stylish enough, smart enough, desirable enough . . .

If only *I* were enough.

Yet despite the calorie counting, hours of cardio, ceaseless self-curation, and valiant attempts at overachievement, I never seemed to actually feel like I was worthy of the love and belonging I desired. As the inner turbulence continued, my anxiety spiraled, trapping me in an incessant cycle of pain.

In hindsight, I call this my Descartes era, in honor of the philosopher who famously declared *cogito, ergo sum*: I think, therefore, I am. Anchored in this over-intellectualizing mantra, I neglected listening to my body and respecting my deeper sense of self (which we might sometimes call the spirit). No matter how much I accomplished, how little I weighed, or what designers I wore, my efforts to escape emotional pain never worked. I *thought* I was doing all the correct things, but I never *felt* worthy as a result.

Living this way is like trying to escape from quicksand—the more you struggle, the deeper you sink into it. However, if you can remember to expand your body and be still, you can actually float to the top. Similarly, it is the struggle against suffering that sinks you deeper into desperation and disembodiment, and it is the willingness to open yourself wide and release the survival impulse that leads to freedom.

So, What Does Your Struggle Look Like?

Sleeplessness. Irritability. Oversensitivity. Whispering doubts telling you that you'll never do enough, achieve enough, or be enough. These are just some of the ways that anxiety shackles you in daily life. These shackles extend from the mental to the physical, knotting your stomach and leaving your body aching with tension.

The insidious part of anxiety is that your efforts to get away from it—to rationalize your fears, to distract yourself from unsettling thoughts and uncomfortable feelings, to stop worrying, ruminating, and beating yourself up—only make it grow stronger. In the next few sections, you'll be examining this vicious vortex to see exactly how it sucks away your confidence, talents, and aspirations.

EXERCISE: Enough Is Enough

Let's start with one of the first questions I ask my clients when they enter the therapy room: "What brought you here?"

Take a deliberate moment and reflect on exactly why you're holding this book in your hands now. Maybe you were looking for a book to support you in your struggles with anxiety and sought this one out, or perhaps you serendipitously saw it on the shelf. (In any case, I'm so glad it was here for you!)

What drew you to this book? What are you hoping to learn? What changes are you hoping to make?

____

____

____

Let's get even more specific.

What is going on in your mind, body, and life that hurts? What are the things that cause you emotional or physical pain? (For example, behaving irritably with family, inability to concentrate at work, headaches, muscle tension, interrupted sleep, thoughts about being worthless or a failure, or fear that your loved ones will leave you.)

____

____

____

Getting clear on the specific struggles and suffering you're experiencing will support you to determine your goals and maintain the motivation to try new strategies.

EXERCISE: Where Exactly Is the Problem?

The next step is to pull out the specifics of everything you've described. Of course, sometimes it's hard to describe what you're feeling beyond "I just feel overwhelmed and on edge, wanting to scream or cry." That's okay! We'll take some time to notice the challenging experiences you're having in your mind and body, such as difficult thoughts, memories, worries, beliefs, feelings, urges, and sensations.

To be clear, it absolutely can be the case that things going on in your life contribute to the suffering you're experiencing on the inside. From bullying in the workplace, to financial pressures, to relationship difficulties, these experiences will naturally impact your internal experience. I want to assure you that we'll look at your life structure and situation later. Right now, though, I want you to focus on your internal experience, within your existing environment, to get clear on the experiences in your mind and in your body that are causing you distress.

For instance, if you sometimes notice a sinking in your stomach but move along quickly from it, it might not feel like a huge challenge. Similarly, if you occasionally think something you said was embarrassing, but you simply laugh it off, it's unlikely to be an issue for you. On the other hand, if those things feel quite painful and stick around for a while, let's note them. Read through the following lists and put a check mark by any of the experiences that are impacting you.

Body	Mind
❒ Breathing difficulties	❒ Fear of losing control
❒ Rapid heart rate	❒ Fear of dying or illness
❒ Changes to body temperature	❒ Fear of judgment
❒ Sweating	❒ Catastrophic thoughts
❒ Tingling or numbness in the arms and legs	❒ Hypervigilance
❒ Trembling	❒ Urge to stay home
❒ Muscle tension in the face	❒ Memory difficulties
❒ Tense neck and shoulders	❒ Difficulties with concentration
❒ Clenched hands	❒ Speech problems
❒ Stomachaches/digestive issues	❒ Other: ____________________
❒ Lethargy	❒ Other: ____________________
❒ Feeling warm	
❒ Other: ____________________	
❒ Other: ____________________	

Now, identify the emotions you feel related to those challenging experiences. You may have already started to do this as you went through the lists, since we experience emotions in both the mind and the body. Write the emotions that come up as painful for you—these might include anger, fear, grief, and so on. (We'll deep-dive into emotions in chapter 6.)

Emotions I find challenging:

____

____

____

The Solution Is the Problem

I'm certain that you've already tried to find some solution for the experiences that cause you pain. Think back to Sarah, who is trying to manage her anxiety by working longer and harder to "get on top of things." Constantly criticizing herself isn't helping Sarah meet the unrealistically high standards she sets for herself. Instead, she becomes more terrified of making a mistake and spends a lot of time worrying about every possible scenario. She believes this will ensure she is prepared. Instead, her anxiety increases, while her self-esteem and confidence erode.

Overthinking every detail of performance isn't isolated to the workplace. Sarah begins withdrawing more and more from social situations. Coffee and sugary snacks get her through to the end of the day, yet she can't seem to sleep, so she reaches for wine in the evening. Unfortunately, the relief is always only temporary, and one glass quickly turns into two. This is how anxiety works. It can pull us into patterns that ultimately leave us feeling worse—vicious cycles.

Now consider Cole and the vicious cycle he is caught in. His experience involves self-monitoring all the physical sensations he experiences, in part to track his digestive issues. His belief that anxiety is bad for his health compels him to constantly track his heart rate and breathing rate. His mind tends to imagine the worst possible outcomes, and he spends increasing hours and dollars at specialists' offices. Sometimes he finds relief, but the symptoms never fully subside. His sensitivity to his heart rate is increasing every time he scans his body looking for symptoms, which means that he is becoming more likely to notice and worry about even normal heart rate variations.

Does any of this sound familiar?

In addition to overthinking our symptoms (a.k.a. worrying), we often try to simply avoid the experiences we find painful. It's incredibly common to seek temporary relief at the bottom of a wine glass, in a pill bottle, or in the ever-captivating scrolling and streaming at our fingertips. Perhaps, while pursuing these numbing or distracting vices, you've found yourself turning down outings and opportunities that, in your heart of hearts, you know would be valuable for your sense of connection and growth.

Imagine this scenario: You have just grabbed your coat to head out the door and meet your friends in the city for drinks. Suddenly, you find yourself feeling flushed. Your heart rate is increasing, and your stomach churns. You have the thought, *I just can't do this*. This thought brings up expectations of how talkative your friends will be about their successful lives and careers and how much money you're likely to spend on this night out—which in turn brings up thoughts of your work responsibilities, filling you with an overwhelming sense of dread. You find yourself scheming ways to cancel the plans before you've even got your arms through the coat sleeves. So you send your friends a quick message with an excuse: Your cat is sick, again.

While your last-minute cancellation might come with a bit of guilt or longing, chances are that you experience relief at this point, not only from the outing but perhaps even from the work deadline. You make a cup of tea and curl up on the couch to get lost in the latest streaming melodrama.

The trade-off is that a sense of anxiety around leaving the house, heading to the city, or meeting friends can intensify in the long term because your nervous system experiences relief when you decide not to go. Essentially, your brain interprets this relief as evidence that the outing really was a dangerous thing, making it more likely that you'll experience even greater anxiety in a similar situation in the future. Your brain learns from the actions you take or don't take, a process known as *neuroplasticity*. And what your brain is learning in this particular scenario will lead to a vicious cycle of anxiety like the one shown here.

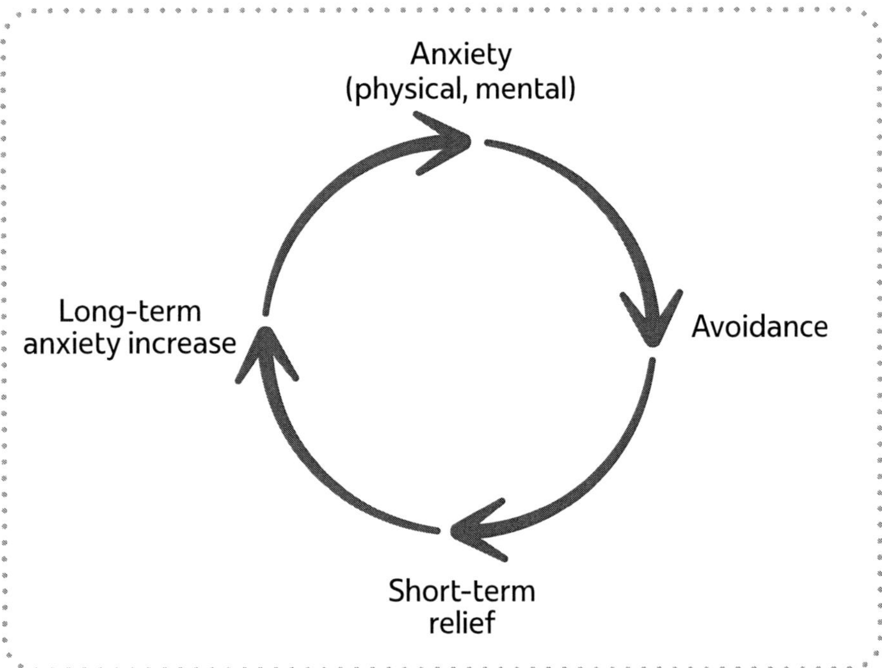

Of course, because we are all unique, there can be different variations of the anxiety cycle. Here's another scenario: Imagine that you have been invited to give a presentation at work. It's a huge honor that has arguably been years in the making. The excitement of receiving the invitation just as quickly turns to dread when "impostor syndrome" kicks in. Your mind starts detailing exactly how you'll make a fool of yourself and imagines the criticism you'll receive from colleagues. You vow to avoid this negative outcome by ensuring your presentation is absolutely perfect, but this only makes you feel more anxious. None of your ideas seem *perfect*, so you don't write any of them down. Instead, you busy yourself with other things and tell yourself that you'll work on the presentation when you're feeling more inspired . . . which never happens. As you run out of time to prepare, you find yourself asking to reschedule the presentation for a later date.

This cycle of procrastination can be mapped out as follows:

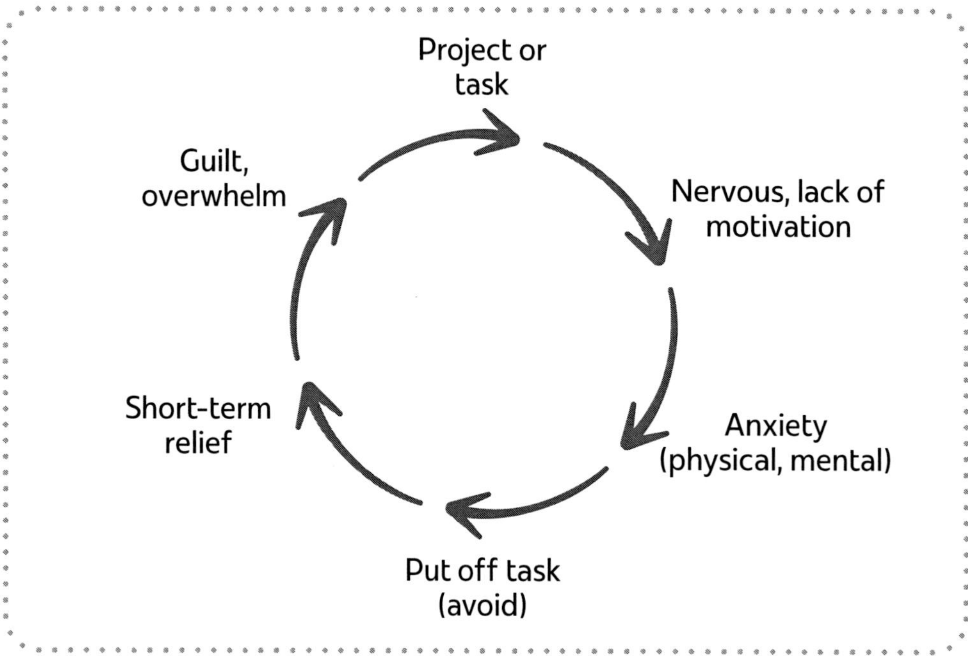

The real kicker in all of this is that anxiety is self-perpetuating. When you're feeling anxious, your brain will have an even lower threshold for signs of danger—you will likely find yourself scanning for signs that something could go wrong, and your threat system will tell you to avoid those dangers.

EXERCISE: Your Anxiety Cycle (Vicious Vortex)

Let's explore whether anxiety has led to any unhelpful cycles in your life. Consider a situation in your life where you experience anxiety. It might be similar to the examples provided, or it might be something else. Write this situation down in the diagram on the next page.

Next, note on the circle any ways you avoid the anxiety related to that situation (e.g., canceling plans, pouring a glass of wine, turning on the TV). Likely, you'll experience short-term relief. However, as you just learned, the downside is that your brain interprets this relief as evidence that the original situation was indeed dangerous, leading you to keep avoiding that situation and others like it in the future. In other words, the "solution" is the problem. Trying to control, suppress, or avoid anxious thoughts and feelings may provide short-term relief, but it can lead to long-term suffering. The cycle becomes self-perpetuating; you cannot escape your feelings.

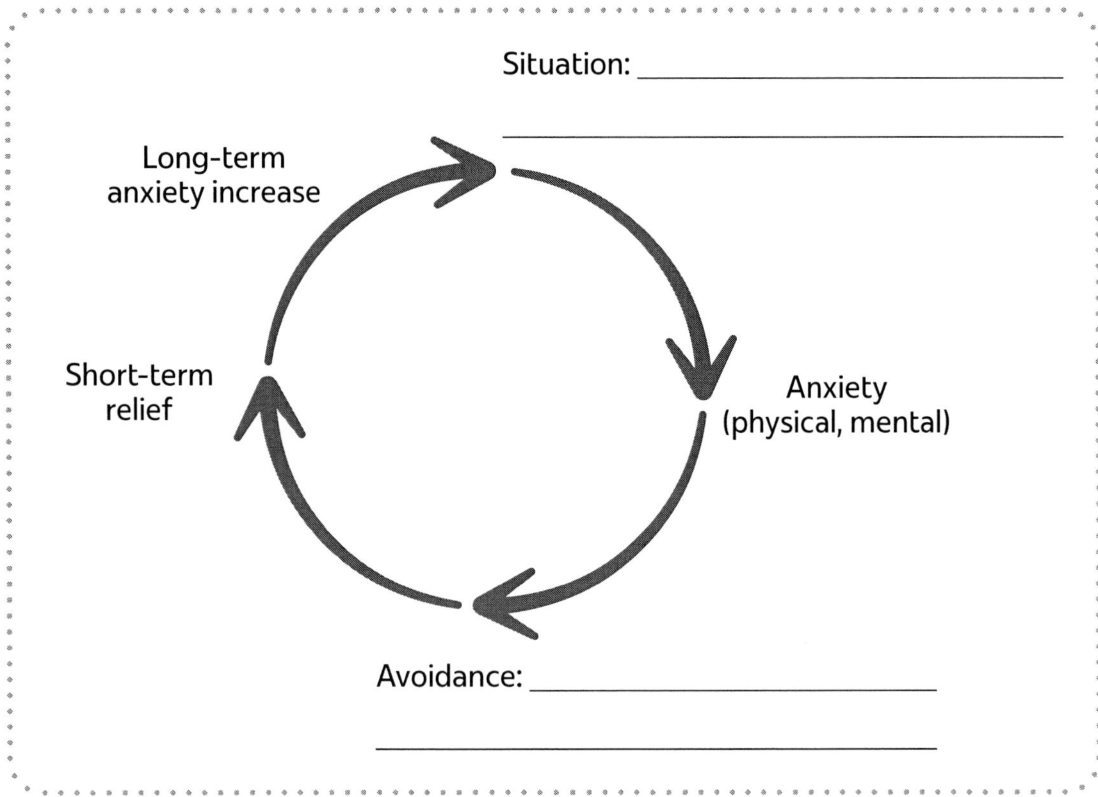

Where Does Your Anxiety Come From?

Let me clarify that the anxiety I'm talking about is not the kind that shows up when a car whizzes past you just a little too close or when you head into a job interview and feel your stomach flip-flop along the way. I'm referring to a pattern where you're experiencing anxiety more days than not and it's impacting your daily life in one way or another.

A major factor in anxiety is what you believe about what you think. So, I must ask: Is everything you think true?

Suppose that, while writing this book, I have the thought that I'm an idiot and that this book will never help anyone. Is that the truth? I can't really know, can I? What I am certain about, though, is that it's not a helpful thought in terms of supporting my desire to write this book. This desire is underpinned by a heartfelt intention to help others, but it will never be realized if I listen to everything my noisy and not-always-nice mind says to me.

I imagine your mind is the same. Maybe you believe it or maybe you battle with it; the underlying fact remains, we cannot possibly evaluate with objective certainty whether what we think is "capital T" true. Instead, it is easier, and a lot more useful, to evaluate whether what we think is *helpful*.

Is This Thought Helpful?

This is the ultimate question in determining how much weight you give to any particular thought. If the answer is yes, brilliant! Go with that thought. If the answer is no, consider that your cue to shift your attention toward something more useful to you. Honestly, even just labeling a thought as unhelpful can make it a little less "sticky."

This isn't the end of the process, though. You see, you have thoughts, including your worries, and you have beliefs about them. These beliefs about your thoughts are called *meta-beliefs*. Anxiety-related meta-beliefs are surprisingly common, so it's important that we bring them into our conscious awareness. Do you relate to any of the following meta-beliefs?

- Worrying is uncontrollable.
- Worrying helps me to cope.
- Worrying could make me go mad.
- Worrying helps me find solutions.
- Worrying helps me understand my problems.
- Worrying is bad for my health.
- Anxiety is bad.
- Feeling anxious is bad for my health.
- If I get anxious, it will overwhelm me.

You can have both positive meta-beliefs and negative meta-beliefs about anxiety. Positive ones (e.g., "Worrying helps me cope") can loop you in ongoing worries, thinking you'll manage better, while the negative ones (e.g., "Feeling anxious is bad for my health") can lead you to feel anxious about feeling anxious—a fear of fear.

Anxiety Sensitivity

Anxiety sensitivity is the fear of anxiety-related bodily sensations, such as an increased heart rate or stomach knots. If you're sensitive to these sensations, it's likely because you believe these symptoms are physically, cognitively, or socially harmful. This unhelpful misinterpretation of bodily sensations intensifies anxiety, which then intensifies the bodily sensations. It also leads to fear-based behaviors, including avoidance. The vicious anxiety cycle then comes into full play, which is why anxiety sensitivity is considered the biggest risk factor for higher levels of anxiety.

Chronic Stress

Chronic stress is another factor that comes into play with anxiety. This is because your body's stress response gets continually activated, leaving you in an ongoing state of high alert that makes you more susceptible to anxiety. Stress influences your body (think digestive issues, tension, and headaches), brain chemistry, arousal level, and thinking patterns, all of which are increasingly common worldwide as our levels of stress rise.

The experience of stress is underpinned by the belief that the demands and pressures you're experiencing exceed or nearly exceed your ability to cope. This belief decreases your feelings of well-being. It has two components: (1) the subjective element—that is, your interpretation and perception of a situation, and (2) the changes that happen within your mind and body and in your behavior. Your experience of stress will be unique because your reaction to a situation is influenced by nearly every variable out there, from your genetics, gender, and age to your psychological history and even your financial resources.

As discussed earlier, the trigger for stress can be anything your mind or body perceives as a threat. Moreover, because the various systems in your body are all connected, health, well-being, and survival are full-body experiences. Your cardiovascular (heart rate and blood pressure), gastrointestinal, immune (inflammation), metabolic (blood sugar), neuroendocrine (hormonal), and nervous systems all respond in concert to an ever-changing environment internally and externally. This full-body response is called *allostasis*.

Allostasis

Allostasis is a fancy word that captures how your body's vital functions continuously fluctuate in response to your environment. From shivering when you're cold to sweating when you're hot, your body is always trying to cultivate a state of internal equilibrium. Though your body will never be static, more intense environments put your organs and tissues under more pressure. It's not surprising, then, that the strain of chronic stress on your body and mind increases "wear and tear" on your various systems, making you more vulnerable to disease.

EXERCISE: What Are You Carrying?

Imagine your stressors as stones that you put into a backpack and carry every single day. A few stones held for a few days will increase your strength and resilience; this is known as *eustress* (*eu* is the Greek prefix for "good"). Just as it is important to have some stress on your muscles so they don't atrophy, some stress in your life can help you grow, perhaps connecting to your sense of drive and passion.

However, just as you typically rest between training days or sets of exercises at the gym, you also need periods of rest from the stress in your life to let your system repair. Chronic stress never allows for this type of reprieve. Instead, it loads your body and mind with "stones" that you can never put down. Without a chance to set the load down, the wear and tear of chronic stress generates ongoing anxiety that eventually starts making you sick.

These stones include both current stressors and long-held patterns of tension resulting from past difficulties and unconscious ways of reacting and responding to challenges in your life. (We won't focus on the historic stones until later in this book, but it would be neglectful not to mention that they're already in that backpack of yours!) Let's look at some examples of the stones that could increase your load:

- **Examples of current stones:** Chronic illness, financial concerns, housing instability, vocational challenges, caregiving for children and aging parents, work deadlines, cleaning your home, life admin tasks (e.g., filing insurance claims, paying bills)
- **Examples of historic stones:** Punitive or perfectionistic parents, bullying, learning difficulties, poverty, loss of loved ones, significant accidents, natural disasters, systemic oppression (e.g., racism, sexism)

Using the diagram that follows, draw in and label the stones you carry in your backpack.

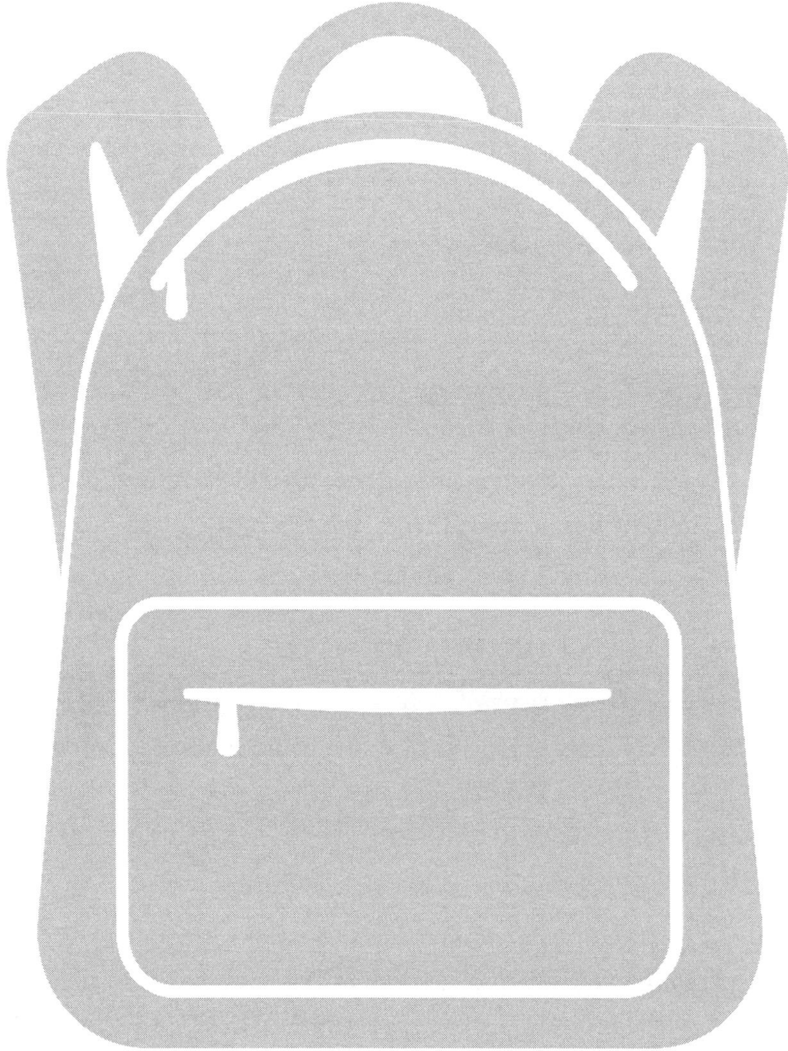

Remember, the experience of anxiety isn't a bad thing. It is a perfectly normal emotional response to a situation or event that is not safe or manageable for you. The problem is when ongoing anxiety gets your nervous system stuck in survival mode, responding to everything as a potential threat, developing patterns of hypervigilance and worry beyond the circumstances in which they are useful.

Do I Have an Anxiety Disorder?

Over the last few years, an increasing awareness and diagnosis of anxiety disorders has led many people to describe themselves that way. While for some folks, it can be helpful to have a definition for their experiences, it also brings the potential to pathologize the human experience. I'll also add that we're learning more and more that the various forms of anxiety and depression are not discrete categories. For these reasons, I generally shy away from sharing clinical diagnoses with my clients, unless I have a reason to believe a diagnosis will offer a sense of connection and clarity. However, in case defining your struggles with anxiety would help validate your experience, I'll explain a few of the common anxiety struggles currently recognized in the *Diagnostic and Statistical Manual of Mental Disorders, Fifth Edition* (*DSM-5*), which is the guide that clinicians use to diagnose clients.

> **Note:** Please remember that a formal diagnosis needs to be made by a trained clinician as they explore your experience against very specific diagnostic criteria in a particular way and consider other health conditions that could influence the symptoms you're experiencing.

In the *DSM-5*, anxiety is generally considered problematic when it interferes with the quality of your life in multiple domains, such as when you're in social situations, at work or school, or at home. It could also be the underlying cause of workaholism, using drugs and alcohol, over-exercising, unhealthy eating patterns, hoarding, and a variety of other behaviors that are essentially efforts to cope. (Remember, the solution can sometimes become the problem.) Returning to your body will allow you to travel back to the root cause of this response and support the healing of historic wounds.

Common Types of Anxiety

- **Generalized anxiety disorder:** Excessive and uncontrollable worry or anxiety about a wide range of everyday concerns and events, interfering with daily functioning, relationships, and overall quality of life.
- **Social anxiety disorder:** Intense fear, anxiety, and self-consciousness about embarrassment or rejection in a social situation.
- **Phobias:** Intense and irrational fear of a specific object, situation, or activity.
- **Panic disorders:** Recurring and unexpected panic attacks characterized by intense surges of fear or discomfort causing significant distress.
- **Post-traumatic stress disorder:** A traumatic event, followed by intrusive reexperiencing of the event (e.g., nightmares and flashbacks), avoidance of reminders of the traumatic event, and hypervigilance or changes in arousal and reactivity levels.

Taking Note of Traumas

Threatening and harmful events, where you experience intense negative emotions or helplessness/loss of control, are *traumatic events*. Chemicals in the nervous system, such as adrenaline, will result in your brain encoding the traumatic event differently from how everyday events are encoded.

While we are not dealing directly with trauma in this book, over 70 percent of people have experienced a traumatic event at some point in their lives (Kessler et al., 2017). This means that, more likely than not, you have too.

When people see the word *trauma*, they often think of the debilitating experience suffered by folks after a perceived life-threatening experience. This is the type of trauma that underpins diagnoses such as PTSD; in-person specialist support is recommended for dealing with its effects. However, there are many other events and situations that can be destabilizing to a nervous system. The experience of trauma is defined less by what happens *to* you and more by what happens *inside* you.

Your Ancestry

Have you ever found yourself responding to a situation in a way that doesn't make sense to you? Perhaps you go into a tailspin when a friend doesn't respond to your text (*What did I do to make them mad at me?*) or when you accidentally overcharge your credit card (*Will my credit score ever recover?*). It's as though your brain knows these are overreactions, but your body is convinced that they are threats to your survival.

Trying to deny or brush off these out-of-proportion responses doesn't resolve them, much less stop them from causing further damage to your body and mind. The fact is, your responses don't have to make sense for you to listen to and honor them. They may be coming not from your own personal experience, but instead from the experiences written into your cells from your ancestral lineage.

This influence of your ancestors isn't limited to your experience of being raised by your parents, nor is it the basic genetic code passed down through generations that decided, say, the color of your hair or the shape of your nose. It's found in your *epigenome*, a modifier of how your DNA is expressed (the prefix *epi* means "on top of"). In other words, your epigenome tells your body which cells to turn on or turn off—specifically, cells related to health and well-being, or those related to illness and disease.

Your behavior today literally changes your epigenome, casting votes for the future you'll have tomorrow. Choices that foster health and well-being open the door to positive changes in your epigenome, while unprocessed stressful experiences and unhealthy behaviors leave you more vulnerable to negative changes in your epigenome. The truly wild thing is that the associated epigenetic changes can be passed down to your kids and even later generations.

One experiment that captured just how influential our family history is involved mice and cherry blossoms (Dias & Ressler, 2014). The researchers took a group of mice and released a cherry blossom odor while simultaneously shocking them. Unsurprisingly, the mice, for the rest of their lives, had a fear response whenever they smelled cherry blossoms. What might surprise you is that their offspring had the same response to the smell, and so did their offspring's offspring. Sensitivity to this smell was passed down through generations of mice with a fear response. This is how generational trauma works—a burden of stress, fear, and anxiety is passed down through families as a biological legacy.

If you are sensitive to certain experiences without knowing why, the reason may lie within experiences endured by your parents or others still further down the ancestral line. Breaking intergenerational patterns is real work and requires accepting that you likely won't know all the elements that have influenced your anxiety in this lifetime. However, you can still gain insight into your unique experiences and successfully find ways of healing yourself and any generations that may come after you. After all, trauma isn't the only thing that can be transmitted through your biological lineage. Your epigenome can also hold, for example, deep intuition and knowledge beyond your lived experiences. You can be a conduit of ancestral wisdom and resilience, developing a vision and resources that support healing and thriving.

EXERCISE: Magic Wand

Imagine that I have a magic wand that can make everything "better." One flick and—*Abracadabra*!—you have your dream life. What does it actually look like?

Are you out laughing with friends? Cuddling at home with children or kittens? Working on an amazing research project or a stunning piece of pottery? Cooking a nourishing meal? Speaking out about a cause that you believe strongly in? Volunteering your energy or knowledge to support your community? Spending time with your elderly relatives? Going for a walk, run, or hike? Sitting in the sunshine with a good book?

I know that you want to feel happy and successful. Everyone does. But rather than just noting that on your ideal day you wake up feeling happy or you that you're successful in a particular venture, I encourage you to write about what you would actually be doing, specifically, in the morning, afternoon, and evening. You can start with something as mundane as what time you'd wake up in the morning, where you'd go once your feet swung out of bed and hit the floor, and go on from there.

____

____

____

____

____

____

Psychological Flexibility

Chronic stress and anxiety can diminish our capacity to choose behaviors that lead us toward a dream day like the one you just described. So what refuels our ability to choose those behaviors? The answer is *psychological flexibility.*

Psychological flexibility is the capacity to fully engage with the present moment as a conscious human being and adapt your actions to align with your values and goals. It is fostered by six abilities (Hayes et al., 2006):

1. **Present-moment awareness:** Connecting with the here and now, breath by breath
2. **Values:** Clarifying and connecting with your heartfelt values
3. **Committed action:** Setting goals and taking actions that are consistent with your values
4. **Self as perspective:** Tapping into a more transcendent sense of self to take perspective on who you are and your experiences
5. **Defusion:** Detaching from distressing private experiences (thoughts, feelings, bodily sensations)
6. **Acceptance:** Practicing nonjudgmental acceptance of difficult and painful experiences

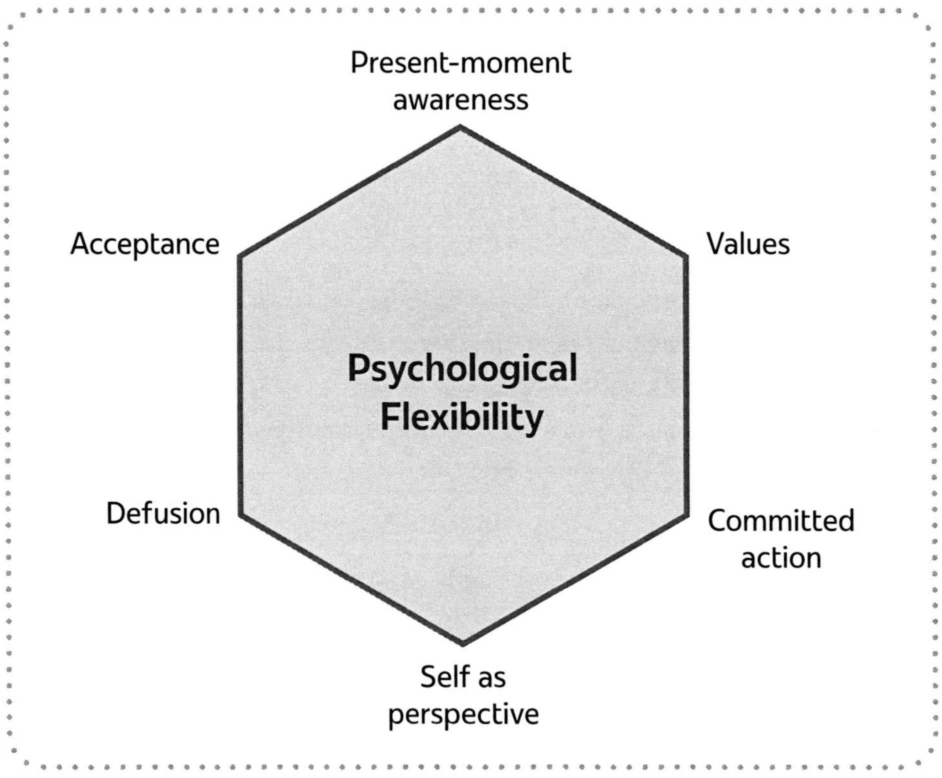

This can be simplified even further as the three pillars that frame the sections of this book: awareness, openness, and engagement. While we're starting with awareness, psychological flexibility skills are not linear in nature. They all connect to each other, and you'll find that we do somewhat dance between them within the pages of this book. You'll most certainly be dancing between them in your life, as this modern mindfulness-based approach is going to resource you beyond anxiety, beyond survival.

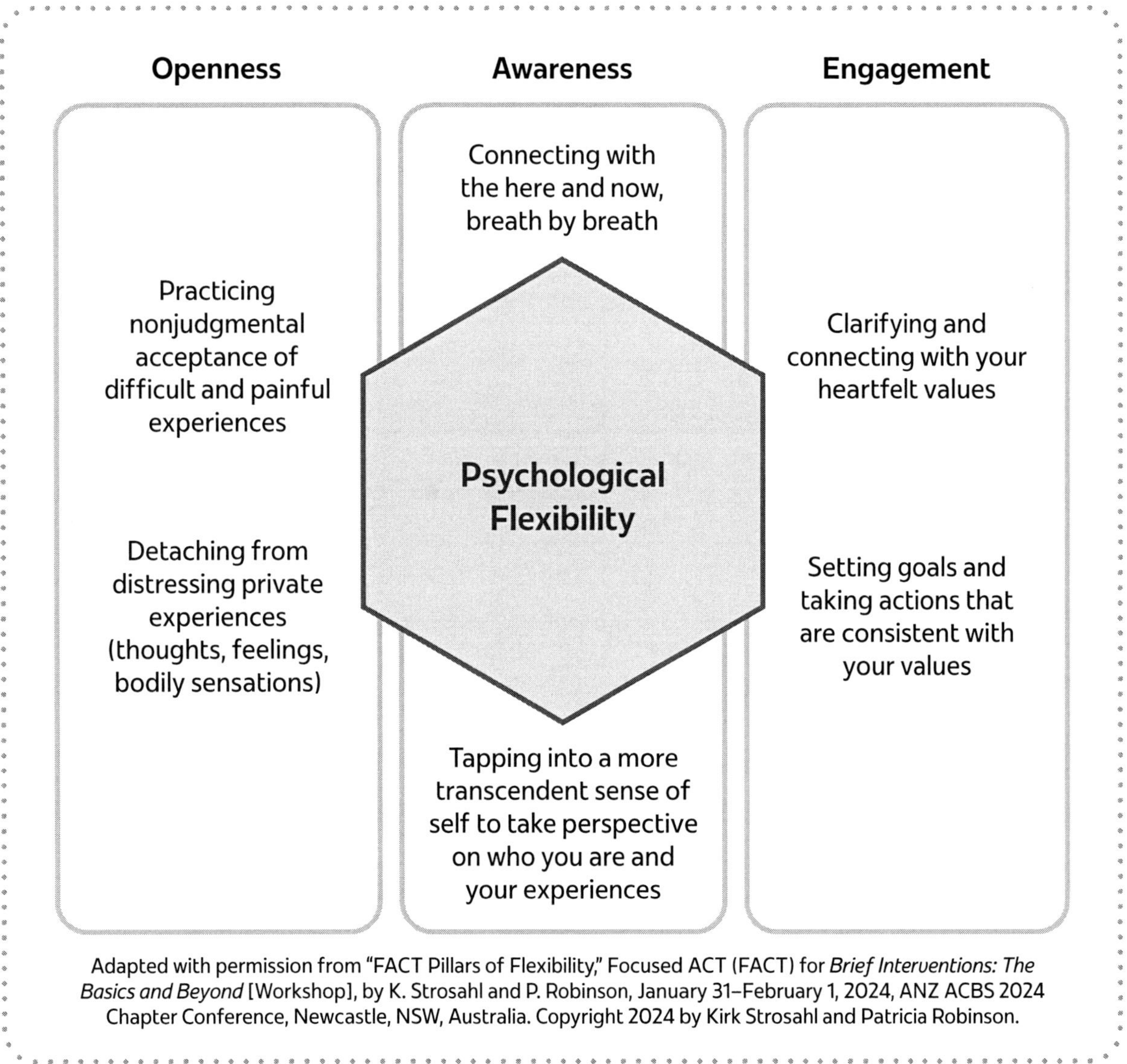

Adapted with permission from "FACT Pillars of Flexibility," Focused ACT (FACT) for *Brief Interventions: The Basics and Beyond* [Workshop], by K. Strosahl and P. Robinson, January 31–February 1, 2024, ANZ ACBS 2024 Chapter Conference, Newcastle, NSW, Australia. Copyright 2024 by Kirk Strosahl and Patricia Robinson.

Psychological flexibility is a *transdiagnostic target*, meaning it is a useful skill to build regardless of which specific diagnosis you might have or which particular experiences you're struggling with. It also asks us to set a goal not for eliminating anxiety altogether, but for skillfully reducing its impact so that we build capacity for working through our challenges and leading a rich and meaningful life.

So, where is your psychological flexibility at right now? Complete the following questionnaire, and you can track your progress on this journey from surviving to thriving!

EXERCISE: Acceptance and Action Questionnaire

Instructions: Below you will find a list of statements. Please rate how true each statement is for you by selecting the appropriate option.

		Never true	Very seldom true	Seldom true	Sometimes true	Frequently true	Almost always true	Always true
1	My painful experiences and memories make it difficult for me to live a life that I would value.	1	2	3	4	5	6	7
2	I'm afraid of my feelings.	1	2	3	4	5	6	7
3	I worry about not being able to control my worries and feelings.	1	2	3	4	5	6	7
4	My painful memories prevent me from having a fulfilling life.	1	2	3	4	5	6	7
5	Emotions cause problems in my life.	1	2	3	4	5	6	7
6	It seems like most people are handling their lives better than I am.	1	2	3	4	5	6	7
7	Worries get in the way of my success.	1	2	3	4	5	6	7

Reprinted with permission from "Preliminary Psychometric Properties of the Acceptance and Action Questionnaire – II: A Revised Measure of Psychological Inflexibility and Experiential Avoidance," by F. W. Bond, S. C. Hayes, R. A. Baer, K. M. Carpenter, N. Guenole, H. K. Orcutt, T. Waltz, and R. D. Zettle, 2011, *Behavior Therapy*, 42(4), p. 676–688 (https://doi.org/10.1016/j.beth.2011.03.007).

Add up your answers to get your total score. A lower score (from 7 to about 24) suggests that you already have a good amount of psychological flexibility. A higher score (from about 24 to 49) indicates that you have less psychological flexibility and are more likely to be experiencing symptoms of anxiety.

Rest assured that it doesn't matter if you are psychologically inflexible right now. In every moment you have a chance to be reborn, so to speak. In fact, acceptance and commitment therapy (ACT) was developed as the result of its founder, Dr. Steven Hayes, suffering from panic disorder. With panic attack after panic attack, he found himself avoiding more and more situations and locations, and his suffering and despair increased. Eventually, panic found him in his own home. A panic attack can happen anywhere because it is an experience that unfolds in our mind and body (which, of course, we cannot escape—like anxiety generally). This is that vicious cycle of anxiety we talked about earlier. Dr. Hayes found his way out of the cycle through cultivating psychological flexibility. Essentially, he started focusing on cultivating emotional openness, awareness, and his ability to do what matters to him in life. It's the same path you're taking now by following the steps in this book.

The Pain Is the Cure

To show you what somatic psychology can do for you, let's fast-forward the stories of Sarah and Cole. How did their experiences with anxiety lead them to somatic psychology, and how are they feeling now, after integrating practices like those found in this book into their day-to-day lives?

Sarah's body was constantly on high alert, trying to protect her from an old, familiar feeling: the sense that she was fundamentally unworthy unless she was achieving marvelous things. Having picked up this message from her loving but perfectionistic parents, she had always gotten through the feeling by gritting her teeth and putting her head down, which left her unable to relax or to truly enjoy the fruits of her labor. Eventually, the feeling of unworthiness grew to the point that she was too overwhelmed to find the motivation or focus to work on important projects.

Fortunately, Sarah recognized that she needed to make a change. She learned to slow down enough to identify and make peace with the parts of herself that had pushed her busyness beyond her capacity. Simultaneously, she used somatic practice to process the overwhelm stored in her nervous system. This supported Sarah in reconnecting to a felt sense of peace and joy, allowing her to rebalance her life. Today, she continues to integrate joyful practices and cultivate a healthy lifestyle. She is delighted to feel truly present with her family, finally.

Cole's story is similar. During his childhood, schoolyard bullying and his parents' divorce left him increasingly lonely. He developed a fear that if anyone ever got close to him, they would discover the devastating truth of how deeply flawed he was. His efforts to heal through spiritual seeking, reciting positive affirmations, practicing meditation, and healthy living had only widened the gap between Cole and the connection he longed for. He wouldn't go to gatherings that didn't meet his strict dietary preferences, and he avoided conversations with friends that he thought could become uncomfortable because he worried about experiencing "negative" emotions.

Somatic psychology practices have supported Cole in opening more gracefully to painful thoughts and feelings. He has shifted his affirmation practice to align with his heartfelt intention to gently sit with all of his inner world, including the loneliness he stills feels at times, and he uses movement practices to release the pain he'd been suppressing. As he has integrated his wounded parts, he's found it easier to be more flexible in his lifestyle. He's in a new relationship that doesn't evoke the unhealthy chemistry of the past and has instead helped him find the courage to honor his own emotional needs and boundaries.

Are you ready to start looking forward in your life? It starts with identifying positive goals for how you want to live, think, and feel.

EXERCISE: Somatic Psychology Goals Checklist

The following are some common goals that folks have when starting their somatic psychology journey. Consider whether they apply in your own life. Tick off any of the following experiences that would support you to live the dream day you envisioned earlier:

- ❐ Rejuvenating your sense of energy and vitality
- ❐ Easing the burdens of chronic stress symptoms
- ❐ Enhancing your physical well-being
- ❐ Releasing stored tensions and aches from past stressors
- ❐ Strengthening your resilience
- ❐ Fostering flexibility to respond gracefully to life's challenges
- ❐ Trusting your gut instincts with confidence
- ❐ Safely connecting with and expressing your emotions
- ❐ Nurturing a healthy and compassionate self-relationship and improved connections with others
- ❐ Amplifying your comfort and safety within your own skin
- ❐ Reducing daily stress and feelings of physical overwhelm
- ❐ Achieving goals that resonate with your authentic self

EXERCISE: Your Intention

With your ideal day in mind and a richer understanding of anxiety's vicious spiral, let's set an intention for the work ahead. We know why you're here and how you're suffering. This is your chance to summarize how you want to show up in this journey of transformation. You can use this as a guide as we delve into understanding your body better.

Here are some example intentions to help you get started:

- To develop deeper self-awareness—an inner understanding of who I am, including my thoughts, feelings, bodily sensations, and behavior patterns.
- To cultivate a sense of mindful awareness in my life, so that I can be present in my body and experience each moment.
- To enhance my emotional regulation and anxiety management, tuning in to the connection between my bodily sensations and emotional experience and developing strategies for managing challenging emotions.
- To improve my bodily awareness and honor my body's wisdom so that I can listen to its signals.
- To treat my body with kindness and compassion, recognizing its inherent intelligence.

____

____

____

____

____

Closing Reflections

As we close this first chapter, please take another moment to reflect on the following key areas before moving forward.

What are the things in your life that bring you the most suffering?

____

____

____

____

Consider your anxiety cycle—is it surprising to you that the things you do to try to feel better may ultimately leave you feeling worse?

____

____

____

____

Are there any stressors (stones in your backpack) that you can shift, or are they more chronic in nature?

What are your thoughts on psychological flexibility? Is it a concept you've explored before?

What do you know about your ancestors and family history?

Takeaway Messages

- Life is full of suffering, and emotional and physical pain are unavoidable.
- Avoiding anxiety results in increasing anxiety.
- Chronic stress increases your anxiety and the wear and tear on your body.
- Your ancestry impacts your psychophysiological responses, but you can shift your epigenome away from illness and disease and toward health and well-being.

CHAPTER 2

The Building Blocks of Your Mind-Body Experience: Nervous System Awareness

"Life doesn't make any sense without interdependence. We need each other, and the sooner we learn that, the better for us all."

—Joan Erikson

You Evolved to Be Anxious

Every painful experience you go through in your life imprints on your brain, body, and nervous system, influencing what you feel and how you think. This imprint is generally outside of your conscious awareness. Left unprocessed, it locks you in the exhausting cycle of anxiety and avoidance, resulting in psychological, emotional, physiological, and spiritual consequences.

Remember that some 200,000 years ago, our ancestors faced a world fraught with immediate, tangible dangers. The unforgiving landscape of the Stone Age required nervous systems to be vigilant for threats that might spell doom. Human brains and bodies evolved around one primal principle: safety first. That ancient version of you who was picking berries, acutely attuned to any unusual rustles or shifts in the shadows of the bushes, is a perfect example of the primal vigilance needed to stay alive. Your nervous system was constantly scanning for signs of lurking predators on the horizon—always on high alert, always prepared for the worst.

Millennia later, this survival strategy reverberates through us in the danger-warning default of our minds and bodies. A chorus of anxiety, caution, and fear serve as our internal alarm systems. The echoes of our caveman past reverberate in our thoughts: *Beware! Danger lurks everywhere—tread carefully!*

But here's where evolution takes an intriguing twist. In the Stone Age, replaying harrowing encounters with tigers and rival clans was essential for survival. It was the mind's way of cataloging lessons learned from brushes with disaster, preparing us for future perils. For example, remembering the way the tiger leapt out from the brush might remind ancient you to observe your surroundings more carefully before you begin gathering berries next time. Yet, in the bustle of our modern lives, we often find ourselves dwelling on painful memories even when there's no practical lesson to glean. The reason why it feels like your mind is compelled to worry is because . . . it is!

To make matters worse, this compulsion is insatiable. In those prehistoric days, your mind's drive for more—more food, more water, better weapons, safer shelter—was a survival strategy that ensured a longer life and more offspring. Today, this drive can manifest as unquenchable desires, a never-ending greed for more than we actually need: more shoes, more social media followers, more of the latest tech, more wealth, and so on.

The drive for more is often intensified by a desire to impress others. As mentioned in chapter 1, humans should not be at the top of the food chain. We have no sharp claws or fangs, no great size or strength, no exceptional skills that help us escape from danger; we are defenseless when alone. What allowed our ancestors to survive the challenges of the prehistoric world was banding together. In those ancient clans, fitting in was a matter of life and death; being rejected from the group meant an inevitable demise. Thus, our human mind evolved to constantly compare ourselves to others, ensuring that we adhered to the group rules and norms. What kept us in check? The same feelings we experience today—guilt, shame, and fear.

Of course, social cohesiveness isn't entirely borne of painful emotions; love, compassion, and connection also evolved to keep us together. Alongside our mind's capacity for fear and shame, we've also evolved sophisticated brain structures that support emotional co-regulation and hormonal changes that promote bonding and caregiving activities. So, while we are primed for vigilance, we are also capable of boundless compassion for others and even for ourselves. In the next chapter, we'll explore in more depth how to harness this innate capacity to soften our inner dialogues. But first, we'll explore the ancient fears that fuel our modern social anxieties.

EXERCISE: Unworthiness Reflection

Do you ever feel unworthy, like you are somehow less than others? Does this sense feel distressing to you? Do you believe that this is a normal human experience or that you're alone in feeling this way?

____

____

____

We're about to unpack your nervous system in more detail. Don't worry, you don't need a refresher course in biology to understand it. The point of this section is to ensure the intellectualizing part of your mind has the material it needs to make sense of the anxiety you experience. You might also find that understanding the nervous system cultivates compassion and connection because you'll see how connected we all are in our feelings of loneliness, other-ness, and insecurity. You are *not* alone.

A Quick Nervous System Refresher

Your nervous system comprises two main parts:

- The *central nervous system* includes your brain and spinal cord.
- The *peripheral nervous system* controls your voluntary and involuntary movement.

Within the peripheral nervous system, there are two more branches:

- The *somatic nervous system* allows your brain to control your voluntary movement through your muscles, joints, tendons, and ligaments. This is exactly how you turn the pages of this book and how you will practice the somatic exercises you'll find in the pages ahead.
- The *autonomic nervous system (ANS)* controls involuntary processes, like your heart rate, blood pressure, digestion, bodily fluids, and breathing. While the ANS is always active, it operates below conscious awareness. This system is vital to understanding the struggles that brought you here and how to release the burdens of the past.

Finally, the autonomic nervous system also has two branches of its own:

- The *sympathetic nervous system (SNS)* is like a vigilant guardian, activating the fight-or-flight response when danger is perceived. It prepares your body for action, heightening your senses and mobilizing energy for survival. This is where your experience of stress arises.
- The *parasympathetic nervous system (PNS)* is a soothing presence, responsible for promoting rest and relaxation. It's like a gentle embrace, calming your heart rate and supporting restoration.

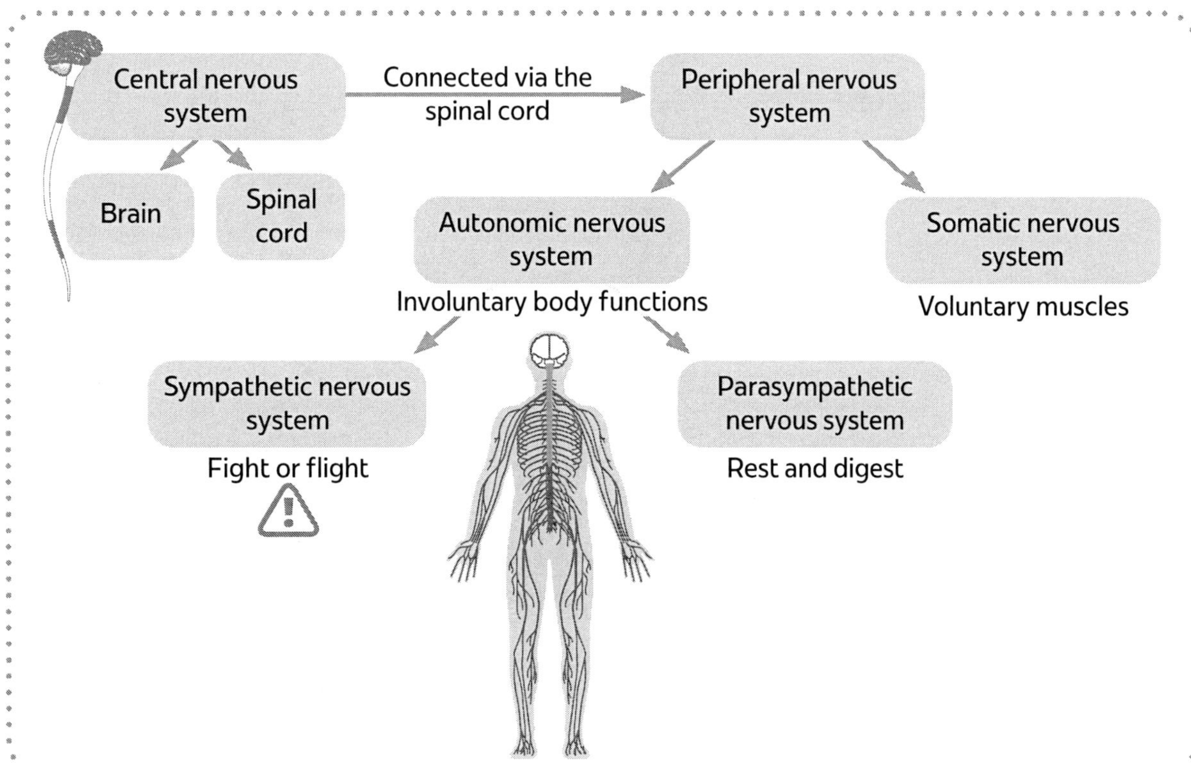

When I first learned about these systems in Psychology 101, one crucial piece of the puzzle was missing. That piece was the *vagus nerve.* Flowing through your upper body like a wandering vagabond (for which it is named), the vagus nerve travels from the nape of your neck down to your heart, lungs, stomach, gut, and reproductive organs, all areas that your nervous system controls. Just as a smoothly flowing river indicates a healthy ecosystem, a well-functioning vagus nerve (scientifically known as *high vagal tone*) is a marker of a strong parasympathetic nervous system—in other words, no resistance to entering the rest-and-digest response.

Measured through heart rate variability, which captures fluctuations in the moments between heartbeats, higher vagal tone indicates stronger stress resilience, emotional regulation, and ability to maintain focus and calm. This is an example of a *biobehavioral* system in which biology influences behavior and behavior affects biological functioning in turn.

Back in the 1960s, a researcher named Dr. Steven Porges at the University of Chicago noted that subjects with lower vagal tone showed heightened responses to stress, including anxiety, lack of focus, and difficulties with emotional regulation, while those with higher vagal tone were seen to move through a stressor more quickly, maintaining focus on the tasks they were given and returning to a state of relaxation and social connection (Porges, 2011). At the time, the scientific community was firmly entrenched in a mind-body dualism, and Dr. Porges's emerging theory of an integrative relationship between body and mind was highly controversial. But when Dr. Porges focused on the freeze response—that is, the slowing down and shutting down of key organs when your nervous system senses life-threatening danger—it yielded a light-bulb moment for his research and led to the development of an important new theory that united physical markers with psychological health.

Polyvagal Theory

In 1994, Dr. Stephen Porges presented his academic community with polyvagal theory, which posited that there are two branches to the vagus nerve that influence different mental and behavioral reactions.

Most of us understand that nerves operate within the body similarly to how electrical wires operate in our homes. Just as the light switch beside my doorway transmits a signal that turns the lights on and off, the body's nervous system transmits signals in the form of sensations—such as smell, temperature, and pain—to guide our physical movements and bodily functions. In other words, nerves are the channel of brain-body communication. This communication works incredibly quickly; brain signals are sent through your nerves so fast that many of the physical reactions they provoke are unconscious.

Now, the light switch beside my doorway includes two buttons. If I hit the top switch, I turn on the living room lamps, while if I hit the lower switch, it turns on the light in the hallway. In the same way, Dr. Porges proposed that different types of stimulation activate different branches of the vagus nerve, each of which yields a different type of response.

The *dorsal vagal* branch is the lowest-level "switch" on our evolutionary ladder—it evolved early in vertebrate history, and it's the first one we're able to access in human development. It primarily controls physical function below the diaphragm; for example, it can slow down your heart rate and digestion. Behaviorally, it's associated with shutdown, energy conservation, and the freeze or fawn responses.

The dorsal vagal response develops first because it is primarily controlled by the unmyelinated vagus nerve. Unmyelinated nerves don't have a kind of insulation known as myelin coating them, which means signals move slower. Myelination is an evolutionary development that only mammals have, one that is critical for the effective transmission of your nervous system's electrical signals. The number of myelinated nerves you have keeps increasing from fetal development until well into adulthood. Babies begin building myelination primarily in the first 3 to 12 months of life, supported by the experience of spending time with an attuned, regulated, and safe adult. However, it is also worth noting that adults can build myelination by engaging in activities that enrich their well-being, such as exercise and meditation.

Once the myelination process begins, the next "light switch," the sympathetic nervous system, begins to develop. Again, this system is what activates our fight-or-flight response, or the state of *mobilization*, as it's sometimes called. It's connected to various organs along our spinal cord, which explains why it tends to cause increased metabolic activity in our stomach and other parts of the digestive system.

The top "switch," the last sub-branch to evolve, is the *ventral vagal* branch. This branch of the vagus nerve activates your *social engagement system*, which is essentially a sense of social connection and caregiving responses mainly connected to your face, throat, and chest. As this develops in babies, they're able to sense and respond to safety, gentleness, and warmth expressed through smiling faces, lullaby singing, rocking, and slow rhythmic breathing.

Science moves slowly, and polyvagal theory is still being evaluated by the scientific community. Regardless, the theory is incredibly useful in making sense of our unconscious reactions and motivations. Just as you can flick on the light switch and instantly see, your nervous system and its various branches facilitate communication between your brain and body at near-instant speed, taking in sensory information about sights, smells, sensations, and temperature and transmitting messages and signals that guide physical movements and bodily functions.

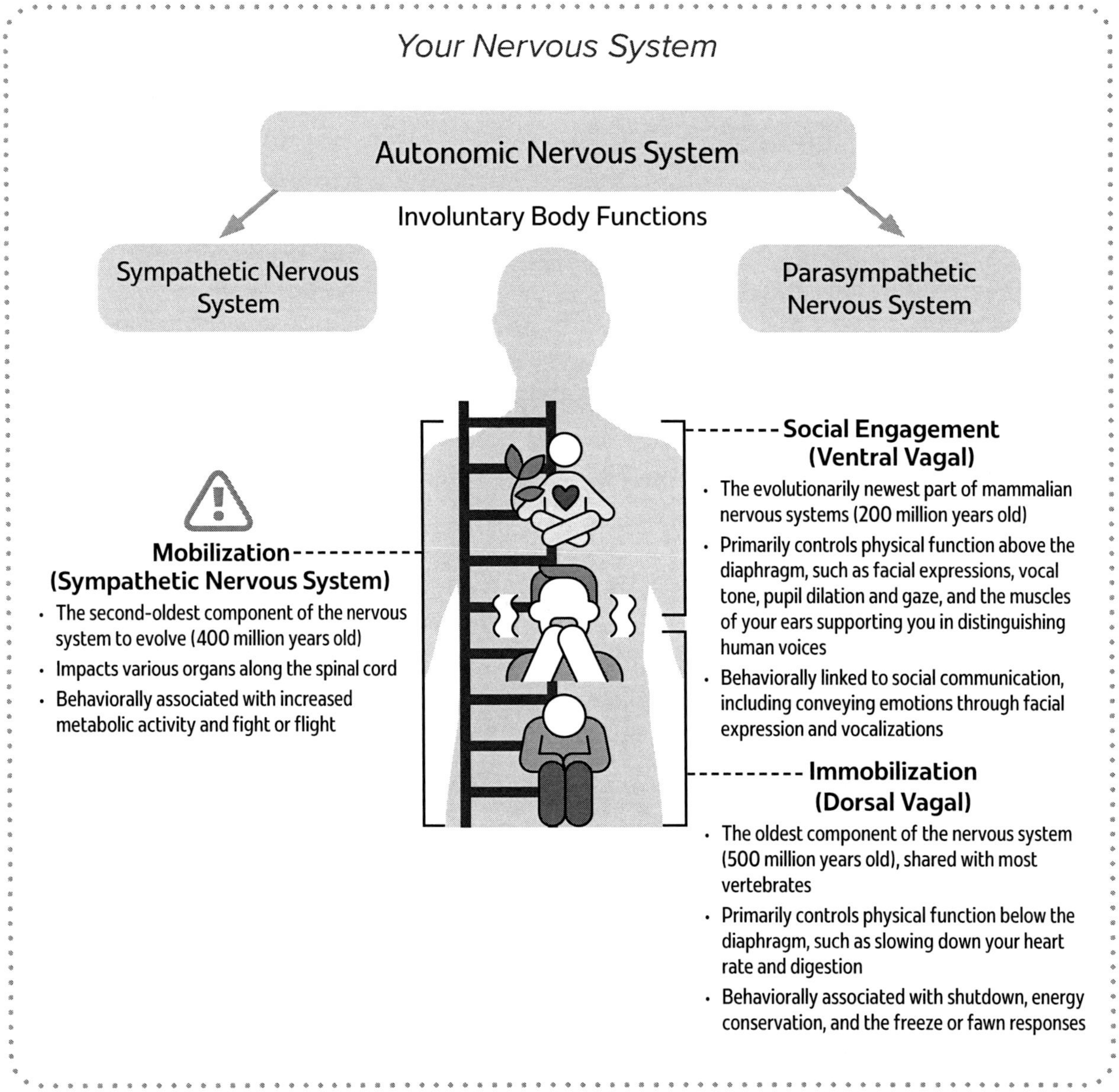

Your Nervous System

Autonomic Nervous System

Involuntary Body Functions

Sympathetic Nervous System

Parasympathetic Nervous System

Mobilization (Sympathetic Nervous System)

- The second-oldest component of the nervous system to evolve (400 million years old)
- Impacts various organs along the spinal cord
- Behaviorally associated with increased metabolic activity and fight or flight

Social Engagement (Ventral Vagal)

- The evolutionarily newest part of mammalian nervous systems (200 million years old)
- Primarily controls physical function above the diaphragm, such as facial expressions, vocal tone, pupil dilation and gaze, and the muscles of your ears supporting you in distinguishing human voices
- Behaviorally linked to social communication, including conveying emotions through facial expression and vocalizations

Immobilization (Dorsal Vagal)

- The oldest component of the nervous system (500 million years old), shared with most vertebrates
- Primarily controls physical function below the diaphragm, such as slowing down your heart rate and digestion
- Behaviorally associated with shutdown, energy conservation, and the freeze or fawn responses

EXERCISE: Mapping Out the Ladder

While we all have similar wiring, our lived experiences shape our biophysiological responses in unique ways. That's why, along with understanding your nervous system from an evolutionary perspective, you need an individualized felt-sense map of exactly what you experience in the various states of nervous system activation. Let's start by mapping out your responses to everyday life situations.

Self-Care Reminder: When doing this exercise, please take care of yourself. It's best if you focus on situations for which you've had some processing time already, rather than on the most difficult situations in your life. The latter would undoubtedly benefit from being explored with a therapist.

While having this individualized map is important, it can be tricky to know where to start in the early stages of your nervous system awareness. I would encourage you to first consider whether you feel more familiar with the fight-or-flight experience or the freeze-or-fawn experience. Once you know your default response, start the exercise with that. Then you can work out the other nervous system response you might be less familiar with, and finally you'll do the safe and social state at the end (it's a nice way to wrap up the exercise!).

If you struggle to identify the unique elements of what is going on inside your skin during this exercise, that is okay! I'm going to support you in building this inner awareness along the way. For now, please do your best to note any observations and reflections you have.

Instructions

1. Close your eyes or soften your gaze and take a few slow, deep breaths.
2. Bring to mind a specific situation where you felt like you were in fight, flight, freeze, or fawn. As you connect to this memory, you may or may not visualize it.
3. As you recall the situation, focus on your body. How did your body react in that moment? Pay attention to the physical sensations. Notice if your body tensed up, if your heart rate changed, how your stomach, chest and throat felt, or any other physical reactions.
4. Now remember the emotions you experienced during this situation. Try to identify and name these emotions. Were you feeling fear, anger, frustration, irritability, nervousness, or something else?
5. Reflect on any urges or impulses that you had during the situation. What did you want to do? Were there specific actions or behaviors that you felt compelled to engage in during that moment?
6. Focus on the thoughts that were racing through your mind at the time. What were you thinking about? Consider any thought patterns or beliefs that might have been present.
7. When you're ready, open your eyes more fully and take a few deep breaths. Reflect on the insights you've uncovered around what sort of situations and inner experiences are related to the fight-or-flight or freeze-or-fawn response. Write down your reflections in the chart that follows.
8. Repeat the previous steps of this exercise for the next survival response in the chart (either freeze-or-fawn or fight-or-flight).
9. Finally, repeat the steps once more, this time reflecting on a situation where you felt safe and social.

	Situation	Bodily Sensations	Emotions	Urges	Thoughts
Safe and Social (Ventral Vagal)					
Fight or Flight (Sympathetic Nervous System)					
Freeze or Fawn (Doral Vagal)					

Reflection

When doing this exercise, did you notice a particular state was more familiar to you?

____

____

____

Can you think of other situations when you've experienced this same state?

____

____

____

Neuroception

Outside of your conscious awareness, your nervous system evaluates every environment you're in to determine whether it's safe or dangerous. This is the concept of *neuroception*.

Neuroception is the hand that intuits which light switch to flick, so to speak. It is not the awareness that comes with conscious perception; it is a subconscious threat detector that allows for automatic responses, the way your hand instinctively knows where to find and flick the right switch when you walk into a familiar room even when it's too dark for you to see. This means that your autonomic nervous system can trigger a defensive response before you rationally consider your safety. Perhaps you startle at a loud noise that turns out to have been a book falling to the floor after you had set it too close to the edge of your desk earlier. Or maybe, thinking you are home alone, you scream when you turn around from filling up the tea kettle to see your housemate in the kitchen. Neither of these situations warrants a defensive response, but you respond that way nonetheless. In some situations, you can't afford to think. Your life (and possibly the lives of others) depends on instantaneous reaction.

Of course, these examples show that neuroception, like conscious perception, isn't always accurate. An inability to determine whether an environment is safe or a person is trustworthy can leave you feeling anxious and disconnected. This is why enhancing intuition by healing ineffective neuroceptive responses is part of your journey ahead.

In many ways, I consider intuition the ability to bring the unconscious to conscious awareness. It's a resource you can develop through cultivating awareness of the circumstances that elicit heightened reactivity in your nervous system when a situation is not objectively dangerous. Essentially, situations that have a significant negative impact on your mental and emotional well-being, particularly early life experiences, leave an imprint on your nervous system. This imprint evokes *procedural memory*—that is, patterns of thinking, feeling, and behaving that you can't consciously explain.

Why You Don't Fit in Boxes

Perhaps you've noticed that not all of your nervous system experiences fit exactly into their designated box, so to speak. For example, in a freeze or fawn response you can still be running around busily taking care of others, while you might be horizontal on the couch watching a TV program at a time when you're feeling safe and social. That's fine. Your nervous system states are a little more complicated than simply having three light switches in your hall.

Let's look at the past experiences of Cole, who feels stuck in life and whose stomach is constantly in knots despite having tried every juice cleanse and elimination diet under the sun. Cole's early years were marred by bullying in school. He has always been a sensitive and artistic soul, for which he was mocked by some of his more callous classmates. The taunts and sense of disconnection caused him to withdraw into himself whenever he confronted challenging situations. As if the bullying wasn't enough, Cole's parents then separated. Not understanding the adult nature of their rupture, he blamed himself for it.

Cole has struggled to find his place in the world throughout his adult years. He's jumped from one job to another, ever seeking a sense of belonging and purpose. While he has plenty of good friends around him, he deeply fears nobody really likes him and that they'll eventually want to get away from him because he's "too much." This drives him to spend a great deal of time and effort trying to care for others and earn their approval.

These patterns of becoming acutely attentive to the needs of others (fawning) and disconnecting from and feeling numb toward his own needs (freezing) patterns are exhausting. Moreover, they hold him back from aligning with a sense of purpose in his life. It is also an example of a *blended state*, where different parts of your nervous system simultaneously engage. I look at this like having the lights on in both the hall and the lounge.

Blended States

Blended states result from different vagal states being activated simultaneously. They include the following.

Fixate

This blended state of feeling mobilized (SNS) and immobilized (dorsal vagal) can be described in many ways. You might say you feel "hooked by," "caught by," "stuck on," or "fused with" a distressing thought, feeling, or urge. In other words, you feel like you can't take your attention away from what is unfolding in your mind or body.

Intimacy

This blended state of safety (ventral vagal) and immobilization (dorsal vagal) is found in peaceful and healing experiences, creative or meditative flow, and connection with others or with your own sense of self.

Play

This blended state of safety (ventral vagal) and mobilization (SNS) is the foundation of active play experiences, from dancing to playing a sport to just goofing around. The emotional quality of this state—joyful, cheeky, free—differentiates it from drive, a similar blended state described next.

Drive

This blended state integrates safety (ventral vagal) and mobilization (SNS), motivating you to achieve, pursue, and seek in challenging situations that you find personally meaningful or rewarding. (This state is often described with the word *eustress,* which you learned back in chapter 1; however, since the word "stress" typically implies a negative experience, I prefer using the word "drive" for this blended state.)

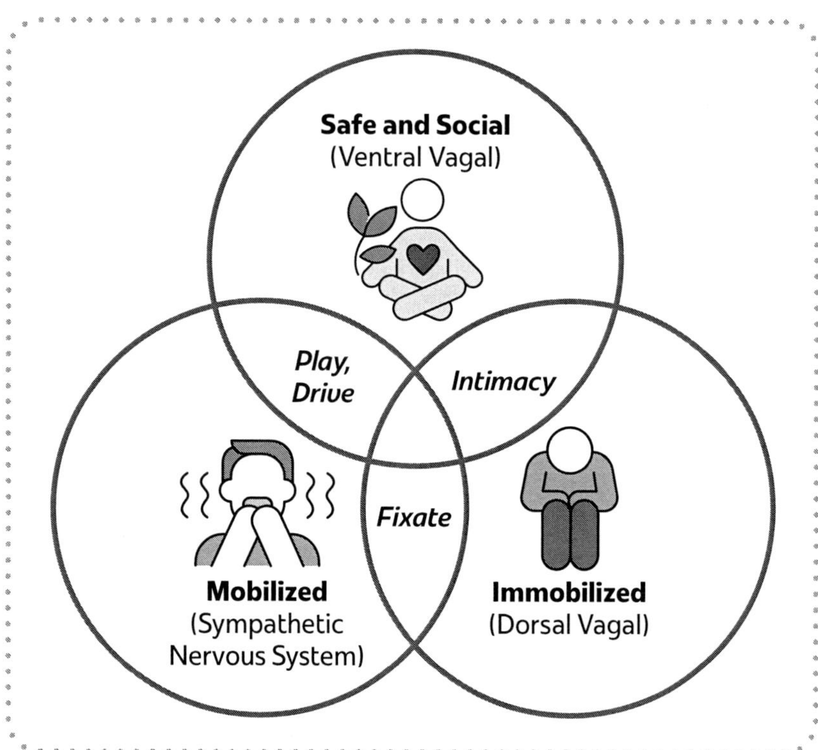

How Do You Even Know What You Are Feeling?

Just as you use different forms of sensory perception (sight, smell, touch, etc.) to access external information, you also have an ability to perceive your inner experience. Throughout the day, you pick up on everything from hunger, thirst, pain, and level of fatigue or alertness to the experience of anxiety, anger, sadness, excitement, joy, and the like. This ability to observe what is unfolding in your physical and emotional body is known as *interoception*, though we sometimes refer to it as your "felt sense." A healthy level of interoception supports you in detecting and evaluating cues of biophysiological stress responses as well as safety.

Everything we do in our journey here is going to support you in accessing the inner wisdom of your felt sense so that you can build a trusting relationship with yourself and meet your own needs. Let's start by measuring your level of interoception—you can use the following questionnaire or, for a version that will automatically calculate your score, head to https://just-digital.github.io/maia-2 or www.drkaitlin.com/maia.

EXERCISE: How Well Do You Know How You Feel?

Below you will find a list of statements. Please indicate how often each statement applies to you generally in daily life.

		Never					Always
1.	When I am tense I notice where the tension is located in my body.	0	1	2	3	4	5
2.	I notice when I am uncomfortable in my body.	0	1	2	3	4	5
3.	I notice where in my body I am comfortable.	0	1	2	3	4	5
4.	I notice changes in my breathing, such as whether it slows down or speeds up.	0	1	2	3	4	5
5.	I ignore physical tension or discomfort until they become more severe.	5	4	3	2	1	0
6.	I distract myself from sensations of discomfort.	5	4	3	2	1	0
7.	When I feel pain or discomfort, I try to power through it.	5	4	3	2	1	0
8.	I try to ignore pain.	5	4	3	2	1	0
9.	I push feelings of discomfort away by focusing on something.	5	4	3	2	1	0
10.	When I feel unpleasant body sensations, I occupy myself with something else so I don't have to feel them.	5	4	3	2	1	0
11.	When I feel physical pain, I become upset.	5	4	3	2	1	0
12.	I start to worry that something is wrong if I feel any discomfort.	5	4	3	2	1	0
13.	I can notice an unpleasant body sensation without worrying about it.	0	1	2	3	4	5
14.	I can stay calm and not worry when I have feelings of discomfort or pain.	0	1	2	3	4	5
15.	When I am in discomfort or pain I can't get it out of my mind.	5	4	3	2	1	0

		Never					Always
16.	I can pay attention to my breath without being distracted by things happening around me.	0	1	2	3	4	5
17.	I can maintain awareness of my inner bodily sensations even when there is a lot going on around me.	0	1	2	3	4	5
18.	When I am in conversation with someone, I can pay attention to my posture.	0	1	2	3	4	5
19.	I can return awareness to my body if I am distracted.	0	1	2	3	4	5
20.	I can refocus my attention from thinking to sensing my body.	0	1	2	3	4	5
21.	I can maintain awareness of my whole body even when a part of me is in pain or discomfort.	0	1	2	3	4	5
22.	I am able to consciously focus on my body as a whole.	0	1	2	3	4	5
23.	I notice how my body changes when I am angry.	0	1	2	3	4	5
24.	When something is wrong in my life I can feel it in my body.	0	1	2	3	4	5
25.	I notice that my body feels different after a peaceful experience.	0	1	2	3	4	5
26.	I notice that my breathing becomes free and easy when I feel comfortable.	0	1	2	3	4	5
27.	I notice how my body changes when I feel happy/joyful.	0	1	2	3	4	5
28.	When I feel overwhelmed I can find a calm place inside.	0	1	2	3	4	5
29.	When I bring awareness to my body I feel a sense of calm.	0	1	2	3	4	5
30.	I can use my breath to reduce tension.	0	1	2	3	4	5
31.	When I am caught up in thoughts, I can calm my mind by focusing on my body/breathing.	0	1	2	3	4	5
32.	I listen for information from my body about my emotional state.	0	1	2	3	4	5
33.	When I am upset, I take time to explore how my body feels.	0	1	2	3	4	5
34.	I listen to my body to inform me about what to do.	0	1	2	3	4	5
35.	I am at home in my body.	0	1	2	3	4	5
36.	I feel my body is a safe place.	0	1	2	3	4	5
37.	I trust my body sensations.	0	1	2	3	4	5

Scoring Instructions

Take the average of the items on each scale.

Note: (R): reverse-score (5 – x) items 5, 6, 7, 8, 9, and 10 on Not-Distracting, and items 11, 12, and 15 on Not-Worrying.

1. **Noticing:** Awareness of uncomfortable, comfortable, and neutral body sensations

   Q1____ + Q2____ + Q3____ + Q4____ / 4 = ____

2. **Not-Distracting:** Tendency not to ignore or distract oneself from sensations of pain or discomfort

   Q5**(R)**____ + Q6**(R)**____ + Q7**(R)**____ + Q8**(R)**____ + Q9**(R)**____ + Q10**(R)**____ / 6 = ____

3. **Not-Worrying:** Tendency not to worry or experience emotional distress with sensations of pain or discomfort

   Q11**(R)**____ + Q12**(R)**____ + Q13____ + Q14____ + Q15**(R)**____ / 5 = ____

4. **Attention Regulation:** Ability to sustain and control attention to body sensations

   Q16____ + Q17____ + Q18____ + Q19____ + Q20____ + Q21____ + Q22____ / 7 = ____

5. **Emotional Awareness:** Awareness of the connection between body sensations and emotional states

   Q23____ + Q24____ + Q25____ + Q26____ + Q27____ / 5 = ____

6. **Self-Regulation:** Ability to regulate distress by attention to body sensations

   Q28____ + Q29____ + Q30____ + Q31____ / 4 = ____

7. **Body Listening:** Active listening to the body for insight

   Q32____ + Q33____ + Q34____ / 3 = ____

8. **Trusting:** Experience of one's body as safe and trustworthy

   Q35____ + Q36____ + Q37____ / 3 = ____

Higher scores indicate higher levels of body awareness. Make a note if you score less than an average of 2.5 in any domains, as these are areas you will particularly focus on enhancing through the course of our time together. Then, come back and redo this assessment when you've finished reading this book to see how your scores have changed.

Your body is always seeking to remain balanced and functional, which requires adjustments in response to changes in your environment or inner conditions. What is important to understand here is that your mind and body are connected in a biobehavioral system. So, if you miss body-based signals, your brain and behavior will also shift, and vice versa. For instance, if your blood sugar starts dropping but you don't pick up on the interoceptive signals telling you that you need to eat, they'll find another way to express themselves. Often, it's through increased irritability; we've even coined a word—"hangry"—to describe this biochemical emotional change.

For another common example, let's go back to Sarah's story. She has a massive project deadline coming up, and when she's not working on it, you'd better believe she's thinking about it. Her mind-body system picks up on her anxiety about the deadline and her neural brain activity, perceiving those feelings as the presence of a threat, triggers a fight-or-flight response that activates something called her hypothalamic-pituitary-adrenal (HPA) axis. The HPA axis signals her endocrine glands to secrete stress hormones into her blood, including cortisol. This energy-inducing hormone evolved to keep us alert in situations of ongoing danger or short-term stressors; however, thanks to the chronic stress rampant in our modern lifestyle, many of us live with a constant "drip" of cortisol that results in a cascade of negative health outcomes, including muscle weakness, high blood pressure, and impaired immune function. While the energy it provides keeps Sarah working into the early hours of the morning, day after day, she catches a cold just a few days after meeting her deadline. Her body is demanding its downtime to rest and recover.

It's important to remember that your nervous system didn't only evolve to prompt stressful survival responses. It's also intended to support you in building connection and, ultimately, cultivating health in your mind and body. That's what we'll be focusing on in the pages ahead.

Closing Reflections

Which nervous system response do you spend most of your time in—mobilized, immobilized, or safe and social? Or perhaps a blended state—play, drive, fixate, or intimacy?

____

____

____

What people and places provide you with a feeling of safety and connection?

____

____

____

Is it easy to tap into a sense of connection and compassion? Why or why not?

When do you feel most attuned to the felt sense of your body?

Reflect on how your mind and body influence each other, and what this has meant for your health.

Takeaway Messages

- Your nervous system evolved for survival and controls many of your unconscious responses.
- Polyvagal theory suggests three main responses in your nervous system: your drive to connect socially, the fight-or-flight response, and the freeze-or-fawn response.
- Your nervous system states can be blended, accounting for other states such as play and drive.
- Interoception is your ability to feel what is happening inside your body and respond to these sensations.
- Your gastrointestinal, hormonal, and immune systems are negatively impacted by psychological stress and anxiety.

CHAPTER 3

Resourcing Your Nervous System: How to Survive and Thrive

"You're imperfect, and you're wired for struggle, but you are worthy of love and belonging."

—Brené Brown

We've talked a few times about the importance of "resourcing yourself" for the work ahead in this book. But what does it actually mean? And how do you know when you are (or are not) adequately resourced? Why is it that some days you can feel calm despite the coffee spilling on your shirt and the hectic traffic on the road, while other days, you find yourself in tears and slamming on the horn?

One way to assess your resource level is by using your internal felt sense to determine where you stand on the polyvagal ladder. However, there is another framework that some find more helpful for stress navigation and emotional regulation. It's known as the *window of tolerance.*

The Window of Tolerance

Throughout life, you'll experience highs and lows related to the challenges you go through. Some stressors will push you toward a state of heightened awareness and energy, while others will sap your energy and make you feel fatigued or even numb. For the most part, these stress experiences tend to stay within manageable bounds. You might feel anxious about a looming project deadline or exhausted by the demands of your kids' school schedule, but you can still think clearly, manage your emotions, and make wise decisions. Psychiatrist and educator Dr. Dan Siegel refers to this as your *window of tolerance.*

An unusually stressful experience may push you outside your window, causing you to end up in a state of *hyperarousal* (fight or flight) or *hypoarousal* (freeze). These states can result in symptoms of dysregulation such as panic, shutdown, emotional volatility, or dissociation, all of which make it harder to cope effectively and maintain a sense of control in your life.

When your window of tolerance is smaller, it doesn't take much stress for you to feel as though you can't cope. A bigger window, on the other hand, means greater resilience to stress and more capacity to navigate challenges.

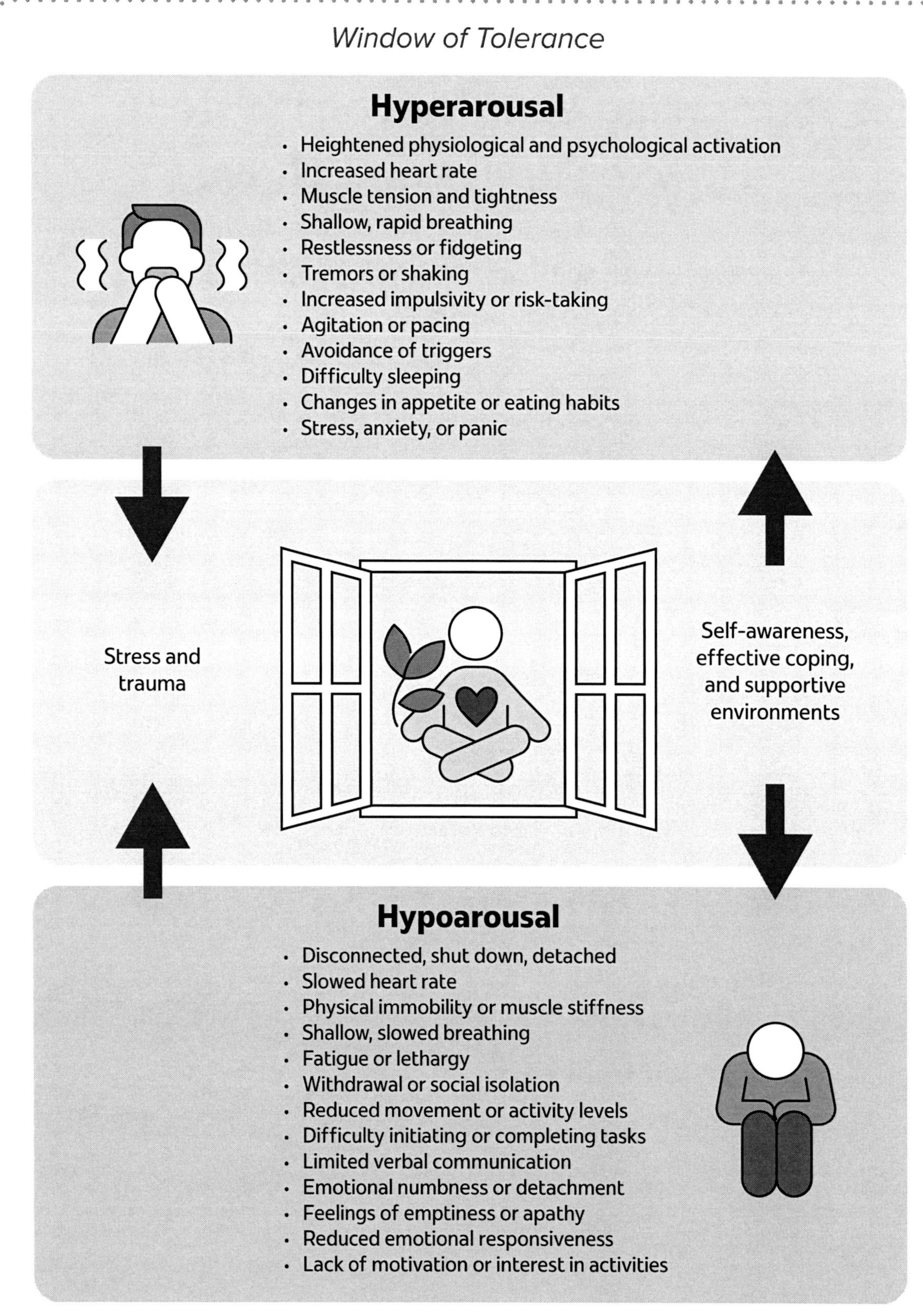

The size of your window is influenced by both your innate sensory processing sensitivity and your life experiences—essentially, a combination of nature and nurture.

In terms of nature, some of us are just more sensitive to sensory input and experience our emotional states more intensely than others. For instance, neurodivergent individuals may be hypersensitive to particular sensory experiences such as bright lights or certain textures. Sensitivity is a beautiful gift, but it requires awareness of your tendencies and your needs in the face of stressors, as well as self-care strategies to meet those needs.

On the nurture side of the equation, if you have a supportive and attuned experience early in life, you'll likely have a larger window and more capacity to navigate challenges. However, if you've had difficult experiences or missed out on your emotional needs being met in your early years, your window of tolerance will likely be smaller.

Fortunately, this isn't the end of the story. Your window of tolerance can be expanded through regular self-care and the use of self-soothing skills that bring you back into regulation when your nervous system is screaming, "Tiger!" The pages ahead will help you develop greater self-awareness around how stress influences your moods and behavior. You will also learn effective coping strategies for releasing somatic tension and improving your general health.

Self-Care Versus Self-Soothing

What is the first thing that comes to mind when you think of self-care? Bubble baths and candles? A pedicure? Maybe a glass of wine? If we go by what we see on social media, these are the cure-alls for everything from a hard day at work to relationship conflict to feeling unsure about where you're going in your life.

There is no inherent problem with these practices. They can undoubtedly soothe us when we're feeling upset, overwhelmed, or just moody. I personally relish crawling into a peaceful bath with Epsom salts to relax my ever-tense muscles at the end of a long day. The thing is, that's all they are: soothing. Once you towel off and head back out to reality, all those stressors, pressures, and emotional-behavioral patterns that brought you to this moment are waiting for you on the other side of the bathroom door.

If self-soothing becomes a way of escaping reality instead of dealing with it, these practices turn toxic. That's why it's important we understand and use self-soothing the way it's meant to be used: as an emergency brake for an overwhelmed nervous system. Self-care, on the other hand, is better understood as an energetic investment you make over the long term. (We'll be covering that topic in chapter 5.)

Even though their effects are temporary, self-soothing practices are nonetheless extremely valuable. They offer a chance to pause and recover so that you can decide consciously what to do next, rather than unconsciously default to survival patterns that could have negative consequences in your life. And if bubble baths and pedicures give you the nervous system reset you need, great!

Sometimes, though, we need something that goes more than skin deep, something that reaches farther into the body and soothes us at the source of our distress.

Self-Soothing Toolbox

Self-soothing can be any sensory experience that changes and regulates your nervous system state in the here and now. When you find yourself spiraling into a panicked or distressed state, the following practices can not only pull you back into your window of tolerance, helping you become grounded and calm again, but also allow blood flow to return to your "thinking brain" (the prefrontal cortex we talked about back in the introduction) so that you can make rational decisions about what to do next.

Given that the thinking brain won't be performing at its best in the moments when you need self-soothing strategies, it's important to have these strategies mapped out for yourself in advance. That way, when a moment of distress arises, you won't have to think about what to do—you can just reach for your "toolbox."

EXERCISE: Belly Breathing

Your breath rests on the border of the conscious and the unconscious, making it an incredibly powerful tool for navigating stress. In chapter 4, we'll go deep into the science behind our breathing and build practices for a variety of effects. Right now, though, we'll start with the basics: learning to deepen the breath and slow the exhale. This breathing style is associated with your social engagement system, the rest-and-digest response of your parasympathetic nervous system. Given that the different components of your nervous system all work together, as your breathing rate slows, you'll experience other state changes too. For instance, your heart rate will also slow and more blood will return to your digestive system.

Here's how to practice belly breathing:

1. Sit in a comfortable chair with both feet flat on the floor. Alternatively, you can lie down with any supports you might need.
2. Place one hand on your chest and the other on your upper abdomen, just below your rib cage.
3. Inhale through your nose, drawing the breath down toward your abdomen to pull your diaphragm down.
4. Hold for a count or two.
5. Now exhale, slowly drawing your abdomen back in and allowing the diaphragm to move back up.
6. Repeat this cycle 5 to 10 times. You should feel your belly going out with the inhale and in with the exhale. Your chest should stay still.

7. Now try extending the duration of your exhale so it is longer than the inhale. You might try a rate of a 4-second inhale to a 5-second exhale. This promotes relaxation.
8. Finally, try to lengthen the whole breath cycle, still keeping the exhale longer than the inhale. For example, you might work your way up to a 6-second inhale and an 8-second exhale.

When you start this exercise, it might feel like you are working hard to control your breath. Through the practice, you're looking for the breath to feel more easeful at the slower rate. This ease will extend through the rest of your nervous system, resulting in a release of stress and a lessening of its negative effects.

EXERCISE: The Dive Reflex

You have an innate physiological response known as the *mammalian dive reflex* that is remarkably useful in times of psychological distress. This protective mechanism supports your body in surviving water submersion by triggering changes that conserve oxygen. The heart rate slows; blood flow is redirected to vital organs like the brain and heart, reducing circulation to your arms and legs; and the lungs constrict to prevent water from entering the respiratory system. In short, this reflex is essentially the physiological opposite of the fight-or-flight response.

Evoking your dive reflex in a time of distress can be life-changing. It can help you break out of panic mode and regulate yourself enough to think clearly about what action (if any) to take next.

So how do you evoke the dive reflex? Easy—hold your breath and submerge your face in cold water. There are no "best practice" guidelines on exactly how long to submerge or what exact temperature the water should be. You can simply fill a big bowl with cold water, submerge your face, and hold your breath for as long as you safely can. You might need to submerge a couple of times to get the relief you're seeking. You can also try this exercise with a soft ice pack. Simply tilt your head back, put the ice pack over your eyes and nose, and hold your breath.

> **Note:** Please ensure that your medical doctor signs off before you try this exercise. Slowing the heart rate is not safe for everyone, particularly those with heart conditions.

EXERCISE: Cold Plunging

In 2007, while I was on a trip to Russia with some university friends, we decided to visit a *banya*, or bath house. In a dark art nouveau–style building with a musty smell, we found our way to a room with a sauna, cold-plunge pool, and birch tree branches. We were amazed by the ease with which the banya-going ladies moved from gently slapping their limbs with the birch branches in the sauna to the freezing water of the plunge pool. I was not so graceful.

I have never responded well to being cold, and I thought that would be the last time I endured such an experience!

However, my tune has changed in recent years, as an expanding body of research (Knechtle et al., 2020) connects cold-water submersion to a variety of health benefits, from decreasing symptoms of anxiety and depression to improving mood, blood pressure, lipid and insulin metabolism, endocrine function, and immune responses. I've given the cold plunge another go and found it to be worth the momentary shock. I've also found it to be less shocking when I integrate deliberate breathing. In fact, some of the practice's benefits may arise from the breathwork it involves.

If you're interested in trying a cold plunge, consider what that might involve for you. You can absolutely try it at home. Turn the shower on its cold setting and set yourself a goal of standing in the cold water for three breaths, or maybe up to 10. You do not have to be under the cold flow for long! In fact, I would encourage you to start with just a few seconds and build your capacity through consistent practice. You can also practice intermittently—start with the cold water running down your face, neck, and chest, then turn on the warm water for a little reprieve before you turn around and let cold water flow down the back of your body.

You could also look at whether there are any cold-plunge facilities near where you live. They are becoming more common in gyms and spas, and often come with access to an infrared sauna. While I have not seen any birch branches on offer in the facilities near me, self-massage is a good alternative to support blood flow.

Note: Before trying this practice, make sure you get your physician's sign-off. In addition to the potential risk of slowing your heart rate, hypothermia can be a danger if you're in cold water for an extended period. Please also consider that there is currently a gender gap in research on the benefits of ice baths, and women should be mindful of how cold exposure interacts with their menstrual and hormonal cycles. Track how your body responds to cold-exposure exercises, and if something feels straining rather than soothing, that's a clue that it might not be the most effective exercise for you at this point. Our aim is always to ensure you're supporting your health rather than inadvertently disrupting it.

EXERCISE: Sauna

Cherished in many traditional cultures, sauna bathing has long offered practitioners a warm sanctuary that can provide transformative benefits for mind, body, and spirit (Peräsalo, 1988). Those benefits are now being unpacked by modern science (Davis-Cheshire et al., 2023). Along with providing a natural mood boost through the cascading benefits of an endorphin release that brings a sense of relaxation and mental clarity, regular sauna sessions may be helpful for high blood pressure, heart failure, headaches, and type 2 diabetes.

Emerging research also indicates infrared rays may support your body's natural healing process through detoxification.

> **Note:** While saunas are amazing if you're feeling depressed and are in a freeze state, some people find that entering a hot, enclosed space while in a state of panic is not particularly helpful for mind or body. My general recommendation is to use cold plunges when you're hyperaroused (agitated, anxious, panicked) and saunas when you're hypoaroused (lethargic, depressed, numb). You can always move back and forth between the two, depending on your inner experience.

EXERCISE: Dynamic Exercise

Just like a sauna gets your heart rate up, so too can dynamic exercise. In fact, exercise is well established as an anxiolytic and antidepressant (Rebar et al., 2015). The physiological changes associated with moving your body and getting your heart rate up can offer instantaneous stress relief (Bernstein & McNally, 2017). There are many forms of exercise that involve dynamic movement, so you can choose the activities that work best for you. Some ideas include walking, jogging, swimming, cycling, yoga, and dancing.

EXERCISE: Massage

Physical touch can support body awareness, enhance emotional regulation, and release emotional tension and distress held in the body. Massage helps tense muscles relax by increasing blood flow to areas of discomfort. In the process, endorphins are released, and the relaxation response is evoked with a slower heart rate, lower blood pressure, and reduced cortisol.

If massage isn't accessible to you at the moment you need it, or you simply don't want to be touched by others, self-massage is a great alternative. Find a quiet, comfortable space, put up your feet, and apply a skin-friendly oil (scented or unscented) to your skin with firm but gentle pressure in long strokes or circles. You could even use the palm of your hand and perform a massage for your arms, hands, neck, and calves—wherever it feels soothing to you.

EXERCISE: Rocking and Swaying

Rocking a baby is generally known to help them calm down and fall asleep. This soothing effect is thought to be due to the vestibular stimulation and is being explored as an anxiety management strategy (Kumar Goothy & McKeown, 2023). You can make use of this regulation strategy too. Whether you're sitting or standing, you might find that swaying from side to side in a gentle motion might help you evoke a relaxation response.

EXERCISE: Grounding Through Your Five Senses

This is a 5-4-3-2-1 exercise. As you follow along, you might like to hold up your hand with your fingers outstretched and close one finger with each category that you count down. Look around you and notice:

- Five things you can see
- Four things you can feel
- Three things you can hear
- Two things you can smell
- One thing you can taste

Repeat the exercise as necessary.

Anxiety Aids

When we are struggling with our mobility, we might benefit from a cane or walker. Similarly, when we are struggling to manage our stress or emotions, we can benefit from using objects designed to assist in self-soothing. Anxiety aids are wide-ranging, from masseuse hands to specially designed tools like acupressure mats and weighted blankets.

Acupressure Mat

This tool, which typically looks like a doormat covered in blunted plastic spikes, is designed for you to lie down on for an engrossing sensory experience. At first, your muscles will tighten up against the stimulation of the spikes, but since they cannot hold full tension for an extended period, they will eventually release the contraction and, along with it, any tension they were previously carrying. In addition, the sensory stimulation from the spikes shifts your attention from the thoughts, feelings, and other experiences unfolding in your awareness.

Weighted Blanket

Increasing research is demonstrating that the pressure experienced under these blankets can activate your relaxation response and trigger vagus nerve activity (Yu et al., 2024). They've even been found to reduce the perception of pain (Baumgartner et al., 2022) and improve sleep quality. Just be mindful that the weight of your blanket is appropriate for your body size; in addition, note that these blankets are not safe for small children to use.

Heating Bags

The evidence for heat bags, hot-water bottles, rice bags, and other warm, weighted options is developing. So far, they show promising results for both anxiety and pain relief (Kim et al., 2019). You can try them and see if they give you the warmth and comfort you might need to support relaxation, as well as pain relief.

Aromatherapy

Aromatherapy (using scents to evoke a therapeutic response) is backed by a developing body of research. Whether it is smelling an essential oil right out of the bottle or dabbing it on your wrists, a tissue, or another object that has meaning to you, you might find a sniff results in a stress reduction (Freeman et al., 2019). Different scents can evoke different feelings; some options that are often experienced as calming include lavender, chamomile, sandalwood, clary sage, and ylang-ylang. Be aware that some people experience irritation or allergic reactions to certain essential oils, and some oils are toxic to pets or harmful for pregnant individuals or those trying to conceive. Please check with your health care provider to determine which scents are best for your circumstances.

Time in Nature

It's well established that spending time in natural spaces decreases anxiety and improves mood (Bratman et al., 2019). Whether it's a visit to the beach, a hike in the forest, a walk in the park, a few minutes sitting on your back patio, or even cultivating a plant in your home, nature has a soothing effect (Deng & Deng, 2018). Getting outside on a regular basis is great for maintaining your mental and emotional health and can be immensely healing when you're overwhelmed. I recommend mixing in some extra sensory stimulation by taking off your shoes and feeling the sensation of your feet on the ground.

EXERCISE: Vagus Nerve Activations

Most activities that improve your mood and your health will enhance your vagal tone, and vice versa. But there are some specific exercises that focus on stimulating and releasing anxious tension in your neck area, where the vagus nerve is located. The pressure they apply to your vagus nerve triggers a relaxation reflex.

Try each of the following vagus nerve activations for two to three minutes, taking note of how you feel before and after. Use a scale where 10 is the highest level of distress and 0 is no distress, or you can simply reflect on your sense of your capacity to cope before and after.

- Sucking (you can use lollipops or lozenges, or drink from a straw that requires heavy suction)
- Chewing (e.g., carrots, cucumbers, apples, gum)
- Long gargling
- Longer exhales
- Controlled vocalization (e.g., singing, humming, chanting)

Along with being useful for self-soothing in times of distress, these exercises can enhance your vagal tone when practiced regularly, much like strengthening your muscles by lifting weights. Increasing your overall vagal tone will support you to move from a state of dysregulation to regulation more quickly.

EXERCISE: Vagal Release Sequence

While this exercise doesn't have the intensity needed for self-soothing when you're outside your window of tolerance, it is highly effective for daily vagal toning.

Assessment

Begin by assessing your neck's range of motion. Gently rotate your neck to the right, keeping your chin level, and stop at the point where you feel slight resistance, without causing strain or discomfort. Note any sensations of pain or strain. Return your neck to the center and then proceed to rotate it to the left, again noting any discomfort or limitations in movement.

Exercise

Find a comfortable position, either lying on your back or sitting with an upright spine aligned with your head. Interlace your fingers and place them firmly behind the back of your head, allowing yourself to feel the support against the back of your head.

Keep your head straight and in line with your spine. Moving only your eyes, turn your gaze to the right. You might use your right elbow to focus your gaze. Maintain this gaze for about 30 to 60 seconds until you notice signs of relaxation from your autonomic nervous system, such as a sigh, yawn, or swallow.

Return your eyes to the center. While still maintaining the interlaced fingers behind your head, shift your gaze to your left elbow until you experience a similar relaxation response.

Upon completing this exercise, release your hands from the back of your head and redo the assessment to gauge improvements in your neck's range of motion, strain, stiffness, or discomfort.

Mental Distraction

So far, we've focused mainly on body-based emotional regulation techniques. But we can't overlook the close connection between your body and your mind. When your body feels flooded with stress that results in hyper- or hypoarousal, distraction can support you by redirecting your mind. While there are plenty of cognitive strategies you can use, I'll introduce just two here:

- **The Alphabet Game:** Mentally list items or words that begin with each letter of the alphabet in sequence. Choose a category to work with (e.g., animals, countries, fruits and veggies, people's names), then start listing one example of that category that begins with each letter of the alphabet. For instance, if you've chosen fruits and veggies as your category, you can start with apple and move sequentially to zucchini. If needed, start back at "A" with a new category.
- **Serial 7s:** Start at 100 and subtract 7, then subtract 7 again, and again until you feel more regulated. I'll start you off: 100 . . . 93 . . . 86 . . .

Rituals to Resource Your Inner Being

In the same way survival is written into your cells, so too is a sense of your personal potential. However, you cannot be free to focus on your inherent drive for personal development until your basic needs are met. The well-known hierarchy of needs developed by Abraham Maslow (1943) shows how our human needs emerge from physical to personal.

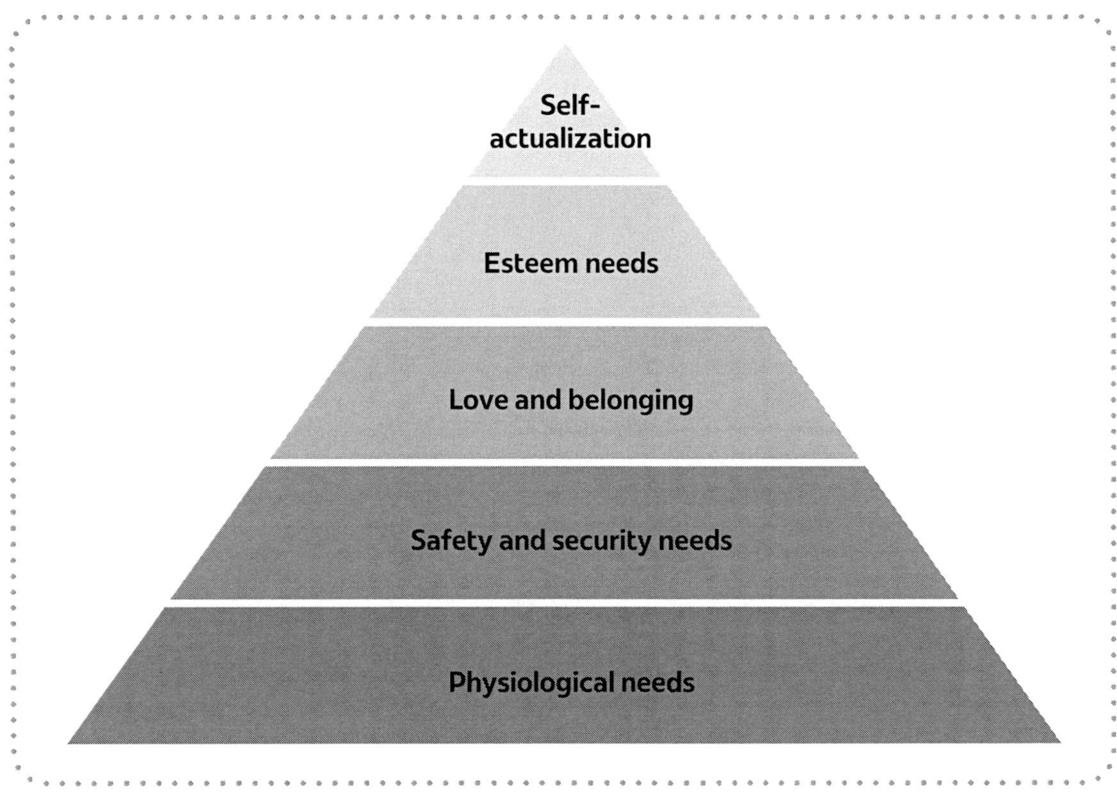

- **Physiological needs:** These are the fundamental requirements for human survival, including air, water, food, shelter, clothing, sleep, and reproduction.
- **Safety and security needs:** We also seek safety, stability, and predictability in life. This includes personal security, financial security, health, and safety from accidents, illness, and unexpected events.
- **Love and belonging:** This category involves the need for social belonging, affection, and love. People seek connections, friendships, intimacy, and acceptance within their family, friends, and other social groups.
- **Esteem needs:** This area includes feelings of accomplishment, recognition, respect, self-confidence, and independence. Esteem needs can be divided into two categories: esteem from yourself (self-respect, confidence) and esteem from others (recognition, reputation).
- **Self-actualization:** This is where you seek personal growth, fulfillment, and realizing your full potential. It involves the pursuit of personal growth, creativity, problem-solving, morality, and the desire to achieve your goals and dreams.

Maslow's original theory was that you could only move up the hierarchy by satisfying the needs within each level in order—for example, you would not be driven to focus on your social and emotional needs until your more basic physical and safety needs were met. This ranked hierarchy has not stood up to evolutionary biology and contemporary psychological theory, but Maslow's foundational concept remains true: When your needs are met, it is generally easier to show up in the way you want to. Most of us find it much harder to be kind, patient, and rational when we're not well-nourished, grounded, and energized.

With this in mind, we'll now focus on strategies for meeting your physical and psychological needs each day to ensure that you are well-resourced for the deeper healing work in the chapters ahead. The following exercises are focused on resources and routines to support you in navigating challenges inside your skin, so that you are better equipped to work on releasing the struggles of the past.

EXERCISE: Cocooning

I'm a massive fan of what I have jokingly called "pity parties." I've heard this same experience more gently termed "cocooning." Both terms refer to a conscious choice for quiet, comforting, solitary activities over going out and socializing.

My cocooning comes with proper party catering: nonalcoholic Shiraz, avocado spread on crackers, cut-up carrots, a small bag of gummy lollies, a heat pack, and a subtitled European drama. If I find myself distracted by doomscrolling on my phone, I pivot to sending check-in texts to elderly relatives and old friends before returning my attention to my cocoon.

It's worth noting that cocooning is about creating a refuge for yourself to balance overstimulation and general exhaustion during busy seasons in your life. If you find that this is no longer a balanced activity—for instance, if you are forgoing more and more social activities or meaningful pursuits in favor of vegging out alone—it is time to consider whether your comfort cocoon is instead becoming a pattern prison. So please, practice cocooning responsibly. Try to be honest with yourself about whether you are doing it as a way of balancing your busy schedule or as a way of hiding from problems that need to be faced.

EXERCISE: Cinematherapy

If your preferred method of cocooning includes watching a movie, that's a great opportunity to practice cinematherapy. Yep, this is a thing, though it's not just about watching a movie. The therapy part comes from mindfully enjoying a film that helps you connect to your values through plotlines that inspire you and characters you admire. It is an opportunity to slow down, to reflect on what really matters in your life and what traits you want to embody, and to train your brain to notice these opportunities in real life.

These moments of witnessing your potential reflected in someone or something else are known in therapy speak as *glimmers*. Just as your neuroceptive system picks up on environmental triggers that pull you into survival mode, seeing other people (even imaginary characters) show qualities and behaviors you admire can enhance belief in your own capacities. Glimmers might seem fleeting, but the more attention you give them, the more likely you will experience them.

I recommend doing this exercise when you find yourself in need of an activity to start settling and slowing into the evening. This exercise can be done on your own or with a friend or family member.

While you're watching the movie you've chosen, keep checking in on how you're feeling in your body and what emotions you're experiencing. Then, after watching the movie, you'll take a moment to reflect on the main character or another character that inspired you.

You can choose from the following list of films, but there are no doubt many more films out there that would serve the same purpose.

- *The Shawshank Redemption*: Themes of hope, resilience, and the human spirit overcoming adversity
- *Good Will Hunting*: Themes of trauma, personal growth, and the impact of therapy
- *Forrest Gump*: Themes of destiny, life's journey, and resilience
- *The Pursuit of Happyness*: Themes of perseverance, poverty, and the pursuit of success
- *Gandhi*: Themes of nonviolent resistance, social change, and leadership
- *The Green Mile*: Themes of compassion, injustice, and the human condition
- *The Perks of Being a Wallflower*: Themes of mental health, adolescence, and the importance of connection
- *Dead Poets Society*: Themes of heartfelt living, inspiration, and the power of education
- *A Beautiful Mind*: Themes of mental illness, genius, and perseverance

Reflection

What physical sensations did you notice? What emotions did you experience?

____

____

____

____

Describe the main characters in the movie. What are their personality traits, strengths, and weaknesses?

What emotions, thoughts, and bodily sensations do you think the characters experienced during pivotal moments in the film?

What does the main character consider as their primary challenge or problem in the story?

How did the main character attempt to resolve or deal with their challenges or conflicts?

What other strategies or solutions could the main character have used to address their challenges?

What was the main character's relationship with other characters in the movie?

____

____

____

____

Were there specific moments or traits of characters that you particularly liked or disliked? Why?

____

____

____

____

Reflect on what's important in your life, in light of having watched this movie.

____

____

____

____

EXERCISE: Safe Space Imagery

Did you know that our bodies respond to our imagination? We can use this power to our advantage when we are pushed outside our window of tolerance. When you feel anxious, depressed, overwhelmed, or stuck in an environment that doesn't feel nourishing, you can imagine yourself in a safe space and resource your sense of calm and connection. This multisensory process is the same practice that can enhance an athlete's physical performance by simply imagining themselves successfully performing that skill (Dello Iacono et al., 2021). It is theorized that this is because similar areas in the brain are involved whether something is happening in real life or being imagined. So, let's get you started cultivating a multisensory safe space. The more vivid your imagery is, the more impact it will have.

1. Find a quiet and comfortable space where you can relax without distractions.
2. Close your eyes or let them remain open in a soft gaze. Take a few deep breaths to center yourself.
3. Bring a safe and peaceful place to your mind. This could be a real location you know well or an entirely imaginary place. It could be a place in nature that you visited as a child or a cozy café in a city that you would like to go to. The main thing is that it be somewhere that lets you completely drop your guard.

4. Visualize the details of this safe space, engaging all your senses to make the imagery vivid.
5. Look around your safe place, first looking around you and then out toward the horizon. Picture all the colors and shapes of this place.
6. Feel your feet on the ground, or reach your hands out to connect with this safe place of yours. Imagine the tactile experience of this place—its temperature and textures.
7. Take a deep breath and imagine you are inhaling the smell of this safe place. Perhaps it is the scent of pine, ocean air, or fresh coffee—whatever fits.
8. Imagine what you would be able to taste in this place. Maybe there's a special food or drink here. Or you might notice a more familiar or neutral taste.
9. Now take note of the sounds unfolding in your safe space. Perhaps this includes lapping water, birdsong, or the sound of your footsteps as you explore your surroundings.
10. Go through all of your senses a couple of times and give yourself a few minutes to explore and enjoy this safe space. Notice if you can open to a felt sense of calm security. Hold where this sits in your body by gently placing your hands on this place of calm in your body.
11. When you're ready, gently bring your awareness back to the present moment and open your eyes.

Reflection

Where was your safe place?

____

____

____

What do you notice in your body after traveling there?

____

____

____

When and where can you commit to regular practice of this visualization?

____

____

____

EXERCISE: Self-Compassion Practice

Cultivating self-compassion offers yet another path to alleviating psychological distress and enhancing well-being. The more compassion we develop for ourselves, the more flexibility we have to make choices that harness our potential to heal and transform, both ourselves and the world around us.

This simple practice is based on the work of pioneering researcher Dr. Kristin Neff. It's particularly useful for times when you feel isolated, are emotionally depleted, or are struggling with feelings of inadequacy and self-criticism. While you're wired for compassion, offering it to yourself is often the most difficult, so please go slowly with this one.

1. Begin by finding a comfortable position, seated with your spine straight and hands on your lap or lying down with your hands on your abdomen.
2. Soften your gaze and take a few breaths to center yourself.
3. Bring to your mind a situation in your life that is causing you distress or discomfort. To introduce this exercise here, please don't choose the most distressing experience, but something that evokes mild discomfort.
4. Acknowledge and validate the difficulty of the situations and your feelings associated with them. If you notice judgment coming up, acknowledge that and come back to validating that, regardless of any judgment, you are suffering in this moment.
5. Connect to the humanity of this experience. There is no person on this planet who hasn't suffered and struggled. What you are experiencing now is a human experience; in this, you are not alone, even if it feels that way.
6. Place your hands on your heart or hold them together in a way that feels nurturing. Evoke the warmth you would send to a dear friend at a time of need, and offer this kindness to yourself. You might say, "May I be kind to myself in this moment" or "May I be gentle with myself."
7. Take a few moments to hold this warmth and kindness.
8. Consider whether there is any action you can take to embody a gesture of kindness to yourself. This can be anything that fits—perhaps making a difficult phone call that you know is important, sitting back down at your computer to finish a project, cooking a nutritious meal, or heading for a walk outdoors.

Reflection

How did you find this exercise? Note any challenges alongside any benefits.

____

____

How do you feel about this concept of connecting to suffering?

____

____

EXERCISE: Self-Holding

Gently holding yourself provides a felt sense of nurturing connection that helps ground your mental-emotional state. You can explore different techniques of self-holding—wrapping your arms around your body in a self-hug, putting your hands on your heart, or even holding your palms together in a hand-hug—and notice what feels most soothing for you, as well as what is most appropriate for different situations. (For instance, the hand-hug is particularly useful if you're in public and want a little discretion in your inner nurturance exercise.) You can practice self-holding on its own or at the same time as another exercise, such as deep breathing or visualization. It pairs especially well with the previous self-compassion practice.

EXERCISE: Compassionate Resourcing Figure

This is an exercise commonly used in compassion focused therapy (CFT), which was developed by Paul Gilbert. It involves receiving compassionate energy from a remembered or imagined figure. I personally have had many sleepless nights where I was utterly exhausted and yet buzzing in distress, overwhelmed by grief and shame—and what has carried me through has been to feel myself held in the arms of my grandmother. Loved unconditionally. Connected in the times when I've never felt so alone. Safe.

Clients of mine describe benefiting in the same way from visualizing being held in loving-kindness by essences ranging from Mother Mary to Drew Barrymore to their childhood dog. Follow the steps here to try it for yourself:

1. Bring to mind a figure or essence that embodies kindness, compassion, strength, and supportiveness.
2. Visualize this figure in detail, imagining their appearance, facial expressions, body language, and so on.
3. Let yourself be surrounded by feelings of warmth, love, and support flowing to you from your resource figure—knowing that they have an infinite capacity to hold you.
4. Cultivate a sense of connection and gratitude toward this resource figure, knowing that their presence is available to you whenever you need it.
5. When you're ready, gently open your eyes and carry these feelings of connection and support with you throughout your day. (Or perhaps you'll fall asleep in this state.)

Finding What Works for You

Most of the exercises we've discussed up to this point are intended to serve as an "emergency brake" in moments where you're pushed outside your window of tolerance. Finding ways to self-soothe in times of distress allows you to take a pause to re-regulate your feelings and step back from any unhelpful urges or problematic behavior. Once you've found relief, you'll be better able to implement the problem-solving and psychological flexibility skills we'll cover in the chapters to come.

When we are outside our window of tolerance, we don't think clearly. This makes us likely to default back to past patterns that don't serve us. Therefore, you need to increase familiarity with the techniques you seek to integrate into your toolbox. You do this by practicing—lots! Over time, you'll figure out the exercises that work best for you under different conditions. You also won't need to deliberately practice them anymore because they'll become your go-to response when you're feeling stressed.

To help you with this, I've created a chart that lists the self-soothing and resourcing exercises we've gone over and includes space for any notes or reflections about your experiences with them.

My Self-Soothing and Resourcing Practices

Put a tick beside the activities that you would like to practice so they are ready for you to use in times of distress. Next, note your reflections after practicing. Remember, if something doesn't work for you, it's okay to find a different practice that does.

❒ Belly breathing	
❒ Dive reflex	
❒ Cold plunging	
❒ Sauna	
❒ Dynamic exercise	
❒ Massage	

❐ Rocking and swaying	
❐ Grounding through the five senses	
❐ Anxiety aids	
❐ Vagus nerve activations	
❐ Vagal release sequence	
❐ Mental distraction	
❐ Cocooning	
❐ Cinematherapy	
❐ Safe space imagery	
❐ Self-compassion practice	
❐ Self-holding	
❐ Compassionate resourcing figure	

Once you've tried out the different options you were interested in, choose a few of the activities that you found helpful. Grab your calendar and schedule regular practice over the week ahead, ideally multiple times per week per activity. You may or may not need the activity when you've got it scheduled; that's not the point. The point is to increase your familiarity with each of these practices so that you remember to use them when you're feeling overwhelmed. As those exercises become second nature for you to use during times of activation, add or substitute new exercises in your scheduled practice.

You'll also find that different strategies work better for you at different times, depending on which nervous system state you're in and the resources (space, time, equipment, etc.) that are available to you in that moment. For example, when you're in a freeze state, it's unlikely that you'll feel up to going for a run, but maybe you can take a warm shower and gently massage your face until your thinking brain comes back online. On the other hand, if you're in a full fight-or-flight response, sitting with a heat pack could feel like torture, but it could be an excellent time to evoke your dive reflex, take a brisk walk coupled with a breathing exercise, or pop a sour candy in your mouth before you turn on your favorite playlist for a dance party.

Write down your plan here. Remember, try to choose a few different activities, including at least one option for each of the dysregulated nervous system states (fight or flight and freeze or fawn). Note which exercises you will practice this week and at what times.

Hey! Seriously, please do this planning part. We always think we will figure it out when the time comes, but the fact is that we generally don't. Give your future self a little grace by taking two minutes now to create a plan for the next time you need self-soothing.

____

____

____

____

____

____

Your Heartfelt Potential

Back in chapter 1, you spent some time envisioning your dream day. Hold on to that while we take a moment to cultivate a sense of connection to your human potential. This can help you to maintain hope and love in the direst of circumstances and empower you to act with compassion, courage, and selflessness, even when it would be much easier to follow the crowd or keep a distance from others. Being connected to your heartfelt potential will support you in keeping one hand on the top rung of your vagal ladder (which is to say, you are acting from a place of calm and clarity) before coming up with your action plan for taking care of the lower levels.

Closing Reflections

Where have you witnessed the innate human capacity for kindness and compassion?

Thinking of Maslow's hierarchy of needs, are there any lower-level needs you struggle meeting?

Do you think you need to work on expanding your window of tolerance? Why or why not?

What self-soothing exercises most appeal to you and why?

What resourcing exercises most appeal to you and why?

Takeaway Messages

- Compassion has an evolutionarily established role and is the antidote to the threat system.
- The "window of tolerance" describes your capacity to cope effectively. Stressors can bump you outside this window, into hyperarousal (fight or flight) or hypoarousal (freeze or fawn).
- Self-care and self-soothing are two different practices, with self-care expanding your window of tolerance and self-soothing bringing you back into your window when you're dysregulated.
- Practicing multiple self-soothing exercises regularly ensures that they're familiar during times of distress. Regular practice will also expand your window of tolerance.
- Imagination resourcing exercises can evoke a sense of safety, connection, and compassion through the power of visualization.

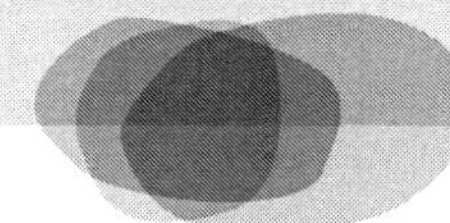

CHAPTER 4

Breathwork: Practices for Energizing and Soothing

"Sometimes the most important thing in a whole day is the rest we take between two deep breaths."

—Etty Hillesum, *An Interrupted Life*

With two kids in the back seat screaming at each other and the rush-hour traffic moving at a crawl, Sarah feels like her throat is starting to close up and her chest is binding her like a straitjacket. She's exhausted, having woken up in a flurry of midnight panic, and now, with her nervous system responding to her kids' constant bickering, she's worried that she's going to have a panic attack. Amazingly, though, Sarah doesn't slam her fist on the horn, nor does she yell back at her kids, "Will you just shut up?!" Instead, she seals her lips and inhales deeply through her nose. With the exhale, she opens her mouth, sticks out her tongue, and makes a loud "Haaaa!" like a lion's roar. And again, and again. Then Sarah starts humming, making a deep rumble like a bumblebee at the back of her throat. When her kids lose interest in their squabble and ask what she's doing, Sarah invites them to join her in making the buzzy bumblebee sound.

Once they all make it home, Sarah gets out of the car and puts her hand on her heart, taking a few deliberate breaths before she opens the doors for the kids. She gets them inside, sets them up with snacks and an audiobook to listen to, pops a frozen lasagna into the oven, and takes advantage of that lull to hop into the shower. More breathwork comes as she counts to 10 with the ice-cold water flowing over her chest. She cycles between hot and cold as she lengthens her spine and envisions Branwen, the Celtic goddess of empathy, compassion, and forgiveness. Sarah chose this compassionate resourcing figure to honor her Irish ancestry, something she has embraced more lately as a way of drawing strength from her epigenetic profile and cultural heritage.

As she dries off in the softest of her towels, she feels Branwen's energy. Sarah notices how her practice of self-compassion is creating an expansiveness in her heart, helping her to extend compassion to others as well. She gets into her coziest pajamas and heads back out to the kids, who have just started to bicker again.

"Hey!" says Sarah playfully. "It's pajama party time!"

Later that week, as Sarah recounts these events in her therapy session, she reflects on the difference her personal work has made. In the past, events like these would have triggered a panic attack that spiraled her into a disastrous evening. She admits that the breathwork practices, self-soothing strategies, and connection to her felt sense didn't make everything "magically" better—they definitely required commitment and effort. But, she says, "The breathing worked. It all worked. I got through it."

The Benefits of Breathing

Chances are that you've recently heard a lot about breathwork. From the seemingly superhuman feats of "the Ice Man" Wim Hoff to the bestselling book *Breath* by James Nestor, more folks are coming to understand that your breath has power—specifically, that effective use of the breath can change the automatic unfolding of various behavioral, neural, endocrine, and immune processes in the body (Hamasaki, 2020).

Just like Sarah, when your nervous system is stressed, you'll likely find yourself breathing faster than normal from your upper chest. This causes your stomach to feel tight and a sense of being on edge to develop. By consciously doing the opposite of that breathing pattern—that is, slowing the breath down and bringing the breath from your chest down to your belly—you can induce a process called *respiratory vagal nerve stimulation* (rVNS), which empowers your body to quickly shift back into a relaxed state after a trigger. (This process underpins the mind-body benefits that are found with practices like meditation, yoga, and tai chi.)

In short, breathing stimulates and tones the vagus nerve (Bordoni et al., 2018). And because your vagus nerve is the biggest nerve in your body and the primary nerve governing your rest-and-digest response, that means your breath holds the key to every other system in your body. So, while you cannot consciously slow your heart rate or improve your immune function, you can influence those functions through your breath. In fact, now that it has been brought to your attention, you're likely more aware of your breathing pattern and may even find yourself changing its flow. Let's try tracking where it is at right now.

EXERCISE: Marking Your Breath

Track how many breaths you take each minute. The easiest way to do this is to set a timer for 30 seconds and count how many breath cycles you have during that period (a breath cycle includes one inhale and one exhale). Then, multiply your result by two.

Write your number here: _____ breath cycles per minute

When relaxed, the average rate is about 12 to 18 breaths each minute. Taking more than 20 breaths in a minute is considered over-breathing.

Breathing in the Therapy Room

Cole sits in my office, his hair falling relaxed at shoulder length. However, Cole himself looks anything but relaxed. He perches on the edge of the lounge chair, the lower portion of his top teeth visible occasionally as he nibbles his lower lip. His right hand seems at first to be playing with his hair, but I'm aware that his fingertips are searching for the right strand to tug out at the root—an unconscious pattern that occupies his fidgety hands and provides a little stimulation and soothing, though it has the unfortunate side effect of producing some bald patches amid his wavy locks. I can see that Cole's chest is making quick and shallow movements up and down; he's breathing in his upper chest.

"I always feel on edge," Cole describes, looking down and defeated. I invite him to place one hand on his chest and the other on his abdomen and to notice which hands he feels moving. Cole only feels the hand on his chest moving; his abdomen is totally still.

I point out to Cole that this isn't a pattern conducive to a relaxed state. When we watch a baby breathe, we see their belly go up and down—their diaphragm contracts to allow the deepening of their breath. This is called *diaphragmatic breathing*. The thing is, it isn't natural to breathe diaphragmatically when you're under stress. Should you need to fight or flee, you need your abdomen engaged. This means the more time your body spends in fight or flight, the more natural chest breathing feels. Your diaphragm becomes conditioned into a restricted range and your abdominal muscles are always engaged. On top of this, you likely heard the term "suck it in" at some point in your formative years, urging you to keep your belly pulled in to conform to mainstream beauty standards. Such unhelpful societal pressure further tugs us away from healthy breathing. This means that diaphragmatic breathing sometimes needs to be relearned.

Cole and I take a few moments to practice drawing every breath down to the belly. Next, I point out that he's breathing open-mouthed. During a fight-or-flight response, you only breathe through your mouth because you need to get extra oxygen into your muscles. Your body doesn't care in that moment if the air has not yet been filtered through the hairs and mucus in your nose. Closing the mouth and drawing breath only through the nose further helps us in slowing down the breath and down-regulating the nervous system.

After practicing diaphragmatic breaths through the nose, we move to the third element—I guide Cole in slowing his exhale. When you are overwhelmed, it feels like you need more and more air, and can't wait for a full exhalation to draw another breath. However, increasing oxygen levels will only intensify your body-based feelings of panic. Your exhale balances oxygen and carbon dioxide levels, inducing relaxation.

Cole leans back into the chair and a softness crosses his face, while his shoulders relax down away from his ears. His hands reach to gently pick up the glass of water on the coffee table as he reflects, "You know, I'd like to work on breathing exercises each day. I want to support my body in remembering its natural breathing pattern."

Designing Your Practice

Along with self-regulating or soothing in times of distress, breathing exercises can be done every day to cultivate your vagal tone. However, different breathing practices are designed to elicit different states in your body and mind. You can breathe to increase energy, to enhance attention, or to calm and soothe yourself by eliciting the relaxation response, as in the session with Cole. The more you practice these breathing exercises, the more familiarity you'll gain with how they impact your mind and body.

How will you know what type of breathing practice you need? Attuning to your felt sense is a good place to start. If you're feeling on edge, like Cole was, you may want to use a practice that helps you down-regulate. If you're feeling flat and lethargic, you probably want a dynamic one that gives you a little gusto for your day.

It's important to note that starting with a practice that presents too much of a step-down for your system can be counterproductive. When your body is in the hyperarousal zone, an intense breathing practice will bring you online and harness your energy, which you can then down-regulate with graded steps. This is why Sarah started with a lion's roar when she was in the car and worked her way down to slower, deeper breathing in the shower. It's the same in the other direction. If you're feeling hypoaroused, start with a gentle breathing exercise and build up to a more dynamic practice.

In the pages that follow, we'll work through a variety of breathing exercises from the most soothing and simple to the more dynamic and complex.

Triple S for Soothing

Remember how Cole and Sarah both worked to create a breathing pattern that was soothing by moving toward a slower breathing into their stomach areas? This is part of the "triple S" approach for your soothing breaths: slow, stomach, and small. I like to think of it as a general principle you can use to check in on your breathing in daily life. It is also the starting point for the exercises you'll be moving into. Here are the triple S principles in more detail:

- Breathe slightly **slower** than might feel normal for you (but not so slow that it creates discomfort).
- Bring the breath from your chest down into your **stomach**.
- Practice slightly **smaller** breaths than you might feel drawn to (again, without creating discomfort).

EXERCISE: Resonate Breathing

Your heart rate increases when you inhale and slows with the exhale. Biofeedback studies indicate that an average of six breaths a minute improves heart rate variability, that marker of vagal tone. Interestingly, many prayers, chants, hymns, and poetry rhythms seem to create the same frequency of breaths per minute. It's like many cultures and communities have been finding their way to evoking healing through breathwork. Perhaps you can find a sense of connection to all the others who have come before as you evoke the resonate frequency. Follow these steps:

1. Sit in a comfortable position. Place one hand on your chest and the other on your upper abdomen.
2. Inhale through your nose to a count of 5, drawing the breath down toward your abdomen.
3. Hold for a count or two.
4. As you exhale to another count of 5, slowly draw your abdomen back in, allowing the diaphragm to rise.
5. Repeat this cycle 5 to 10 times (which means you take 6 breaths every minute).
6. As this becomes more easeful, you can try extending the duration of your exhale so it is longer than the inhale (like you did with the belly breathing exercise in chapter 3).

EXERCISE: Square Breathing

This exercise, which is sometimes called "box breathing," is incredibly common in therapy rooms. The visual focus of the square can be particularly helpful for folks new to breathing exercises, and like all the deep breathing exercises, it's a useful practice for calming your nervous system and reducing stress.

1. Sit in a comfortable position.
2. Imagine a square shape, or look at the image provided. You may find it helpful to slowly trace the sides of the square as you complete the following steps.
3. Inhale for a count of 4 (as you trace the first side of the square).
4. Hold for a count of 4 (and trace the next side).
5. Exhale for a count of 4 (and trace the next side).
6. Hold for a count of 4 (and trace the final side of the square).
7. Repeat the cycle 4 to 5 times.

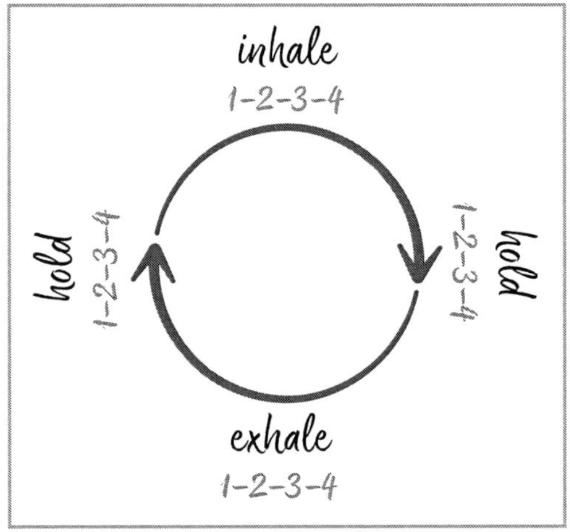

EXERCISE: Energy-Transfer Breath

Building on your belly breathing practices, we'll begin to integrate more felt-sense awareness and healing visualization with this practice. It will support you in noticing and moving areas of felt-sense openness and vibrancy into areas of tension and stuckness. This is a great exercise for when you are feeling very anxious and experiencing bodily tension, or when you're feeling flat and your body feels heavy and listless.

1. Sit in a comfortable position.
2. Come to a relaxed belly breathing pattern.
3. While breathing, scan your body, noticing areas that are more tense and tight as well as those that are more relaxed and open.
4. Turn your attention to one or more of the relaxed areas and notice what they are like. You might associate a color, scent, or texture with these relaxed areas of the body.
5. Visualize gently drawing the energy and openness from these relaxed areas and guiding it to flow into the tight areas of your body.
6. Imagine you are breathing a sense of softening and release from the open areas into the tense areas. Inhale and move the openness to the area of tension, and with the exhale release the tension.

EXERCISE: Alternate-Nostril Breathing (Nadi Shodhana)

Derived from traditional Indian medicine, alternate-nostril breathing involves breathing through one nostril at a time, alternating between the left and right. A finger is used to close off the other nostril. Arousal, attention, and focus is bolstered through this practice, alongside heart rate variability. It also provides bilateral stimulation, which you'll learn about in chapter 11.

1. Sit in a comfortable position.
2. You will be using your thumb and ring finger to alternate between closing nostril sides; you can let your index and middle fingers rest between your eyebrows.
3. Close the left nostril and inhale through the right nostril.
4. Close the right nostril, open the left nostril, and exhale.
5. Inhale through the left nostril.
6. Close the left nostril, open the right nostril, and exhale.
7. Repeat this cycle 5 to 10 times.

EXERCISE: Right-Nostril Breathing (Surya Bhedana)

This practice is thought to energize and warm your body. In fact, the word *surya* translates to sun. In the same way that sauna bathing can be an effective first stage in self-soothing when you're feeling depressed or numb, you might consider this practice at times when your energy is low.

1. Sit in a comfortable position.
2. Use your thumb or another finger to close your left nostril.
3. Inhale and exhale through your right nostril.
4. Repeat this cycle 5 to 10 times.

EXERCISE: Left-Nostril Breathing (Chandra Bhedana)

Chandra translates to "moon," making this practice a balance to the warm sun of the previous practice. In the same way that moving to a cold shower is a good first stage for self-soothing when you're feeling overstimulated or anxious, you might consider this practice at times when your energy is higher.

1. Sit in a comfortable position.
2. Use your thumb or another finger to close your right nostril.
3. Inhale and exhale through your left nostril.
4. Repeat this cycle 5 to 10 times.

EXERCISE: Bee-Humming Breathing

Remember how we learned in chapter 3 that humming is good for vagal tone? I suspect you'll feel it as you practice this exercise, especially if you're feeling a little anxious and need soothing. In fact, it has been found to lower blood pressure and heart rate and even enhance your brain function. All of this is thought to be due to your parasympathetic nervous system coming online.

1. Sit in a comfortable position.
2. Place your lips together, but keep your teeth apart.
3. Inhale through your nose.
4. Make a humming "mmmmhm" sound as you exhale through your nose. You should feel a gentle vibration in your lower throat and hear the humming sound as you exhale. Allow the exhale to go through to its natural conclusion.

5. If you feel comfortable increasing the sensory sound, you may close off your ears and eyes by gently placing your thumbs in your ears and using your fingers to gently close your eyes.
6. Repeat. Start with five cycles, and then build up the duration of your practice.

Paired Breathing Exercises

The following exercises pair breathing with other body movements, such as moving the arms and torso. Paired breathing is common in yoga practice, particularly flow yoga (so called because it creates a continuous flow of breath and movement). Like other forms of breathwork, different paired breathing exercises offer different benefits, such as calming or energizing the body.

EXERCISE: Ocean Breathing (Ujjayi Pranayama)

This dynamic and energizing practice constricts and slows the breath so that it may be paired with flow movements.

1. Sit in a comfortable position, or practice during your yoga flow or while doing other kinds of fluid movements and stretches that feel good to you.
2. Constricting your throat and making a "ha" sound, draw the air in and out through your nose as if you are fogging up a window. (You might practice first with your mouth open, actually making fog on a window or mirror, then practice closing your mouth and using your nose.)
3. Pair the inhale and exhale with your body movements in a way that feels supportive for you.

EXERCISE: Arms of Joy

This practice allows you to utilize simple visual feedback about the rhythm of your breath.

1. Sit in a comfortable position.
2. Reach your arms into a circle in front of you, like you were going to hug a tree.
3. As you inhale, draw your hands in toward your chest.
4. As you exhale, push your hands back out, away from your body.
5. Use the visual feedback of your arm speed to make gentle adjustments to your breathing rate.
6. You may like to visualize healing light coming to your heart with the inhale, and unhelpful energy being released with the exhale. You may also pair a word or mantra with this practice, such as "om" or "I breathe in serenity and breathe out tension."

EXERCISE: Paired Breathing Using Bird Wings

This practice allows you to utilize simple visual feedback about the rhythm of your breath.

> **Note:** Please do not engage in this practice if you have any concerns that your shoulder joint has been injured or gives you any feedback that this movement is not safe. We are *not* taking a "no pain, no gain" approach, and there are other exercises that can be substituted.

1. Sit in a comfortable position with your arms by your sides.
2. As you inhale, reach your arms upward.
3. As you exhale, float your arms back down to your sides.
4. Use the visual feedback of your arm speed to make gentle adjustments to your breathing rate.
5. You may also like to pair a word or mantra with this practice.

EXERCISE: Breath of Fire

This dynamic breathing exercise focuses on cultivating a sense of heat or power in the center of your body. It is one that you should avoid if you are pregnant. It is also advisable to take a break if you get dizzy—this could be a sign that the inhale and exhale are not balancing effectively. Try slowing down in this case, then build back up as it feels more easeful.

1. Sit in a comfortable position—perhaps on a chair, placing your arms on your thighs so that you can use your arms to maintain your balance. Or, if you are able to, you could kneel on the ground, sitting on your heels you can place your hands forward on your knees.
2. You will focus on a forceful exhale through your mouth with a "ha" sound. The inhale will take place automatically through your nose.
3. Relax your belly entirely as you exhale, then contract it back quickly (like you're snapping it in) as you make the "ha" sound exhaling through your mouth. Do this rapidly, with about one exhale every second: "Ha! Ha! Ha!"
4. Try to start with 15 cycles (15 exhales), building up to 30 over time.

EXERCISE: Breath of Joy

This is another incredibly energizing breathing practice you can pop into the morning or in the middle of your day when you need an energy lift. It pairs your breath with the motion of swinging your arms and forward folding. This is a very dynamic exercise; you can build up to it by practicing the arms of joy and breath of fire exercises, which involve similar elements. Once these exercises are more familiar, you can start working on the breath of joy. Start slowly and increase your speed as it becomes more familiar to you with practice.

Note: If you have low blood pressure or struggle with quick postural shifts (moving from being upright to a forward fold), check with your medical doctor about how to practice this exercise safely or how to modify it as needed.

1. Stand with your feet slightly wider than your hips, keeping your knees soft.
2. With your arms at your sides, exhale completely.
3. The next few steps involve a multi-part inhale, so pace yourself accordingly. First, inhale with your lower belly while raising your arms, palms up, forward in front of you until they are about parallel with your shoulders.
4. Let your arms slide back down slightly and inhale with your middle belly while moving your arms up and outward, opening your chest and reaching out to either side of you, your body forming a "T" shape.
5. Let your arms relax back down a bit and inhale with your chest while bringing your arms forward and lifting them up toward the sky, until they are fully extended above you.
6. Exhale with a "ha" sound (breath of fire) as you fold forward at the waist with your knees bent, swinging your arms back down beside and behind you like they're completing a circle.
7. Repeat three times as you increase your familiarity with this practice. Remember, you can slow it down or speed it up depending on what is going to be most helpful to you in the moment.

Integrating Breathwork with Other Activities

You can be creative with how you practice paired breathing. It doesn't have to be limited to a formal yoga practice—you can also pair your breath with your footsteps when walking in nature, with gentle body movements as you sit in the sauna or take an ice bath, or even with your hand movements while washing the dishes. No matter what you do, the intention is to let your breath lead your movement. I would encourage you to include a few different exercises in your weekly routine. That way, they will be familiar when you need them.

Take a moment to write down your design for integrating a breathwork practice into your daily life.

I hope that you now feel like you have more clarity in how you can use your breath for both self-soothing (up-regulating and down-regulating your nervous system) and for regular self-care. In the next chapter, we'll explore other healing lifestyle habits.

Closing Reflections

What breathing exercises do you find most nourishing?

When in your daily life do you find you have the most relaxed breathing?

Which breathing exercises do you find work well to down-regulate you?

____

____

____

____

Which breathing exercises do you find work well to up-regulate you?

____

____

____

____

How will you track your breathing throughout the day to cultivate awareness of your nervous system states?

____

____

____

____

Is there a way you can integrate a sense of sacredness to your breathing practice?

____

____

____

____

Takeaway Messages

- Your breath is the only autonomic (unconscious) body function that you can bring under conscious control, offering incredible possibilities for self-regulation.
- Breathwork exercises can down-regulate your nervous system when you are anxious and up-regulate it when you are feeling down.
- In a state of relaxation, your body is designed to do belly breathing through the nose with an extended exhale: a low, slow flow.
- Breathwork can be practiced every day for vagal tone and nervous system well-being, and it can be used as a self-soothing strategy in times of distress.

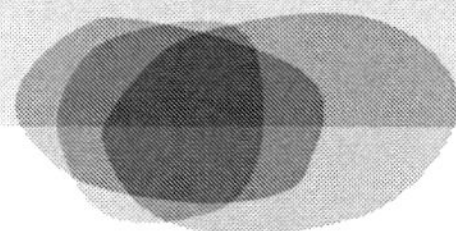

CHAPTER 5

Sustainable Self-Care in Your Lifestyle: Holistic Health

"Self-care is not a waste of time. Self-care makes your use of time more sustainable."

–Jackie Viramontez

Evie walked into my office with downcast eyes that quickly teared up when I asked her what had brought her in for a session. She pulled her knees up to her chest like she was trying to melt into the couch and described being weighed down by a persistent low mood and relentless lethargy. Her university studies had become progressively more daunting, with essays and assignments always looming. While Evie was desperate to tackle her assignments, concentration eluded her and she found herself in a cycle of procrastination. This said, Evie did manage to meet deadlines by sheer willpower, but she tended to find her flow only in the middle of the night, leaving her utterly drained afterward.

"Evie," I said, "when was your last blood test done?" This is a standard question asked by therapists, alongside questions about diet, exercise, sleep, energy, and the like. But for Evie, it came as a surprise.

"Why does that matter?" she asked.

I explained that treating organic causes of mood disturbances is important for mental health treatment to be effective. Without understanding and treating any possible biological foundations for our issues, it is hard to benefit from therapy.

Evie said that it had been years since she had checked her levels. That very afternoon, she visited her doctor, who ordered a comprehensive panel of tests. The results revealed deficiencies in vitamin D, B12, and iron—all of which shed light on her persistent fatigue and low mood.

With her doctor's advice, Evie wasted no time in organizing a B12 shot at the pharmacy and investing in high-quality supplements. Between these efforts and her new habit of heading out into the sunshine first thing each morning (a strategy we had discussed to support her in resetting her circadian rhythm), she found that her sleep and wake cycle started to balance.

When Evie returned to my office two weeks later, her eyes sparkled with tears again—not of despair this time, but of joy and relief. "I wake up feeling refreshed, and my focus has returned to my studies. I even took the leap to return to my favorite dance studio. I finally feel like myself again," she shared, her voice filled with newfound optimism. Then she added, a tinge of regret evident in her voice, "Why didn't I get to this sooner?"

This is the irony, right? When we're caught up in the whirlwind of a busy lifestyle, it's easy to overlook the profound impact of basic health care. But now, with her physical well-being restored, Evie had the capacity to start placing a healthy lifestyle at the top of her priority list. Hers was a lesson we can all benefit from: a small investment in physical well-being can offer immense returns in mental clarity, vitality, and resources for the healing journey ahead.

I'm not guaranteeing that your journey will be like Evie's; it is incredibly rare that the "fix" for our mental health issues is that simple. However, taking care of your basic health needs is a foundational part of self-care, one of the many lifestyle medicine practices we will focus on in the chapter ahead. First, we'll resource your journey forward by reflecting on the positive events in your life to this point.

EXERCISE: Positive Events Timeline

Creating a timeline of delightful, happy, and love-filled memories can be a powerful exercise for cultivating positive emotions. The more time we spend connecting to positive emotions, the stronger our vagus nerve becomes, and the more quickly we can move from dysregulation back to our social engagement system.

Start by setting your intention to connect with your positive emotional state and cultivate inner resilience. Then grab a writing utensil and prepare to create a timeline of your positive memories. You can use the space provided or a separate piece of paper.

1. Reflect on the moments in your life that have evoked a sense of joy, connection, and play. Consider various aspects of your life, such as family, friendships, other relationships, accomplishments, hobbies, and travel experiences.
2. Choose two or three specific events or experiences that are particularly delightful to you and describe them in detail. Include details such as the date or age when the event occurred, the location, the people involved, and why the moment was special to you.
3. Notice how you feel in your body in the presence of these memories and write this down as well. Do your muscles feel relaxed? How is your breath flowing? What is the temperature of your skin and body? Do you feel a state of calm, pleasure, or the like? How able do you feel to connect with your higher self? With others?
4. If an image or icon represents these moments, you might collect it and keep it near as a path to connect with this felt sense of positive emotions.

Positive Events:

Birth

Self-Care

As mentioned back in chapter 3, self-care and self-soothing can overlap greatly in terms of practices. The main difference is that self-soothing is an "emergency brake" measure for when you're overwhelmed or overstimulated, while self-care is a preventive strategy integrated into your daily or weekly routine. The idea is that nurturing your needs on a regular basis makes you less likely to experience the overwhelm that calls for self-soothing strategies. This is why I always check in with clients about how much they've slept, what they do for physical activity, what their diet is like, when they last had their bloodwork done, who their close friends are, and what activities they do to relax. In short, your lifestyle itself can be the therapy you need! This isn't to say that psychotherapy and medication don't have something to contribute, but when you can engage in everyday activities that help you feel shiny and sharp, without side effects, why wouldn't you consider it?

Lifestyle Habits

Your lifestyle strongly influences your life expectancy and your risk of illnesses, such as cardiovascular diseases, diabetes, and cancer. While having a healthy and balanced lifestyle doesn't mean you won't ever get sick, it usually does mean that your body and mind are more resilient and you are better able to engage in any medical treatments and psychological strategies you need to get well.

There are nine evidence-based practices that have come to be termed *therapeutic lifestyle habits* (Walsh, 2011), thanks to their efficacy in optimizing cognitive function, emotional well-being, and general health. As you might have guessed, adequate sleep, proper nutrition, and regular exercise are three of the most essential practices. In fact, physical activity is the most effective anxiolytic and antidepressant out there.

Of course, I'm sure you already know that sleeping well, eating well, and moving your body are important. The challenge tends to be developing or continuing these habits when we are overwhelmed and time-poor. So, in this chapter, we'll look at simple ways to strategically integrate them into your life. In addition, we'll look at how you can develop the other therapeutic lifestyle habits—enjoying time in nature, supportive relationships, recreation, stress management, spirituality, and contributing to your community—so you can enjoy their benefits as well.

Along with the things you begin doing, the things that you stop doing can support your physical and mental health—namely, sitting for extended times, smoking, and drinking alcohol. This, of course, forces us to confront the major challenge with therapeutic lifestyle practices: you must make changes, some of which you might not feel motivated for. This is where we need to start the conversation. Why would you want to do something you don't want to do?

The answer is the trade-off: the lifestyle practice for the vitality. Things like moving your body a little more, eating an apple before you head out to an indulgent lunch, and setting an alarm to get into bed on time may be tricky today, but tomorrow, you may find the same actions a little bit easier. As you start to feel a little more vibrant in your being, day by day, these activities become easier to practice.

If you need more motivation, consider that these activities will make you well-resourced for the more dynamic somatic healing practices ahead in this book. In fact, you might find you don't actually have as much to heal once your lifestyle is nurturing you with supportive habits.

The Two-Minute Rule

Motivation is an unreliable fairy godmother—even if you feel it now, you cannot plan on it always being present. It tends to desert us right when we're on the brink of diving into a new habit. That old *I can't do it* thought creeps in, persuading us that we're somehow broken because this thing seems to be easy for everyone else.

That's why, with any new health habit you're going to be integrating into your life, I recommend starting by practicing it for just two minutes. For most folks, even if they lack motivation or feel overwhelmed by the prospect of big changes, their mind is okay with taking two minutes for something new. (If even two minutes feels like too much, that's fine—start with one minute.) The point is to have a defined starting point that will support action and limit procrastination. Once you can get your mind to get through two minutes of your new habit, it becomes easier to automate that practice so that it becomes a habit, not requiring a sense of effort or even motivation. Then you might find yourself doing three minutes, four minutes, ten minutes . . . and so on.

The "Two by Two" Rule

Along with the two-minute rule, I advise clients to follow a two-day rule: that is, you never miss practicing your habit for more than two days in a row. If you set a goal that you're going to do something every single day, your new rhythm will inevitably be interrupted when life happens. In those moments, your mind may default to all-or-nothing thinking, deciding that you might as well just stop this habit altogether. It's a good practice to accept in advance that you'll likely miss a day or two, so that when it happens, you can pick yourself up, dust yourself off, and start again. Because life is full of slips, stumbles, and falls. That is the only way to learn and grow. Imagine if we gave up our efforts to walk the first time we fell on our bottoms. Not a single one of us would be walking now.

As a kid, I remember deliberately not brushing my teeth on the nights my parents didn't check in. (It seems ridiculous now, until I remember how getting my own kids to brush their teeth takes the effort of climbing a small mountain.) Nevertheless, by the time I was a young adult living on my own, I would stumble home in a wild state, totally exhausted, yet I would never go to bed without brushing my teeth. Your hard-won habits will eventually stick—just give them time.

Therapeutic Lifestyle Habit #1: Exercise

There is nothing so well established in the health science space as the fact that regular exercise improves both physical and emotional health and enhances your cognitive function, making you more efficient at the things you do (Bernstein & McNally, 2017; Mahalakshmi et al., 2020; Rebar et al., 2015). In terms of your mental health, it is one of the most effective anxiolytics and antidepressants out there, not to mention one of the cheapest!

The mental benefits of exercise are so well established that a colleague of mine won't treat clients who don't complete a certain amount of physical activity each week. I get this approach, but I find it to be a bit simplistic. After all, when we're not feeling well it is really hard to start a new activity, particularly one like exercise that often feels daunting. In my view, most of the benefit from this therapeutic lifestyle habit comes from just getting off the couch for a moment, even if it's just to walk to the mailbox at the end of your driveway. Perhaps over time, you'll want to keep moving past the mailbox and work your way up to, say, 15 to 20 minutes of vigorous movement each week. This alone will decrease your mortality risk by 16 to 20 percent, and the benefits grow with every minute, with your optimal dose being about one hour each week (Ahmadi et al., 2022). Remember, this is per week, not per day! Once you get your heart rate up with some moderate physical activity, you'll likely experience an improvement in your mood. From psychological changes, such as feeling more positive about yourself or being more distracted from a negative mood, to neurophysiological changes like an increased body temperature and changes in your brain chemicals and even your brain structure, we know that moving your body impacts multiple systems that offer that feel-good effect (Chan et al., 2019).

If you think for a moment, you might find that you're already regularly practicing an activity that qualifies as physical exercise. For instance, Sarah reported that she didn't exercise at all—she took an occasional weekend hike with her family, but nothing on a regular basis. She was overwhelmed by the idea of trying to add something else into her already full day, and devastated that it felt so hard to do something for her health. However, when we got into the nitty-gritty of her daily routine, we found that whenever she took private calls at work, she would head out of the office and walk while she talked. It turned out that she was getting an average of 15 to 20 minutes of movement each day this way. Needless to say, she was delighted by this discovery!

Success inevitably builds motivation. Sarah decided to maximize this embedded movement in her day by keeping a pair of slip-on sneakers in a drawer of her desk. Whenever she went to take a phone call, she traded her loafers for the quick-moving kicks, popped in her headphones, and deliberately kept a brisk pace while she walked and talked.

Here are some more "action seeds"—small steps you can take to create or build on your existing therapeutic lifestyle habits—related to exercise. You can also add your own ideas to the list.

Action Seeds

- Park your car farther away from your destination or get off one stop earlier when taking public transit and walk the rest of the way.
- Take your morning or afternoon break at a coffee shop that you can walk or ride a bike to.
- Periodically take breaks for exercises or chores that involve moving and lifting.
- Take the stairs rather than an elevator.
- Other: ____

Therapeutic Lifestyle Habit #2: Nutrition and Diet

Nutritional psychiatry is a growing discipline devoted to exploring how nutrient intake influences our mental health. From supplements to the foods we eat, there is an unequivocal link between what we put in our bodies and how we feel in our minds. But, as the story about Evie and her blood panel shows, we sometimes forget what a profound impact nutrition has on our mental health. Then, when we're struggling, it becomes another burden on our ever-growing to-do list, one that typically ends up falling off the list altogether.

Eating a balanced diet isn't just an ideal; it's vital for both your physical and mental well-being. This means ensuring you're eating enough vegetables, legumes, fruit, and healthy grains, and supplementing if your dietary needs or preferences leave out any important nutrients. (For instance, I follow a vegan diet, and I've been advised that it is very important to supplement my B12 intake. I get mine through the fatty acid omega-3, which is found in plant fats such as walnuts and soy, as well as DHA from seaweed-based supplements.)

Remember that just because someone else eats a certain way and takes specific supplements doesn't mean it will be the most effective for you. Your existing health conditions, ancestry, lifestyle, and a myriad of other factors will influence what your body needs at any given time. So please be gentle with yourself, and allow yourself the time to explore and adjust the different foods and supplements you take into your body. It is also worth talking to your doctor or making an appointment with a dietitian.

Action Seeds

- Eat an apple *before* lunch to ensure you're getting some plant-based nutrition and are not in starving mode when you make your choices about what to put on your plate.
- Cut up fruit and veggies right after you buy them to make healthy snacking a little easier.
- Develop two signature go-to meals that are delicious and nutritious, take less than five minutes to prep, and include ingredients that can be stored in your freezer or pantry. Then stock up!
- If you've been recommended daily supplements by a health practitioner, set a reminder in your phone so you don't forget to take them.
- Other: ______________________________

Therapeutic Lifestyle Habit #3: Time in Nature

From decreasing your heart rate and blood pressure to increasing your feel-good hormones and improving your cognitive functioning and attention, spending time in nature—such as around water or in parks and forests—reduces stress and improves your mood (Bratman et al., 2019; Deng & Deng, 2018). You can also integrate other activities into your nature time, perhaps taking your lunch to a park bench, adding hikes and beach walks to your exercise routine, or throwing down a blanket to catch up with friends over a picnic.

You can also bring nature into your home and office. From having an image of a natural scene on your wall (or your screen saver) to cultivating a nursery of houseplants, research shows that even these interior efforts have positive effects (Deng & Deng, 2018).

Action Seeds

- Eat meals outdoors.
- Walk to nearby parks.
- Start a collection of potted plants inside your home.
- Plan to head to a forest or beach once a week.
- Other: ______________________________

Therapeutic Lifestyle Habit #4: Relationships

There is nothing more important for your well-being than meaningful and supportive relationships. They improve physical health, enhance your life quality and resilience, and cultivate a sense of joy. This is even the case in the therapy room, where the biggest predictor of success is not the therapist's credentials or the type of therapy, but the therapeutic relationship. This mammalian need for connection and compassion really is a need, because we are a social species. This is why it is incredibly important to invest in being socially connected to family, friends, or your community. When you have a tough day, your nervous system needs to connect with supportive people, share your distress, and find capacity and perspective.

You also have a need for friends that you can share joy with. Honestly, sometimes it is harder to find these people than those you can call in moments of distress. But these positively oriented relationships are indeed vital. Relationships where the emotional connection is all based on shared pain and suffering can have a negative impact on your mental health. You need people who will also celebrate the good things that happen in your life.

EXERCISE: Relationship Map

Make a list of the people you feel close to and consider which ones are supportive, and in which ways. Because the fact is, not all your relationships need to serve the same purpose, and you don't have one person to meet all your needs. For example, among your friends, you might have some deep and meaningful friends, other friends you meet only for certain purposes (like hiking, crafting, or parties), workplace friends, long-term friends who feel more like siblings, and so on. Which relationships do you want to invest in and strengthen?

If you map out your relationships and realize there are gaps, such as not having someone you can ring up to spontaneously catch a movie or someone who will listen to you when you're angry or sad after a tough day, you may want to focus more on building new relationships than strengthening existing ones. And please, particularly invest in relationships where you can share both joys and sorrows, where you can be seen and loved for who you are.

Take a moment now and draw out your close relationships. You might organize them into groups, such as family members, work colleagues, school friends, and so on. There might be some individuals who count within multiple groups, and there might be "groups" with only one person. For instance, for a long time, I had a friend that I only saw when we were rock climbing—it was always just the two of us, and it was the only activity we did together. She wasn't the person I would call when I wanted to grab a coffee and have a deep and meaningful conversation, which isn't to say I couldn't have. In fact, if I had drawn a relationship map for myself at the time, I might have considered investing more in that relationship. This is exactly the point of this exercise! Go ahead and draw your map in the space on the next page.

One challenge to this lifestyle habit is that not all relationships are equally nourishing. While healthy, supportive, and attuned relationships cultivate your well-being, unhealthy ones are draining and dysregulating. Often people say to me, "I'm in therapy because the people around me are not." In other words, they feel they are being negatively impacted by the unhealthy patterns being lived out by the important people in their lives.

Look back at the relationship map you created. Are most of these relationships nourishing, mutually supportive, and safe? If you have a pattern of struggling in relationships, or seem to mainly "attract" people into your life who are negative or dysregulating, it may be time to invest in healing your attachment wounds—that is, unhealthy relationship patterns that you learned in early childhood environments or through important relationships that unfolded throughout your life.

Your attachment system is characterized by the dimensions of both anxiety in relationships and avoidance of relationships. I think it's helpful to picture it as an axis, as in the following image (based on the work of Bartholomew & Horowitz, 1991).

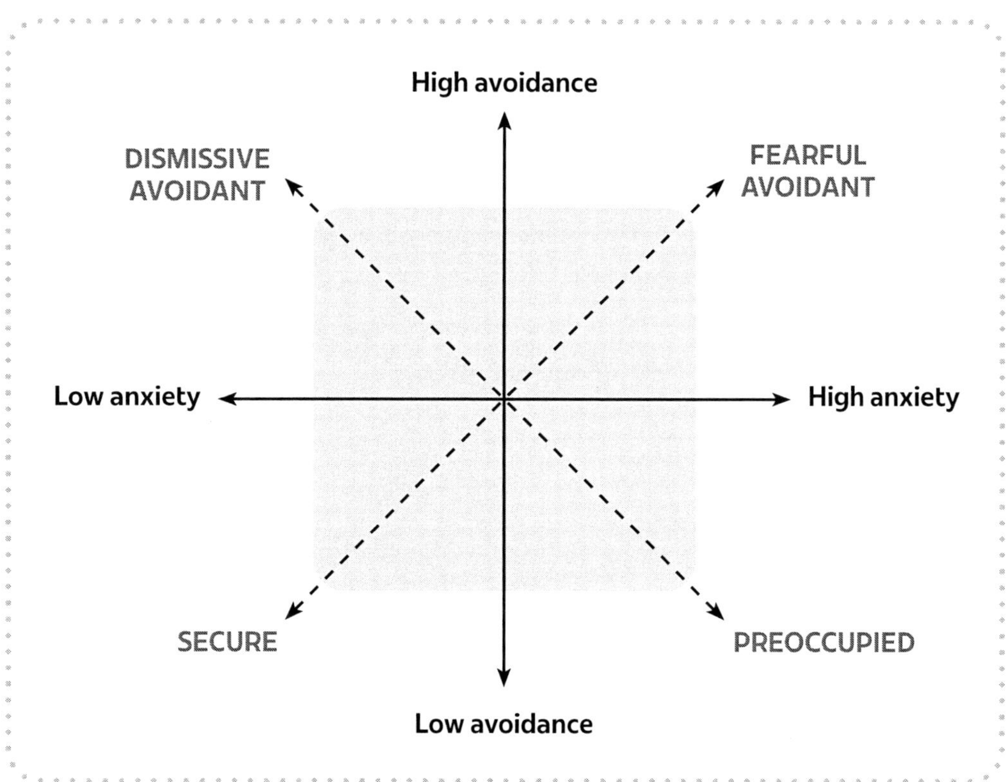

Each quadrant represents an attachment style, or a pattern of behavior you demonstrate in relationships:

- **Secure** (low anxiety and low avoidance): Securely attached people feel comfortable with intimacy and are trusting and supportive in relationships. They feel confident both in giving and receiving love and support.
- **Preoccupied** (high anxiety and low avoidance): People with this attachment style seek intimacy but are anxious and hypersensitive to signs of rejection in relationships. They

struggle with self-doubt and communicating their needs directly. They may respond to being triggered by "acting out"—for example, feelings of rejection may result in behavior aimed at making their partner jealous.

- **Fearful avoidant** (high anxiety and high avoidance): People with this attachment style have low self-esteem and seem to sabotage their relationships by engaging in unpredictable behaviors. They are more dependent than folks with a dismissive avoidant pattern, and have strong fears of rejection along with high levels of anxiety in relationships.
- **Dismissive avoidant** (low anxiety and high avoidance): People with this attachment style downplay the importance of relationships and are incredibly self-reliant. They can be distant and pull back when someone expects vulnerability.

If you find yourself reflected more in one of the non-secure attachment styles, don't be hard on yourself. Your attachment style isn't your fault—it results from the way that your nervous system seeks safety in the felt sense of familiarity. If your early relationship needs were met, your nervous system will experience low anxiety around relationships, and you won't find yourself avoiding them or constantly feeling insecure about them—in other words, you'll probably develop a secure attachment style. If, on the other hand, you had past relationship trauma or caregiving that was inconsistent or over-intrusive, you are likely to feel insecure in relationships.

If you find that your relationship patterns often feature anxiety or avoidance, please know that this isn't the end of the story. Your attachment style can shift, and when you enter relationships with an attuned and responsive nervous system, you'll create a new pattern and move toward security. (This is something we'll focus on in chapters 9 and 10.)

Action Seeds

- Send one check-in message to a loved one whenever you hop onto public transit or get into your car.
- Identify someone from your relationship map that you would like to develop a deeper connection with. For example, if they're currently more of an "activity friend," you might invite them for coffee so you can get to know another side of them.
- Join local Meetup or Facebook groups to build relationships within your community.
- Join groups or activities where you're likely to meet like-minded individuals—for instance, where you might learn a new skill, discuss a shared interest, or play a sport.
- Other: ______________________________

Therapeutic Lifestyle Habit #5: Recreation

In our society, we seem to consider recreation a luxury rather than a need. However, a vital part of your well-being is engaging in hobbies that you enjoy. It enhances your physical health, improves your mood, and reduces your stress. The root of the word "recreation" gives a sense of its deeper benefits: *re* = again and *create* = bring forth. In other words, recreation means doing things that bring back your spark, your energy, your health!

Recreation is one of those things that we all intuitively understand, but it can be tricky to describe. Generally, the defining feature is that it is an activity you do for pleasure. It's joy for joy's sake. Even if your work brings you joy, it still involves striving, that experience of positive stress we call "drive." Recreation is different. It necessarily excludes the pressure involved in work. Recreation can involve performance (such as competitive sports) or effort (like a good DIY project), just as much as it can be a more calming activity like reading a book or an entertainment-oriented activity like going to a concert. The essential thing is that it gives you a break from the pressure of survival and caring for others, and provides a sense of pleasure that refuels your ability to perform and be productive, not to mention your ongoing growth.

Action Seeds

- Schedule opportunities to engage with the activity you enjoy most. Art, sports, music—it really does not matter, as long as you love it! If you're not even sure what you enjoy, think about what you enjoyed in the past, even as far back as your childhood, and let that guide you.
- Play music from your adolescence when you make dinner, and dance to it.
- Buy some beautiful pens and color or write in your journal.
- Set up your home in a way you enjoy, perhaps looking for secondhand treasures.
- Other: ____________________

Therapeutic Lifestyle Habit #6: Relaxation and Stress Management

It might seem like relaxation should be considered part of the recreation category. But recreation isn't always relaxing—just watch the fans in the bleachers at any sports event if you need proof. Many recreation activities involve heavy sympathetic nervous system engagement, and that's perfectly fine! However, true relaxation practices support your body and mind to reduce or release the stressors you experience and cultivate a calm state that helps you better manage the stress you experience.

Remember that chronic stress isn't just a psychological burden; it impacts our bodies at a cellular level, affecting everything from hormone levels to gene expression (Pfeiffer et al., 2018). But despite anxiety and stress being a universal experience in the modern world, many of us lack effective strategies to manage it. Fortunately, ancient mindfulness-based practices such as tai chi, yoga, and meditation are gaining popularity, offering psychological, therapeutic, neurological, physiological, biochemical, and even epigenetic changes that ameliorate the effects of stress-related disorders and improve your quality of life (Calderone et al., 2024; Saatcioglu, 2013; Venditti et al., 2020). They also support interoception, bolstering your somatic skills (Gibson, 2024). These practices can help you cultivate an open curiosity about what is unfolding in the present moment through a focus on your embodied experience, such as your breath or a gentle body movement. (It's worth nothing that more dynamic forms of yoga might be considered more physical activity than relaxation.)

Relaxation can also be the seemingly rebellious act of doing "nothing"—for instance, curling up with a cup of tea and a book you can't put down, lying outside in the sunshine, or taking your time engaging in a multisensory evening skin routine. If your mind insists that you don't have time for it, that's a good sign it's the right form of relaxation for you! The following list offers some practical and accessible relaxation techniques that you can incorporate into your daily routine.

Action Seeds

- Practice the belly breathing exercise you learned in chapter 3.
- Practice the three-minute breathing space meditation or progressive muscle relaxation (described next).
- Try mindful movement practices such as tai chi or yoga.
- Consider what smells, sounds, and sights nourish you, and set up your home accordingly.
- Wear sensory-friendly clothing, especially at home.
- Other: ______________________________

EXERCISE: Three-Minute Breathing Space

Consider an hourglass shape: wide, narrow, wide. This exercise starts by widening your awareness of your thoughts, feelings, and bodily sensations, then narrowing your focus to your breath, and finally widening your awareness again to a sense of your entire body.

1. **First minute:** Take a moment to center, breathing in and out by way of your nose. Bring your awareness to notice what is present with you today. Notice the thoughts here in this moment—any descriptions, judgments, urges, memories, and the like. Notice what sensations are present in your body—warmth, coolness, tightness, openness, areas

connected with the earth and those lengthening upward. Notice what emotions are present here and how you're feeling in this moment.

2. **Second minute:** Next, bring your attention to your breath. To your inhale and exhale. To the sensation of the breath moving in, perhaps a little cooler on the upper lip, and to the exhale, perhaps a little warmer on the upper lip. Allow your belly to expand on the inhale and release on the exhale.
3. **Third minute:** Finally, expand your attention back out to encompass a sense of your entire body, breathing. Breathe through your whole being, right through to the boundary we call the skin, holding in your awareness a sense of your entire being.

EXERCISE: Progressive Muscle Relaxation

This practice is designed to reduce the stress and tension held in your physical body, supporting you in cultivating a sense of ease. Start by finding a comfortable position, either seated or lying down. You may close your eyes or soften your gaze. Take a few breaths to tune into your body in this moment, inhaling through your nose and gently exhaling through your mouth.

You can either follow the instructions here for both the left and right sides of your body simultaneously, or start with your left side and then repeat the sequence with your right side:

1. **Feet:** Bring your attention to your feet. Curl your toes in and tense the muscles. Hold the tension for a count of 5. Then release, saying gently to yourself, "relax." Notice the sensation of the release—the felt-sense difference of tension and relaxation.
2. **Calves:** Move your attention to your calves. Pull your toes upward and tighten the muscles of your calves as much as you can. Hold the tension for a count of 5. Then release, saying gently to yourself, "relax." Notice the sensation of the release—the felt-sense difference of tension and relaxation.
3. **Thighs:** Move your attention up further to your thighs. Contract the muscles in your thighs as tight as you can. Hold the tension for a count of 5. Then release, saying gently to yourself, "relax." Notice the sensation of the release—the felt-sense difference of tension and relaxation.
4. **Buttocks:** Move your attention to your buttocks. Squeeze the muscles tightly. Hold the tension for a count of 5. Then release, saying gently to yourself, "relax." Notice the sensation of the release—the felt-sense difference of tension and relaxation.
5. **Abdomen:** Bring your attention to your mid-body, your abdomen. Tighten your stomach muscles in. Hold the tension for a count of 5. Then release, saying gently to yourself, "relax." Notice the sensation of the release—the felt-sense difference of tension and relaxation.
6. **Chest:** Now move up to your chest. Take a deep breath and hold it as you tighten the muscles in your chest area. Hold the tension for a count of 5. Then release, saying gently

to yourself, "relax." Notice the sensation of the release—the felt-sense difference of tension and relaxation.

7. **Arms:** Bring your attention to your arms. Make fists with your hands and tighten your arm muscles. Hold the tension for a count of 5. Then release, saying gently to yourself, "relax." Notice the sensation of the release—the felt-sense difference of tension and relaxation.
8. **Shoulders:** Bring your attention up to your shoulders. Pull them up toward your ears and hold them as tight as you can, creating tension in your neck area. Hold the tension for a count of 5. Then release, saying gently to yourself, "relax." Notice the sensation of the release—the felt-sense difference of tension and relaxation.
9. **Face:** Finally, bring your attention to your face. Scrunch the muscles up as tight as you can. Clench your jaw and squeeze your eyes shut tightly. Hold the tension for a count of 5. Then release, saying gently to yourself, "relax." Notice the sensation of the release—the felt-sense difference of tension and relaxation.
10. **Whole body:** Now tense your entire body at once. Try to make yourself as tight as you possibly can. Hold the tension for a count of 5. Then release, saying gently to yourself, "relax." Notice the sensation of the release—the felt-sense difference of tension and relaxation.

Conclude by scanning your entire body, from your toes to your crown. If you notice any areas of remaining tension, you might breathe into these areas, imagining letting go of the tension. Allow yourself a few moments to be with the feeling of relaxation before you return to your day.

If you practice this regularly over time, you will eventually be able to simply say "relax" to yourself and your muscles will automatically start to release their tension.

Therapeutic Lifestyle Habit #7: Religious or Spiritual Practices

Most of the world's population connect with a religious or spiritual practice, some 90 percent actually (Koenig, 2009). Whether you call it the universe, your higher consciousness, nature, God, Allah, the Almighty, or Infinite Bliss, engaging in a belief system focused on love and forgiveness can provide a resource when navigating stress and illness and is positively associated with mental health, emotional well-being, and relationship quality (Tuck & Anderson, 2014).

If this area is helpful, you can look at how you regularly connect to a healthy religious or spiritual practice. This might involve attending a sangha, mosque, or church, or you may have a more personal or informal spiritual practice. Whatever practice evokes a sense of enriching connection for you, honor yourself by engaging with it regularly. Engage in practices or services where you feel connected and expansive (and step back from places where you don't feel this).

Action Seeds

- Take a moment to light a candle and align your heart.
- Read poetry or say a prayer.
- Take to a yoga mat or meditation cushion.
- Head out to walk in nature or look up at the stars.
- Other: ____________________

Therapeutic Lifestyle Habit #8: Service and Contribution

Altruism is a win-win for both the receiver and the giver. The benefits are obvious for the receiver, but the giver experiences enhanced positive emotions, self-esteem, and more satisfaction in life (Post, 2005). We're wired for compassion and our system actually rewards us when we enter the social connection state (Gilbert, 2020).

The way you practice service to others can be anything that aligns with your resources. If time is scarce but you're financially stable, consider a monetary donation to a cause you believe in. If you've got more time than money, consider volunteer work. It's worth knowing that volunteers are not only physically healthier and happier; they live longer (Nichol et al., 2023).

One other factor in this lifestyle habit that I find delightful to think about is *social contagion*. While this concept is often discussed in terms of unhealthy behaviors, like how we are more likely to smoke if those within our social circle do, we can also touch many others with the positive social contagion of altruism and cooperation. What you give not only goes to the direct recipients of your generosity but also flows through your social network to evoke similar behaviors in others.

Action Seeds

- Whenever you buy a coffee, transfer the same amount to a donations account.
- Consider a skill you have and figure out how you can give it in a way that is purely for the benefit of others.
- Volunteer for political or social justice causes you care about.
- Do a food drop for a neighbor or a family member that might be struggling.
- If you're going to donate, look into the most effective charities. For instance, www.thelifeyoucansave.org has a list of charities where a significant percentage of donations makes it to those in need, rather than the high administrative costs that come with some organizations.
- Other: ____________________

Therapeutic Lifestyle Habit #9: Sleep

I doubt I have to sell you on the importance of sleep. Many of us already understand that it is fundamental for obtaining optimal physical, emotional, and cognitive health. It is during sleep that your body repairs tissues, restores muscle mass, produces healing immune proteins, replenishes energy, regulates hormones, and consolidates memories.

Changes in sleep patterns are indicative of our mental health, be it sleeping less when your mind spins with worries or sleeping more when your mood is feeling low. On the other side, our sleep impacts our well-being; when we're not well rested, it's harder to regulate our mood and navigate the challenges of our days.

The challenge lies in balancing this seemingly paradoxical relationship. You might be exhausted during the day, which makes it hard to do anything and even pulls you to curl up in bed early, only to find that as soon as you do so, your mind starts spinning in a worry loop and your heart rate increases, spurred by the panic that you'll never get to sleep and won't be able to function tomorrow. You check the time on your phone and start counting down the hours. You sleep poorly and wake still exhausted—and the cycle repeats.

The recommendation I give to every client who struggles with sleep is the same one I follow for myself: get outside! First thing in the morning, get outside (or at least open your blinds) and let that morning sunlight stream directly into your eyes. Your eyes are directly connected to your brain, and they have specialized cells that register the sunlight and start synchronizing your body clock, helping you reset your circadian rhythm to support sleepiness in the evening. This is how you tell your brain to make melatonin in about 14 hours. Meanwhile, your body starts making cortisol to energize you for the day. After all, cortisol is healthy for your body in balanced amounts; the concern is when it's overproduced due to extreme stress.

My other recommendations are to read fiction books and have a warm bath or shower before bed. When you're in the warm water, your body temperature will rise. Then, when you step out into the open air, your body temperature drops. Since your body temperature drops when you fall asleep, your system interprets this temperature change as a sleepiness cue. Curling up with a fiction book helps pull your mind from your current reality into an imaginary world. It's a gentle way of letting go of the day and shifting your brain state so the altered consciousness state of sleep can more easily follow.

Action Seeds

- Create a relaxing bedtime routine to signal to your body that it is time to wind down (for instance, having a cup of caffeine-free tea, practicing relaxation techniques like meditation or breathing, taking a warm bath, or reading a book).
- Develop a consistent sleep schedule. Ideally, go to bed and wake up at the same times every day, even on weekends. Even when you can't get to sleep at the same time, still try to wake up at your usual hour. This helps regulate your body's internal clock.
- Optimize your sleep environment by keeping your room cool, dark, and quiet. This might mean installing black-out curtains or getting a sleep mask, earplugs, or a white noise machine.
- Only use your bed for sleep and sex. This is about paired association. If you watch movies or eat meals in your bed, your nervous system is learning that your bed is a place where you're awake. So, when you hop in at night, you're not going to automatically trigger your system for sleep the way you would if that was the only association you had with your bed.
- Limit your exposure to screens, ideally keeping them out of the bedroom. Some folks like to plan for an hour of screen-free time before bed. If you're not doing this, ensure your devices are on a warm-light night mode to reduce the blue light being emitted. This said, if you can't limit your screen time, consider why. Are you working late at night or scrolling social media? Perhaps these habits are stimulating rather than soothing.
- Limit stimulants in the evening. From caffeine in coffee and chocolate to nicotine, any stimulants will impact your body's ability to evoke sleep. Some of us are more sensitive than others; in fact, lots of folks I know won't drink coffee after 11 a.m. I can get away with it until 4 p.m., whereas my mother can drink it into the evening and reportedly sleep fine. All our systems are different, but if sleep is challenging, try moderating your caffeine consumption.
- Exercise regularly and ideally in the daytime, as it promotes better sleep. Vigorous exercise in the evening can delay your sleep onset, so consider if there are any changes you can make to your schedule.
- Limit your daytime naps. I know it sounds cruel, particularly if you are tired. But if you must nap, plan to take it before 2 p.m. and limit it to 20 or 30 minutes. You could even try the pen strategy. Essentially, you hold a pen in your hand when lying down to go to sleep. You'll tend to drop it when you fall asleep, waking yourself up. It's that relaxing period of drifting off to sleep that is the midday invigoration you likely need; if you sleep longer, you'll likely end up waking up feeling groggy and worse off than before. So save the deep sleep for the evenings when you have more time.

- Establish a sleep-friendly mindset. The fact is, you can survive without a perfect night of sleep. We all do! The more distressed we get about not sleeping, the harder it is for us to actually sleep. So remind yourself that you'll be okay, and get out of bed if you cannot fall asleep after about 20 minutes. Go read a book in a dimly lit room or do something slow and boring until you feel a wave of sleepiness come on. Then get back into bed. This can help prevent further frustration and anxiety around sleep and honor your body's natural rhythm. Sleepiness tends to come in waves, so if you miss one, get out of bed and wait for the next.
- As you lie in bed, try bringing in your resourcing figure by wrapping those loving arms around you with a sense of safety to help you fall asleep.

Note: If you are still struggling with sleep or daytime sleepiness after trying these suggestions, chat to your doctor about getting a referral to a sleep specialist. There can be underlying conditions or more extreme circadian rhythm disruptions that indicate professional help is needed.

EXERCISE: Wellness Wheel

In addition to considering your action seeds in the different domains, it's worth getting an overall picture of how healing your lifestyle is. Enter the wellness wheel, an excellent way to consider the domains you have skillfully established, celebrate your success in them, and track areas that could use a little more attention.

You'll notice that, in addition to the domains we've already looked at in this chapter, I've included an additional category in the wellness wheel: security. This goes back to that old hierarchy of needs. Not having our lower needs met makes it harder to move up the ladder (though not impossible). It is worth considering what in your life impacts your sense of security, and if there are any changes you can make to enhance your sense of stability in this domain.

Take a moment now and consider how well you are doing in each of these domains on a scale from 1 to 10. A higher score indicates greater success, and you would color the wheel from the inside out to the number you've decided on. You might notice that your wheel is imbalanced—for instance, you might have a 10/10 in relationships but a 1/10 in exercise. That's okay! The assessment is intended to show where your wheel is imbalanced, so that you'll know where to devote more energy.

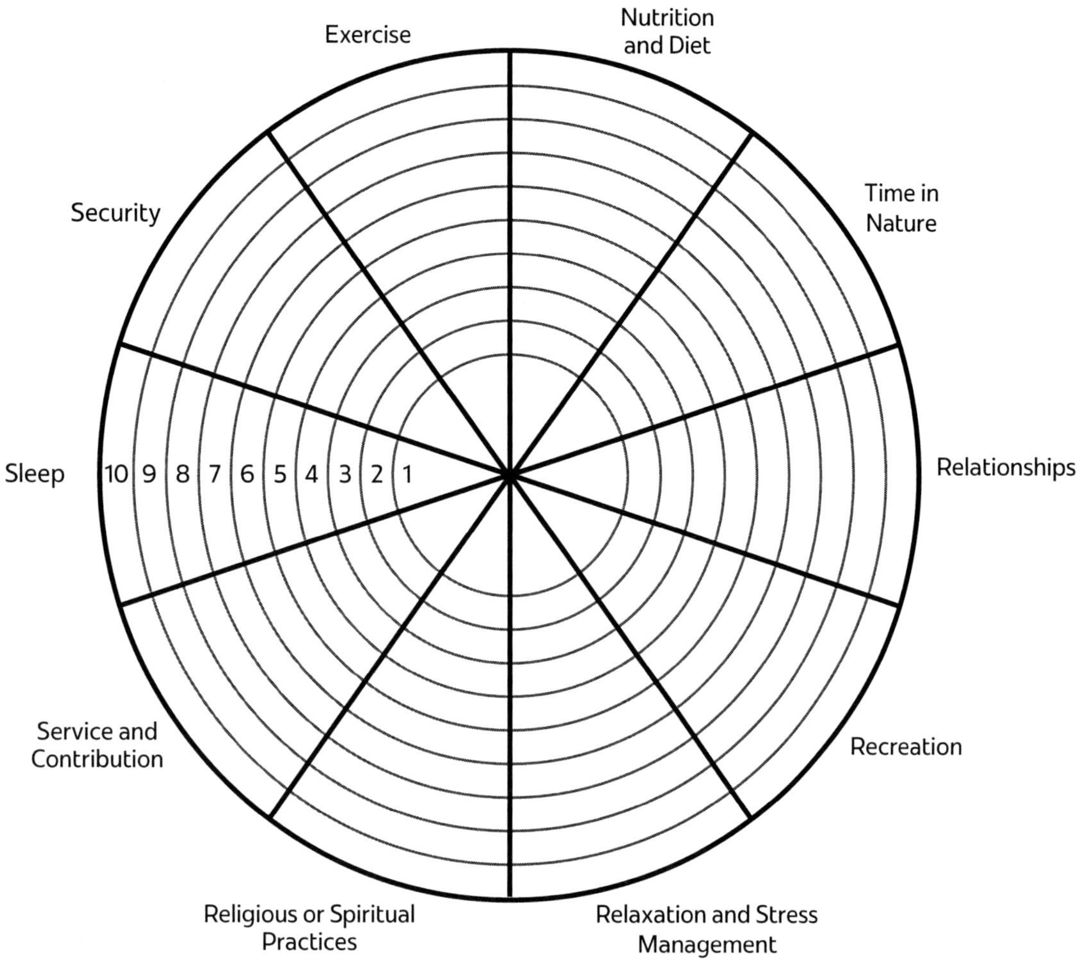

Exercise

Nutrition and Diet

Time in Nature

Relationships

Recreation

Relaxation and Stress Management

Religious or Spiritual Practices

Service and Contribution

Sleep 10 9 8 7 6 5 4 3 2 1

Security

EXERCISE: Resilience Routine

Now that you've identified which areas of wellness you want to focus most on developing, it's time to brainstorm ways to do so. You can review the "action seeds" that were listed for each domain or think of other practices you might like to integrate into your day-to-day life. Be creative, and see if you can think of activities that would meet multiple needs at once to get "more bang for your buck." For example, walking in nature with a friend to have a healthy picnic offers exercise, nutrition, nature, relationships, and a sense of spiritual connection. Jot down all the practices you are interested in starting or building.

____

____

____

____

Now it's time to set up those habits! Consider which practices you'll put into your calendar daily. Then consider which ones might show up less regularly but are also worth doing. For example, if you are looking to get more time in nature, you might plan to go outside for a short walk each day, go for a longer hike each weekend, spend a day at the beach once a month, have a weekend-long camping trip each quarter, and go on a week-long outdoor excursion once a year. If you want to build your relationships, you might plan to connect with friends via messages or calls daily, grab coffee together weekly, go out for dinner monthly, host a quarterly "crafternoon," and make a yearly visit to your hometown or to a dear friend's new city.

My Resiliency Rituals

Daily	
Weekly	
Monthly	
Quarterly	
Yearly	

You've now got a resiliency routine in place to ensure you regularly integrate self-care into your life. This will expand your capacity to manage the ups and downs of life.

Closing Reflections

What does self-care mean to you?

What healthy lifestyle habits have you already established in your life?

Are there any lifestyle habits that you can stack together regularly (e.g., going for a walk with a friend or volunteering outdoors for a national park)?

Do you notice any patterns playing out in the attachment styles of people you've had relationships with (e.g., always dating avoidant folks)?

Takeaway Messages

- Lifestyle medicine is one of the most effective ways to enhance mental and physical health and well-being.
- Physical activity is the most effective anxiolytic and antidepressant (as long as it is not engaged in excessively, indicating an avoidant-addictive pattern).
- Humans are wired for relationships, and developing mutually supportive and connected ones is a huge predictor of your life quality.
- Sleep is commonly impacted by anxiety, and anxiety increases with poor sleep quality, making it very important to practice good sleep hygiene.
- Maintaining a lifestyle medicine–based resiliency routine is imperative for a felt sense of vitality.

CHAPTER 6

Feel It to Heal It: Emotional Awareness

"Emotional intelligence is your ability to recognize and understand emotions in yourself and others, and your ability to use this awareness to manage your behavior and relationships."

—Travis Bradberry, *Emotional Intelligence 2.0*

If you've been in therapy before, you've probably heard the adage, "You've got to feel it to heal it." This advice is based on the way your emotions combine the physical sensations of your body with the stories of your mind to make meaning of your experiences and motivate you to take aligned action. Think of how fear connects the story of a severe storm with an increased heart rate, or how guilt integrates the story that you betrayed a friend with a sinking stomach, or how excitement connects the story of you getting to spend a weekend away with your partner with the butterflies in your stomach. Such emotional experiences are inherently adaptive, supporting your survival and well-being—the fear motivates you to take shelter from the storm, the guilt provokes remorse that helps you repair the friendship, the excitement heightens your senses so that you fully enjoy the romantic getaway. Whether pleasant or unpleasant, comfortable or uncomfortable, emotions serve as felt-sense messengers about what matters to you.

Unfortunately, if you were not taught about emotions growing up, you might not have learned how incredibly useful they are, nor how you can effectively manage the distressing ones. Instead, you might have developed unhelpful beliefs about emotions being unwarranted, unbearable, or unmanageable. These beliefs make emotional regulation tricky, limiting your capacity to live a meaningful life and fostering several psychological struggles.

The Discomfort of Distress

Living in a state of perpetual comfort simply isn't possible. From feeling cold or hot to tired, hungry, or sick, your discomfort sends you messages that support the health of your body and even help you take care of others.

Emotional discomfort is the same. It's an inevitable part of your life designed to communicate the needs of your mind and body. The intensity of the emotions we feel can be strong—say, the absolute fear many folks experience with public speaking or a flash of fury that rises during a heated argument with a loved one—or mild, like the annoyance we might feel when we're waiting on a red light to change or a faint nostalgia as we remember an old relationship.

The interesting thing is that it's typically not the emotion's intensity that predicts the level of suffering you'll experience from it. Instead, it's how willing (or unwilling) you are to experience the emotion, based on how unbearable you believe it to be. Being able to accept your emotions, even those you don't want to feel, makes you better able to manage and regulate them.

Think back to that vicious cycle of anxiety you learned about in chapter 1—when you're scared of your feelings, you try to avoid the situations that cause them, but the avoidance only makes those situations more scary. The same principle applies to any uncomfortable emotions: our unwillingness to be with them increases their intensity.

Trying to avoid feeling your emotions is known in clinical terms as *experiential avoidance* (Spinhoven et al., 2017). It might not surprise you to learn that it shows up more often in folks with chronic mental health struggles such as generalized anxiety and depression. But what might surprise you is that experiential avoidance is itself a major predictor of someone developing clinical anxiety or depression (Ouimet et al., 2016). In other words, it functions as both cause and effect.

Imagine you wake up feeling on edge, your mind crowded with worries about everything that could go wrong in your life, your heart rate increasing as you go through your usual morning routine. Noticing these symptoms could send you into a tailspin—along with worrying about the challenges you're confronting, you're now worrying about how much they're worrying you! You could spend all your energy wondering what this sudden onslaught of fear means for you, trying to mask the anxiety you feel, and hyper-focusing on your heart rate and any other sensation that could predict panic.

On the other hand, you could observe these symptoms with gentle curiosity, accepting that such mental and physical experiences show up from time to time. You could go through your day with a plan to pause whenever the symptoms intensify and take a few minutes to do a breathing exercise or step outside for a walk around the block, recognizing that your body and mind simply need space and time to process something that will eventually become clear. This doesn't mean ignoring the content of your worries—maybe it's a difficult project at work, a large bill that's due soon, or your child's troubles at school—it just means you understand that the anxiety you're feeling is not a problem in and of itself. You will actually be better resourced to deal with that project, bill, or situation if you accept your worried feelings with gentle neutrality.

The fact is that a single day of trying to avoid anxiety symptoms is much more of a mental health risk than experiencing those symptoms regularly and dealing with them calmly and compassionately. Avoidance also predicts ongoing symptoms and relapse (Spinhoven et al., 2017).

In this chapter, we'll deep-dive into the skills you need to regulate your emotions effectively. First, though, we need to make sure you have the capacity to safely introduce your nervous system to the sensations that unfold within your body.

Flooding

If you've spent your whole life trying not to feel your feelings, having them kick in can be overwhelming, consuming the entirety of your inner space and taking you outside of your window of tolerance so that you cannot think clearly. This is why chapter 3 focused on exploring and practicing self-regulation skills like evoking the dive reflex, sucking on sour candy, engaging in intense physical activity, or practicing compassionate figure imagery. While you always have these practices to bring you back inside your window of tolerance and get through distressing times, they don't necessarily increase your felt-sense awareness or your capacity to hold your inner experience without resistance. For that, you need to expand your window of tolerance—in other words, build your capacity to be with what you're feeling.

When we're trying to increase our physical strength, most of us know we can't go from couch-potato mode to bench-pressing 200 pounds in our first session—we'd get squashed! Instead, we build up our muscles by starting with small weights, doing several rounds of a few repetitions and taking breaks in between. It's the same with developing mental and emotional strength. Just as a fitness trainer will help you find the right balance of ease and challenge with a weight exercise and guide you in starting and finishing safely, a therapist will help you find the right balance of exposure to a distressing emotion or sensation, guiding you into and out of the felt sense as needed. A gym coach encourages you to push your muscle fatigue without straining you to the point of injury; a therapist helps you work to the edge of your emotional capacity, expanding your window of tolerance without becoming flooded and losing your connection to the present.

I want to make sure you have the skills to monitor this yourself, so that you can take yourself safely into and out of your inner experience. (And remember, you can pull the emergency brake and use your self-soothing toolbox anytime you need it.) To do this safely, you need the processes of *titration* and *pendulation*.

Titration

This term comes from the field of chemistry, where it refers to blending substances drop by drop until the expected dose or balance is achieved. In the emotional context, titration is the slow and steady method of exploring physically based sensations and emotions. By approaching your sensations slowly and deliberately, ensuring you maintain a sense of safety, you build your confidence and capacity to get in touch with sensations you might instinctively avoid because they feel overwhelming or scary. Drop by drop, your system will learn that you can be with and respond to these sensations skillfully.

Pendulation

Like the pendulum of a clock moving from side to side, your capacity to be with discomfort can be developed by shifting between exposure and resourcing, arousal and calm. Through this rhythm, your inner system learns to increasingly relax and allow the discomfort of certain inner experiences, rather than tensing and contracting in an effort to keep the experience at bay. This cultivates belief in your capacity to make space for all your sensations, regardless of their pleasantness or unpleasantness. As you learn unpleasant sensations won't overpower you, they become less scary.

EXERCISE: Sensation Pendulation

This exercise assists you in regulating your autonomic nervous system by noticing what is unfolding in real time, as your body changes moment by moment in difficult situations.

Part 1: Noticing Sensations

Think of a mildly stressful or triggering event (on a scale of 0 to 10, choose one that is a 5 or less). Pay attention to any physical sensations that arise in your body and use the table that follows to document these sensations, including the level of distress you experience and any associated emotions or thoughts. Remember, you're just getting a profile of the sensations right now; if your mind pulls you to further thoughts or memories, gently come back to the sensation with an intention of curiosity. If you notice your distress creeping up to a 6 or 7, stop and move to part 2.

Sensation	Body Location	Distress (0–10)	Emotions, Thoughts, Memories
Tightness	Throat	5	Anxious, "I can't handle it," disagreement with boss

Part 2: Shifting Focus (Pendulation)

Alternate your attention between the sensation arising with the painful memory (activation) and a neutral or pleasant sensation somewhere in your body (deactivation). Your hands or feet can be a useful anchor for your attention when you are seeking to deactivate, because they are generally less likely to be triggering. Observe the differences in the intensity and nature of these sensations as you move back and forth between them.

Distressing Sensation	Deactivation (Neutral or Pleasant Sensation)
Tightness in throat	Warm right foot, sensation of sock

Tips for Practice

- Start with a brief period of focusing on the uncomfortable sensation, then switch to the pleasant or neutral sensation.
- Notice any changes in your overall sense of well-being as you practice shifting your focus.
- Take your time with each shift, allowing yourself to fully experience each sensation before moving to the next.

Emotion Regulation

Emotion regulation is a series of strategies used in response to your emotional experiences, all of which are underpinned by your beliefs about emotions. The strategies are:

1. **Awareness:** Being able to recognize your emotions in real time.
2. **Understanding:** Comprehending underlying causes, triggers, and patterns of emotions.
3. **Acceptance:** Acknowledging your emotional experience without resistance or judgment.

Sounds simple, right? But, as you likely know, these practices can sometimes be elusive when you need them most, particularly in moments when you feel sad, mad, or scared. So let's dig deeper into what they really involve.

Strategy #1: Emotional Awareness

A common saying among therapy providers is "Name it to tame it," which is to say, when you label your emotions, the intensity will often decrease. Ambiguity hurts because your feelings are more likely to feel confusing and unexpectedly flood you. This is why emotional regulation starts with developing your emotional awareness—your ability to recognize your emotions in real time.

Emotional awareness involves noticing what is going on in your body and in the environment while you're feeling a difficult emotion. It is influenced by your neurobiology—how your specific nervous system has developed to respond to stimuli—as well as the emotional education you've received in your lifetime. This education often involves instances when an emotion is labeled, which teaches you to categorize your experiences and develop your felt-sense awareness within them. If, as a child, you smacked your sibling for grabbing the toy you wanted and your caregiver said, "You're feeling angry," you would have learned that "anger" means a warm flush, gritted teeth, and an urge to hit, coupled with a circumstance where something you want is taken from you.

However, if your caregivers had difficulty labeling your experiences because they struggled with emotional awareness, or if you were told "You're fine," "Don't be so dramatic," or "Just stop your crying!" when you had big feelings, you likely got the message that your big feelings were a problem and you should shut them down or, better yet, not feel them at all. Past generations often believed that this way of dealing with emotions made people stronger; in fact, it makes us less skilled at processing and regulating our emotions, a condition known by the clinical term *alexithymia*. With alexithymia, you not only miss noticing your own emotional states, but you also have more difficulty recognizing what others might be experiencing.

Fortunately, even if you had less than optimal emotional education as a child, you can develop your emotional awareness on your own. Your first step is to learn the emotion categories. If you've struggled to specifically label what is going on for you, it can be helpful to use an emotions wheel where you move from broad categories into more specific emotional states.

EXERCISE: Emotions Wheel

Saying you are "glad," "sad," "mad," or "scared" is a good start, but the more sophisticated and precise you can be in labeling your emotional experiences, the less distressing they will feel. Start practicing by noting exactly what you are feeling right now, in this moment. Review the wheel provided and consider which emotion best captures your inner experience.

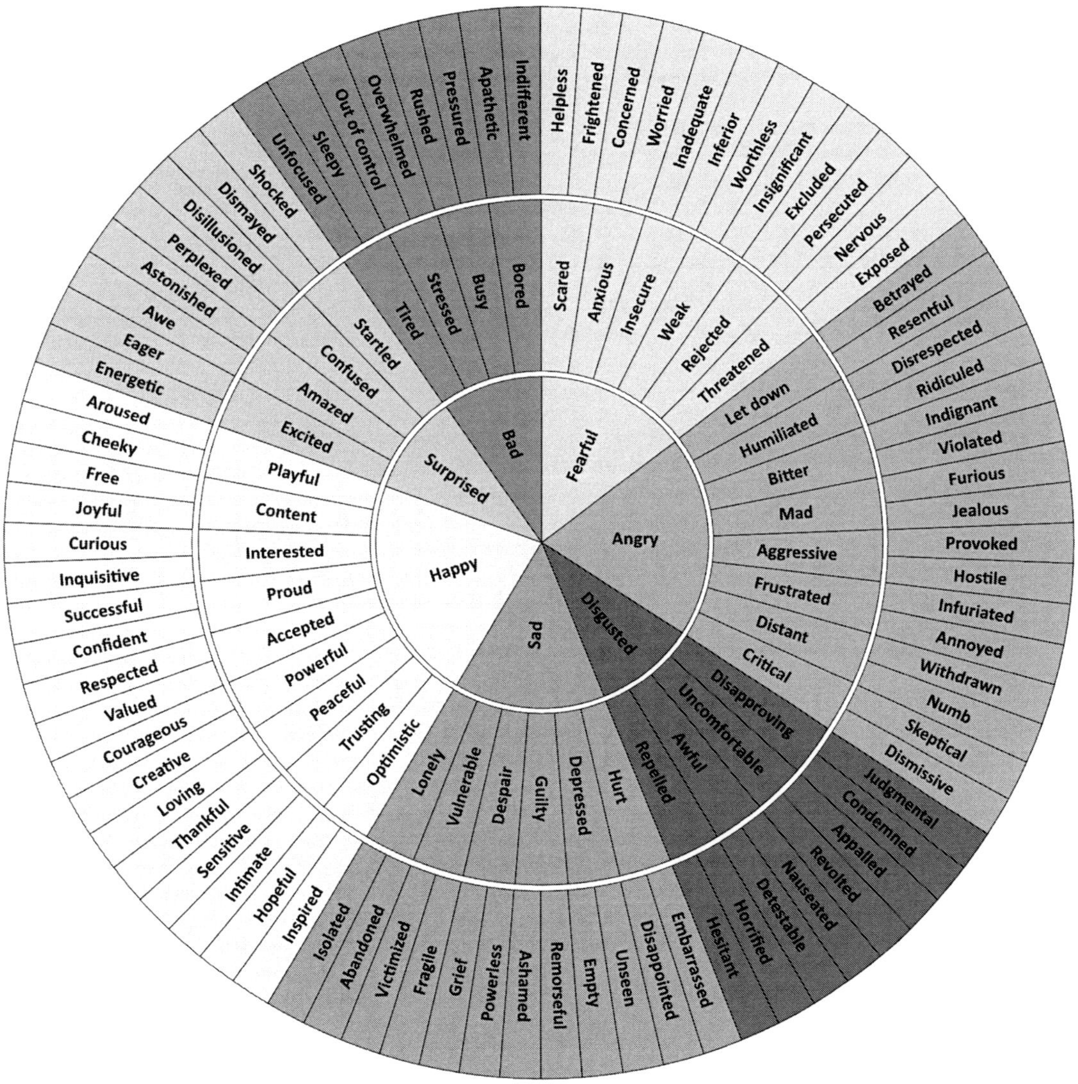

Now, set an alarm to go off two more times today, and each time it goes off, use the wheel to notice exactly what you are feeling. I recommend doing this practice three times per day for the next three to five days (or more) to keep developing your emotional awareness.

While the emotions wheel works from the top down, moving you from what you process in your mind to the sensations in your body, there is another model that works from the bottom up, supporting you in cultivating the interoception (internal felt sense) you need to mentally identify your feelings. This model, known as the *circumplex of affect* (Russell, 1980), supports you in interpreting your body's sensations to get to the underlying emotional concept.

In the image that follows, you'll see a horizontal axis for valence (the positive to negative spectrum of your inner experience) and a vertical axis for arousal (the intensity of your inner experience, from low to high). As you can see in the image, happiness and excitement are on the positive end of valence, while anger and sadness are on the negative end. Meanwhile, excitement and anger are in the high end of arousal, whereas calmness and exhaustion are on the low end.

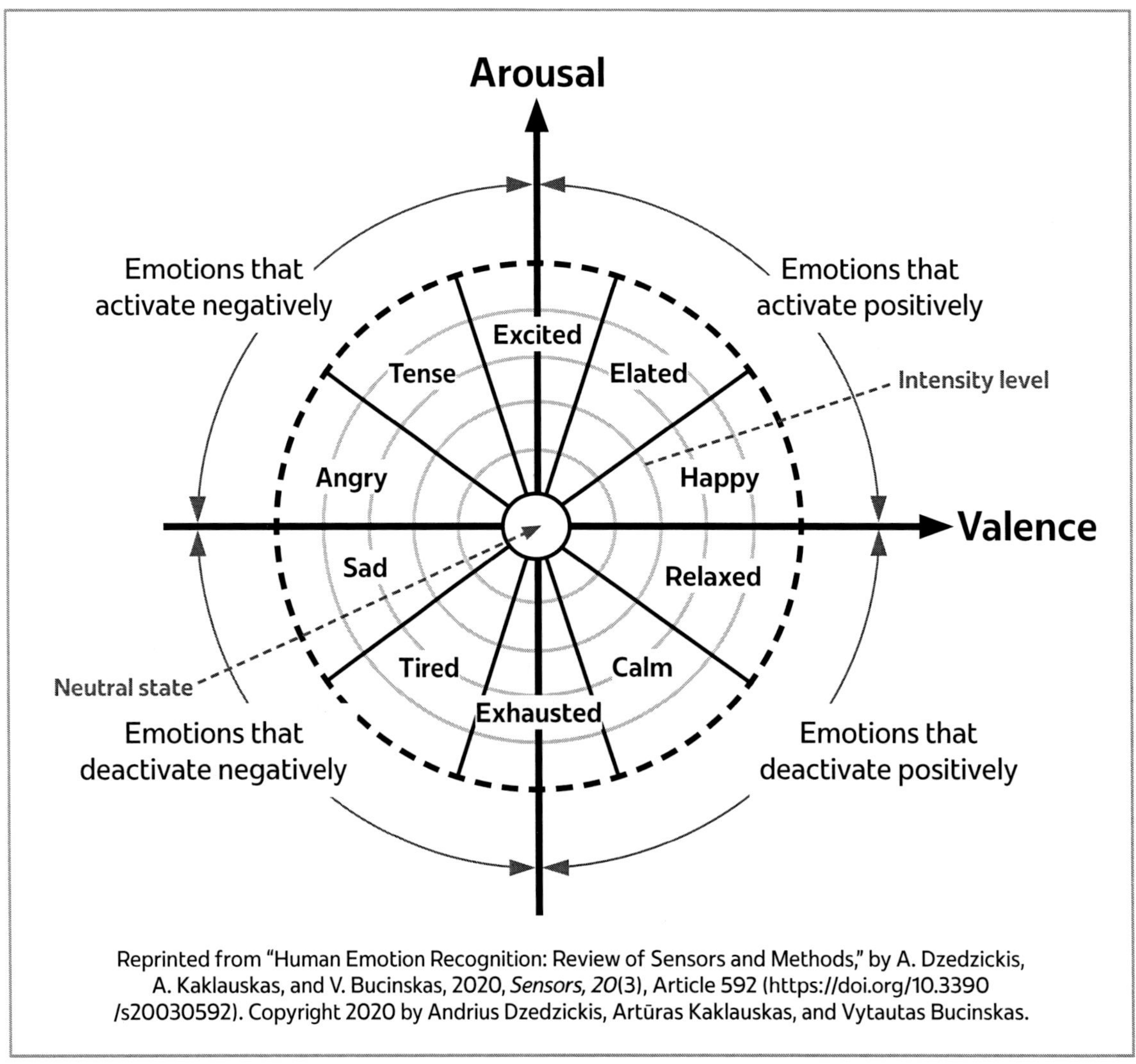

Reprinted from "Human Emotion Recognition: Review of Sensors and Methods," by A. Dzedzickis, A. Kaklauskas, and V. Bucinskas, 2020, *Sensors, 20*(3), Article 592 (https://doi.org/10.3390/s20030592). Copyright 2020 by Andrius Dzedzickis, Artūras Kaklauskas, and Vytautas Bucinskas.

Essentially, each emotion can be understood as a combination of valence and arousal. Your mind interprets these inner experiences in the context of what you perceive to be happening to you right now and what you perceived happening to you in the past. In the next section, we'll dig deeper into how this interpretation process happens—why the same level of arousal can lead to either positive or negative emotions. But first, let's take a moment for you to practice identifying your emotions using the concepts of arousal and valence.

EXERCISE: Plotting Your Affect

Take a moment to plot how you're feeling right now on the quadrants below. What level of arousal and valence are you experiencing?

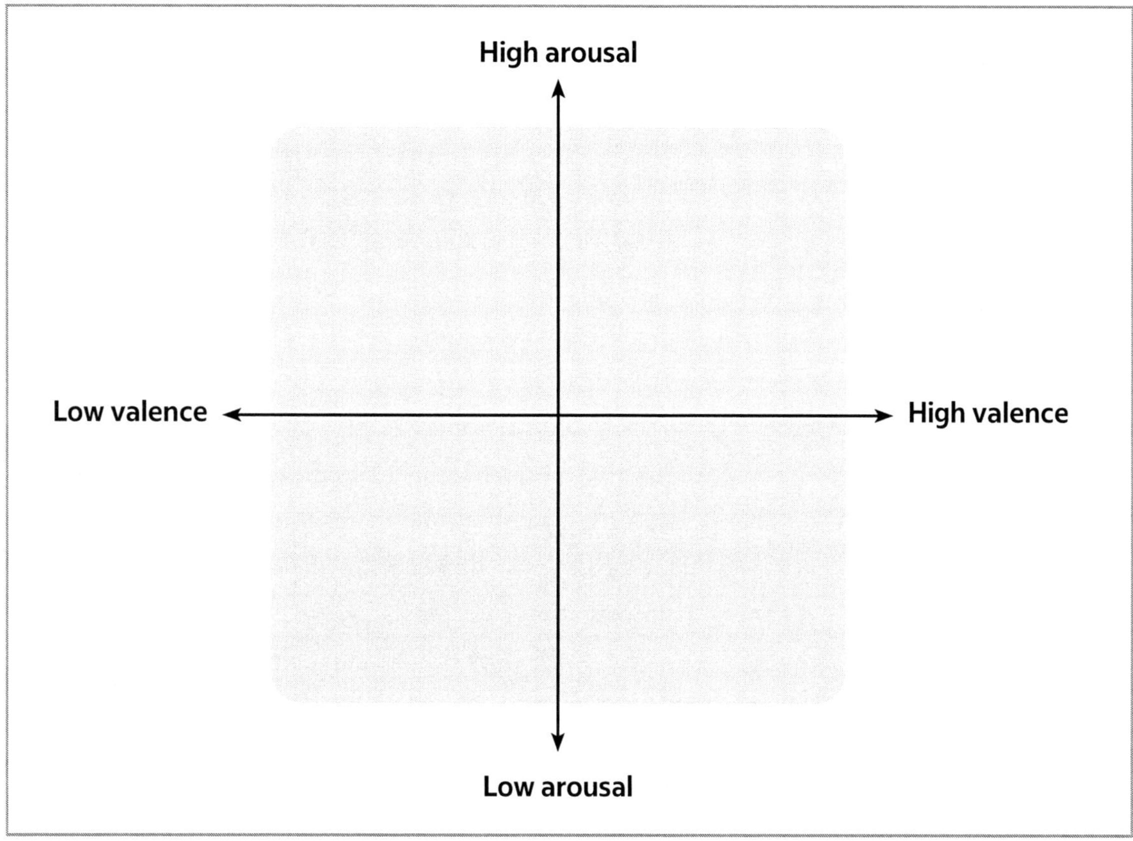

Now label the point you plotted using a feeling word or two to describe your current experience (e.g., excited, tired). You're not limited to the words from the circumplex figure—you can also use the emotions wheel from the last exercise to help you label the feeling more precisely.

Set an alarm for two more times today, and when it goes off, revisit this exercise and plot your emotional state on the quadrants. I recommend doing this emotional identification practice three times per day for three to five days to help you develop emotional awareness.

Strategy #2: Understanding Your Emotions

In addition to getting clear on *what* you're feeling, it is helpful and healing to gain clarity on the *why*. Identifying the reason behind your emotional response involves exploring both the current context of the feeling and your personal history around it. As you better comprehend the underlying causes, triggers, and patterns of your emotions, you build your capacity to act with wisdom in managing those emotions and responding to the situations where they arise.

If you search "emotions" on the internet, you'll probably encounter an image with a row of faces—smiling, frowning, open-mouthed surprise, tears, scowls, maybe more—referred to as the "universal emotions." The implication is that we all look, feel, and do the same things when we experience emotions. This is the emotional education many of us received as children; I know I was certainly taught this way. And yet it's possible for someone to smile sadly or to appear angry when they're simply concentrating. The truth is, we don't all express our emotions in the same way—and we don't necessarily *feel* our emotions in the same way, either.

It turns out that the way we experience emotions is not so simple or universal after all. It's not just a matter of positive events making you smile while negative events make you frown; instead, your past experiences influence how you perceive, feel, and respond to this current moment. Nobel laureate Gerald M. Edelman (1989) referred to this as "the remembered present." In other words, when it comes to your emotions, the past and present coexist, with your brain drawing on your previous experiences as well as your current bodily sensations and the situational context to inform what you are feeling in the here and now. I envision these various pieces of information (past experiences, bodily sensations, situational context) as blocks that the brain stacks to construct a given emotional experience: a colorful pillar of happiness, a narrow and teetering tower of fear, and so on.

Imagine that you're at a party with your friends, dancing to a playlist of all the fun and upbeat songs of your youth. Your brain takes in information like your increased heart rate and shortness of breath caused by dancing, the rich memories evoked by the nostalgic music, and your feeling of safety from being surrounded by people you love and trust, and assembles them into a construct, which it then compares against your more recent experiences: *This seems like happiness—does it resemble happiness as I understand it now? Yes, I am happy.*

Now, take one of those same pieces of information—say, increased heart rate and shortness of breath—and insert it into another situation, like walking alone down a dark alley. In this context, you would likely feel tense, even afraid. Your brain might recall frightening memories or news reports related to the different elements of this situation.

As Dr. Lisa Feldman Barrett, the developer of the constructed theory of emotions, says, "Heart rate changes are inevitable; their emotional meaning is not" (Feldman Barrett, 2017, p. 33). Emotions are the tools we use to make sense of our inner and outer experiences and find guidance for how to experience and behave in each situation. At the party, happiness tells you to keep dancing. In the alley, fear tells you to keep a close lookout and walk fast.

As you sit here reading this book, your cardiovascular, immune, gastrointestinal, and every other body system are in action alongside your interoceptive sense system and your mind. All of this yields a vast amount of information your brain is processing. There's too much information for your brain to give every data point the same amount of attention, so it learns to prioritize and focus on certain cues.

For example, look up from this book right now and find five blue items in the space around you. Got them? Now, while looking down at the book again, I want you to recall everything in your environment that is shaped like a circle. That second task was more difficult, right? When you were actively looking for blue things, your brain wasn't primed to notice circular things. I just had you intentionally focus on a specific aspect of your environment, but your brain also chooses specific things to pay more attention to even when you're not consciously aware of it. What your brain decides to pay attention to is based on what it believes is important based on past experiences that are similar to what is unfolding in the present moment.

Let's go back to that evolutionary example from the introduction: the rustle in the bush. Given the past experiences that you (or your ancestors) have had with tigers and warring clans, that original sense data is going to mobilize you for fight or flight, even before you consciously consider the situation. Your brain is simulating what the situation might involve—like an unconscious movie preview—and preparing your body for this predicted scenario. This is because if you wait any longer to get more information about the rustle you heard, you lose the advantage of early escape. This is neuroception in action. And it's not just the heart rate change that evokes the response; it's your brain using emotion to create meaning in the situation: *Rustle* ⇨ *fear* ⇨ *run!*

As we've already discussed, differentiating between emotions at a strictly physiological level is quite tricky. Is that tightness in your chest anger, anxiety, or excitement? Is that coldness in your extremities surprise, shame, or depression? That's why, in addition to the felt-sense data from your body, your brain uses other data to construct which emotion you'll feel. As I've already mentioned, it considers your current context and compares it to past experiences. But other than the situation you're in, one of the biggest predictors of the emotion you feel is your existing mood when the new emotion arises. That mood, in turn, is contingent upon your *allostatic load*, also known as your "body budget"—that is, the level of stress and pressure your body is carrying on a regular basis, balanced out by things like nutrition, hydration, sleep, movement, energetic reserves, immunity, hormone cycles, and the like.

Your emotion construction is also influenced by the mental concepts you carry. These are essentially the frameworks your mind creates to capture an understanding or representation you have about the world. They include beliefs, desires, emotions, your sense of time, textures, colors, and so on. Mental concepts are the neural pathways that are created based on your prior experiences and worldviews—in other words, the blueprints for how you feel about what.

Mental Concept
- Neural pathways
- Prior experiences
- Worldview

Body Budget
- Allostatic load
- Body state
- Interoception

Affect
- Mood
- Arousal (intensity)
- Valence (positive vs. negative)

Emotion Constructed
- Simulations
- Predictions
- Brain's goal: survival

As we saw with the rustle in the bushes example, your emotions are associated with urges. It makes sense—your emotions exist to guide your behavior. However, while following these urges may occasionally help you survive a situation (like running for shelter from a dangerous storm), much of the time, it causes you to react impulsively and ineffectively (like shouting at someone when you are frustrated). That's why our second strategy for emotional regulation is learning to understand these emotions before you follow their guidance. Another way to say this is learning to respond instead of react. Instead of immediately following the emotional urge, you pause to consider where the emotion is coming from and whether it's accurate to the situation you're in, then take thoughtful and intentional action.

A great way to start cultivating the awareness you'll need for this process is through a body scan. This can help you step back from your mind's tendency to automatically categorize your experiences into good/bad or right/wrong, which tends to motivate all-or-nothing thinking and impulsive, thoughtless action. If you can step back from the situation for a moment to witness what you're feeling, you'll be more likely to respond to the situation with wisdom.

EXERCISE: Felt-Sense Focused Body Scan

1. Sit or lie down in a comfortable position. Ensure your back is straight and your body is relaxed. Close your eyes gently.
2. Take a few deep breaths, inhaling deeply through your nose and exhaling slowly through your mouth.
3. Now allow your breathing to return to its natural rhythm.
4. Set an intention to be open and curious about what you may feel in your body. This is about exploration and understanding, not judgment or fixing.
5. Start by bringing your attention to your feet. Notice any sensations or lack of sensations there. These might include tension, discomfort, warmth, coolness, tingling, and so on.
6. Gradually move your awareness up through your body, from your feet to your legs, hips, abdomen, chest, back, shoulders, arms, hands, neck, and head. As you scan through your body, note any areas that stand out to you. Again, these might be areas of tension, discomfort, warmth, coolness, tingling, or any other sensation.
7. Choose one area or sensation that feels significant or noticeable. Focus your attention on this sensation and describe it:
    - Location: Where exactly in your body do you feel this sensation?
    - Size and shape: How big is the sensation? Does it have a defined shape?
    - Temperature: Does it feel warm, cool, or neutral?
    - Density: Does it feel heavy, light, dense, or airy?

- Movement: Is the sensation static, or does it move or shift?
- Color: If you were to give this sensation a color, what color would it be?

8. Notice if any emotions are associated with this sensation. What feelings come up as you focus on it?
9. Give yourself permission to fully experience the sensation without trying to change it. Just observe and feel it, allowing it to be.
10. Take a few breaths and imagine directing your breath to the area of the sensation. Notice whether this changes anything.
11. If it feels appropriate, you can ask the sensation questions like "What are you trying to tell me?" or "What do you need?"
12. After spending some time with this sensation, gradually expand your awareness to include your entire body again. Notice how your body feels now compared to when you started.
13. Gently bring your attention back to your surroundings. Wiggle your fingers and toes. Take a few more deep breaths and, when you're ready, open your eyes.

Take a moment to reflect on your experience. What did you notice? How do you feel now compared to before the scan?

____

____

____

____

____

Strategy #3: Acceptance

By developing a deeper awareness and understanding of your body and emotions, you are well on your way toward emotional regulation and overall well-being. The final step in learning to move through uncomfortable emotional experiences is accepting your feelings—that is, to feel them without reacting in an unhelpful way or disconnecting from the situation.

Shark Music

Even if you haven't seen the movie *Jaws*, you likely know its unsettling theme song (*duuuun dunn . . . duuuun dunn . . .*). It's become the universal musical accompaniment for something bad about to happen. You can even play the music over an innocuous and delightful scene—say, little mermaids dancing around with clown fish—and still, you'll find yourself scanning the perimeter of the scene, expecting something to go terribly, terribly wrong.

"Shark music" has also become shorthand for what your nervous system does when an emotional state primes you for fight, flight, freeze, or fawn. Even when your thinking brain recognizes that everything is fundamentally safe, your emotional state suddenly has you startling at shadows and quick movements, struggling to respond rationally to what's actually happening.

Certain emotional states can make us feel incredibly uncomfortable and afraid, even when we are in perfectly safe situations. Moreover, it's not always the emotions you expect that create these intense reactions. For example, a moment of happiness may suddenly evoke deep anxiety, like you're just waiting for the other shoe to drop. Remember, it is the experiences from your past that are telling you to be uncomfortable with a feeling. Perhaps when you expressed happiness as a child you were shamed for being "overexcited" or "too much," and so feeling happiness as an adult continues to bring up a sense of discomfort for you.

Identifying your shark music emotions can support you in understanding why you might feel shame or fear associated with those emotions. As a child, that shame or fear motivated you to try to get away from your shark music emotions so that you could feel safer with the adults around you. The challenge is that all emotions are not only safe, but essential to be able to experience if you want to maintain connection with people around you (Cooper et al., 2009). When you can notice the shark music playing, you can recognize that particular emotional experience as a trigger and slow down enough to focus on meeting the real need under the emotion. Essentially, you learn to notice your shark music as just that, rather than an actual shark.

EXERCISE: Shark Music

What are your "shark music" emotions? Reflect on some of your recent experiences of being outside your window of tolerance (being in a fight, flight, freeze, or fawn state). What emotions did you feel right before you left your window of tolerance? You can use the emotions wheel from page 113 to support you in identifying these feelings. List any emotions that tend to evoke a distress sense for you.

____

____

____

____

____

____

EXERCISE: Sitting with Your Emotions

Now that you've reflected on your shark music emotions, practice sitting with your emotions.

Note: Remember, you can use titration and pendulation (as described on page 109) as needed. While you are working to learn to be with your emotions, there will be times when it is very sensible to seek some reprieve and space. When you experience an intense emotion that threatens to overwhelm you, go back to your self-soothing skills and resource skills.

1. Choose a quiet, comfortable place where you won't be disturbed. This could be a cozy corner in your home, a quiet park—any space where you feel safe and at ease. Arrange pillows, blankets, or any other items that make you feel comfortable. Dim the lights or light a candle if it helps you relax.
2. Take a moment to ground yourself. You might want to set an intention for your practice, such as "I am here to explore and nurture my emotions."
3. You can choose to sit, lie down, or engage in gentle movement like yoga or stretching as you complete the next steps. Whatever position you choose, ensure you feel supported and comfortable.
4. Start by bringing attention to your feet and slowly move up through your body, noticing how each part feels, until you finally reach your head. This can help you become more present and aware of bodily sensations.
5. Now focus on your breath. Take slow, deep breaths, inhaling through your nose and exhaling through your mouth. Let your breathing anchor you in the present moment.
6. Witness any physical sensations in your body. Notice areas of tension, warmth, coolness, tingling, or any other sensations. Approach these sensations with curiosity and without judgment. Acknowledge them as they are without trying to change them.
7. Notice the thoughts that arise as you tune into your body. These might be worries, memories, or random thoughts. Label these thoughts simply (e.g., "planning," "worrying," "remembering"). This helps to create a bit of distance between you and your thoughts.
8. Become aware of any emotions that are present. These could be directly linked to the sensations in your body or the thoughts you're having. Give a name to each emotion you identify, such as "anger," "sadness," "fear," or "joy." Naming the emotion can reduce its intensity and help you understand it better.
9. Allow yourself to fully experience each emotion. Notice how it feels in your body and where it is located. Practice accepting the emotion without trying to change or resist it. Understand that it's okay to feel this way and that it's a natural part of the human experience.
10. Reflect on whether the emotion feels manageable or overwhelming. If the emotion feels too intense, use self-soothing techniques like deep breathing, grounding exercises, or gentle movement to bring yourself back within your window of tolerance.

11. Consider what you might need in this moment. This could be rest, a comforting activity, reaching out to a friend, or simply taking a breath.
12. Speak to yourself with kindness and understanding. Acknowledge the difficulty of what you're feeling and offer yourself the same compassion you would offer a friend. Use affirmations to support yourself, such as "It's okay to feel this way," "I am doing my best," or "I am here for myself." Express gratitude to yourself for taking the time to sit with your emotions and for the insights gained from this practice.

By following these steps with detailed attention, you can create a nurturing space to accept how your emotions are trying to help you survive by guiding you toward taking action, while at the same time choosing instead to respond wisely. This compassionate, careful process is what leads to greater emotional resilience and self-awareness.

Discharging the Emotion

The saying "feel it to heal it" can be interpreted in different ways. Being with emotions safely can build our capacity to experience them without dysregulation. However, it's not always the case that we can safely be with our feelings. There are certainly times when I notice an intensity in my feelings at an inopportune time for "being with them." Maybe I have to go pick up the kids, maybe I have a project do, or maybe I'm already utterly exhausted—in all these instances, I know that right now is not going to be an effective time to experience my feelings in full. Sometimes it's better to immediately discharge the emotion by expelling energy or to distract yourself from the feeling of it. That is okay! Sure, it's a "kick the can down the road" type of thing—I know those emotions I've chosen to get away from in the moment may come back to me a little muddier when I do go to pick up the can. But sometimes, it's worth the trade-off.

You can use the techniques from chapters 3 and 4 or find other healthy ways to discharge intense emotions. Here are a few ideas; what else can you add to the list?

- Exercise—go for a walk or run, practice yoga, swim, dance it off, or similar
- Distract yourself with a favorite book, show, or movie
- Engage in a creative outlet such as art, music, or journaling
- Use a stress ball or fidget toy
- Scream, cry, or laugh into a pillow
- Write an unsent letter to a person you're experiencing difficult feelings about
- Use a punching bag or visit a rage room
- Other: ____________________

Making Note of Moods

Up to this point, we've been focusing on emotions—that is, brief states of feeling. Moods are emotional experiences that last for longer periods of time, though at a lower intensity. For instance, on some days you might wake up feeling bright and cheerful for no apparent reason; specific things might happen that make you feel angry or anxious for a moment, but you gravitate back to that happy mood. Other days, you might wake up on the wrong side of the bed. Throughout the day, you might have moments where you feel joy or delight of some sort, but find yourself drifting back to that feeling of sadness or irritability. This is normal, even if it often defies explanation.

Like emotions, moods are effective signals of how you're traveling through each day or season and can yield useful data in planning how you will balance stressors, implement boundaries, and nourish yourself mentally and physically. Sometimes, there is a hormonal or seasonal pattern to your moods; recognizing this predictability can definitely help you take the edge off by prompting you to devise strategies for managing that mood or just by reminding you that it's bound to pass eventually. However, if that unpleasant mood sticks around for an extended period or if the flare-ups are concerningly intense, it's a sign that some sort of change or support might be needed.

Tracking your mood supports your emotional awareness and reminds you to engage in activities that promote your well-being. It is helpful to engage in this reflection alongside tracking the things you are grateful for each day—this supports you in balancing the brain's natural negativity bias, something you'll learn about in the next chapter. For now, the important thing to know is that your brain registers the negative experiences that happen more strongly and recalls these experiences more readily than any positive experiences. This makes it valuable to deliberately focus on the positive events that occur each day, to ensure that you notice and remember them. Recalling them again in your journal allows you an opportunity to relive positive moments in your life, even the smallest ones, like a warm cup of tea or the birdsong you hear as you take the garbage bins out.

EXERCISE: Mood Monitoring and Gratitude Tracking

In this exercise you'll develop a visual tool to track your mood through the days of the month, allowing you to notice any patterns. The shape you'll be using is a circle, or it could be considered your monthly mood mandala. Mandalas signify transformation, and while we are not looking to transform your emotions themselves, my hope is that you are experiencing a transformation in how you view and respond to your feelings, using all of the tools here to cultivate a sense of peace with your mood state, whatever it is.

Additionally, you'll be engaging in gratitude tracking. This may seem to pair with your mood in times of joy, or you might notice how you can experience a challenging mood state and still evoke a sense of gratitude. Both can be present, giving you access to multiplicity of the human experience (which I like to call the "both/and").

1. First, create a key for your mood mandala. List the mood states you would like to track and choose a color to represent each. Choose emotional states that are impactful for you. Some examples are calmness, anxiety, fear, amusement, sadness, craving, and interest. Yes, these are emotion names. Remember that what differentiates moods and emotions is their durability—that is, how long they last. What you're tracking here is the overall feeling you have that colors your experience of the day.

2. Each evening, reflect on the predominant mood of your day. Then fill the associated color into the outer ring of your mandala.
3. Reflect on the delightful moments experienced in your day, no matter how small (such as the sunlight through your curtains or the smell of your body wash). Choose one to note in the pie slice space for the day.
4. Continue this practice every day for a month, until your mandala is complete.

Reflection

Reflect on your completed mandala. Do you notice any patterns? Does anything stand out to you as surprising or significant?

We have talked a lot about emotions, and about how emotional awareness supports your healing and general well-being. Because cultivating this awareness is the first step in regulation, you've looked at practices to support you in safely allowing your inner experiences and understanding how these experiences are created. A lot of these exercises have had a mindfulness component to them, but now it is time to really deep-dive into mindfulness because it is ultimately the single best way to build your emotional awareness, as it enhances your present-moment awareness. This is exactly what we'll be covering in the next chapter.

Closing Reflections

When you were a child, what did you learn about emotions?

How does it feel to tune into your body and use those clues to identify your emotional experience?

Was learning about the way your past experiences, bodily sensations, and situational context all contribute to your emotions helpful for you in understanding your inner experience?

Do your shark music emotions relate to what you learned about emotions as a child? How so?

Which patterns do you notice in your mood states, and how can you use this knowledge to better support your healing and well-being?

Takeaway Messages

- Emotions evolved to motivate actions, and even the uncomfortable feelings are important.
- You can use titration and pendulation to practice being with uncomfortable bodily sensations and emotions safely.
- Regulating your emotions involves enhancing your awareness, understanding, and acceptance of them.
- The constructed theory of emotions demonstrates how your mental concepts, body budget, and affect all influence your emotional experience.
- Your mood states are more pervasive ways of feeling, while emotions generally arise for a shorter duration.

PART 2

Opening

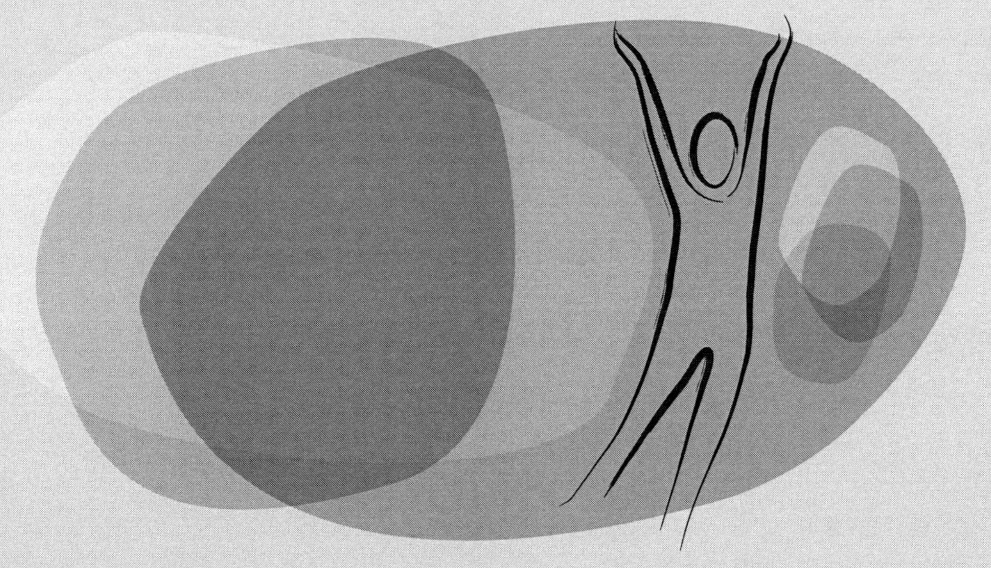

CHAPTER 7

Embodied Presence: The Art of Mindful Awareness

"I want to know if you can sit with pain, mine or your own, without moving to hide it, or fade it, or fix it."

—Oriah Mountain Dreamer, *The Invitation*

"The lifestyle medicine you talk about doesn't work," said Cole.

"I'm curious—what do you mean by that?" I asked, softening my voice in response to the edge in Cole's.

"Well, if eating the right foods, spending time in nature, and exercising regularly really was the elixir of well-being, I should be on cloud nine," he replied, his voice breaking. "I literally do all the right things. I've tried so hard."

"I know," I affirmed. "You've invested so much in aligning your lifestyle with your intention for health and well-being. Unfortunately, there is often this notion out there that if you follow the 'rules' perfectly and do all the supposedly 'right things,' you will feel amazing. But in reality, taking care of your physical body is just the prerequisite to managing anxiety and balancing your mood. The fact is, you can run miles, meditate, and drink all the spinach smoothies in the world, and still feel worthless and overwhelmed."

Like Cole, lots of us experience increasing distress when we have done all the "right" things and still don't feel well. What we may not realize is that sometimes, being so rigidly focused on being "healthy" can end up creating *more* worry and anxiety. This doesn't mean that caring for yourself is a waste of effort. However, we need to make sure that our efforts are balanced between healthy behaviors for our body and healthy management of our minds.

While your body is a physical structure, it is heavily influenced by the mental processes that result in your thoughts, beliefs, memories, desires, and emotions. Your felt experiences are created in part by your unconscious mind. This is why it's helpful to have a practice that allows you to witness your mind-body relationship. Enter the practice of mindful awareness, which is our focus in this chapter.

What Are You Thinking About?

Most of us have had the experience of noticing that a loved one looks unsettled and asking them what they are thinking about, only to receive the response, "Nothing." We've also probably given that response ourselves, at least on an occasion or two.

In reality, your mind is never doing *nothing*. When we answer this way, it's for one of two reasons: Either we don't want to share what we were thinking about at that moment, or we were unaware of what our mind was thinking about. The second reason is the more likely explanation. Studies show that you are barely present for half of your day; the other half (47 percent, to be specific), you're somewhere other than the here and now (Killingsworth & Gilbert, 2010). I'm sure you've experienced those moments when you arrive home and don't remember anything about the drive, or you've missed getting off at your bus or train stop because you were "somewhere else." Apart from the inconvenience, such experiences might seem inconsequential. However, a famous research study by Harvard psychologists Matthew Killingsworth and Daniel Gilbert (2010) demonstrated that your mood suffers when you're not present.

Here's an example: Taking out the trash is not often ranked as a highly pleasurable activity, yet if you were to practice presence during chore time, you might notice the sensation of the plastic knot of the garbage bag in your hands, tension in the forearm you're holding the bag with, the shifting light on the driveway's pebbles, and the feel of the breeze against your face as you walk to the bin.

As an alternative, let's take a stereotypically pleasant activity: a bubble bath. Imagine sitting in a luxurious spa with ylang-ylang-infused Epsom salts soothing your tired muscles and a cool glass of sparkling wine in your hand . . . all while running your mind over the outline for tomorrow's meeting. Suddenly, you realize that you've downed your drink, and your increasing muscle tension is giving those salts plenty of work to do.

I'd go so far as to say there's a good chance you'd rate your mood lower in the bubble bath scenario than in your experience taking out the trash. Presence is the key!

EXERCISE: Minding Your Mind

This exercise builds on your work in the last chapter developing emotional awareness. Set an alarm for three times per day; each time it goes off, make a note in your phone or journal about what you are thinking, along with a rating of your mood on a scale of 1 to 7, where 1 is poor and 7 is fantastic. Another option is to check in on your thinking and mood each time you reach for your phone. Since most of us look at our phones multiple times per day, creating this paired association is a wonderful opportunity to check in with yourself, though it will undoubtedly require a little practice. It may help to set up your phone screen with a reminder.

After three days of these check-ins, look at the data and see if you notice any patterns. Compare your mood rating at times when your thoughts were grounded in the present moment against times when you were thinking about something else. What do you notice?

____

____

____

____

The Default Mode Network

If it feels better to be present, why don't we naturally connect with the moment? Why do we instead spend so much time worrying about the future and ruminating on the past? Once again, it comes back to survival.

When you are not actively engaged in a specific task, your brain has evolved to use the lull to figure out who you are, where you are, and how you will survive. This is thanks to your default mode network (DMN), a group of different brain regions that includes your prefrontal cortex, posterior cingulate cortex, and parts of the temporal lobes; all of these are the self-referential parts of your brain.

The DMN is responsible for creating a concept of self (these personal ways you perceive, feel, and think), evaluating your social characteristics (whether you are relatively clever, desirable, etc.), and mental time traveling (remembering the past and imagining the future). As the place of learning, reasoning, and planning, your DMN uses reflection on your past to consolidate knowledge you've gained, which it then uses to help you anticipate the future. However, the DMN can also cause pain when unhelpful patterns of thought start circulating, such as predictions of impending failures, social doom, and rejection.

This is the cruel irony of the DMN. It teaches us about our patterns and allows us to plan while also holding us hostage to the pain of the past and fostering worry about a future that has not yet unfolded. These tendencies of the DMN were very useful in times past, supporting humans in considering whether going out from the cave at dusk was safe or whether they should travel through another clan's territory. In the modern world, however, higher DMN activity is connected to depression and anxiety (Broyd et al., 2009).

Your Negativity Bias

If your brain is always looking for something to focus on, why wouldn't it gravitate toward your positive memories or the joys you can look forward to? After all, if you have a half-decent life, there ought to be plenty of delightful moments for your brain to revisit, right?

It's a good question. Think back to that exercise in the last chapter where you took note of five blue items in the room, then tried to remember how many circular things were there. Your brain does not see reality as it is, or as you might want it to be. It sees what it predicts. And what it predicts is generally a catastrophe—failure on every front. Your brain evolved to prioritize survival over contentment and joy, which compels it to constantly scan for dangers in your environment. From a survival perspective, enjoying the scent of a beautiful flower is less critical than keeping your ears keen for a rustle in the bush behind you . . . or, for that matter, replaying the last time you heard a rustle in the bushes as you determine whether that path is safe to take again tomorrow.

That's not all. Your brain is also biased in how it interprets information and experiences. This bias even changes how you experience reality. (This is why eyewitness testimony is largely considered one of the least reliable forms of evidence in court.) We see the world not as it is, but as we think it is; moreover, every time we remember something, we mentally reconstruct the event according to our bias, unconsciously adding and omitting details, and ultimately changing our memory of what happened.

Understanding that your brain has a negativity bias is helpful in finding effective ways to manage your limited energetic and attentional resources. Without conscious awareness, you'll naturally give more attention to negative experiences, emotions, and information. In the modern world, this might mean that even if most people you interact with today act neutrally or kindly toward you, you will remember the one person who spoke in a tone you found rude or behaved in a way that upset you. Driven by survival and negativity bias, your mind will make that story the focal point of your day. In all likelihood, your brain will replay it repeatedly, as your DMN searches for lessons it can learn from the experience and tries to anticipate how you'll handle such situations in the future.

Imagine you're walking through your local park on a sunny afternoon when you spot one of your friends sitting on a park bench reading a book. You haven't seen this friend in a few months, and you feel excited for this opportunity to catch up! You raise your arm and start waving an enthusiastic hello.

Your friend momentarily looks up from their book, quickly turning their head back down. No smile. No wave.

What might you feel in your body at this moment? What emotions and thoughts would likely arise? Would you walk toward your friend, or away from them?

It is totally possible that your first thought is that your friend didn't see you. But if you're like many of us, your first thought comes courtesy of your negativity bias: *They don't want to see me. I've done something wrong.* This perceived rejection hurts, sometimes even viscerally—you may feel it like a knot in your stomach, a sinking in your chest, or a slap to the face. It doesn't end there; as you go about the rest of your day and even beyond, your brain's DMN will send you time traveling back to that moment, replaying it again and again. You'll find yourself anticipating the next time you'll see this friend and trying to unpack what their response was all about and what it means for you in the future.

Your Inner Symphony

I think of the DMN as music of your mind, arising from an inner orchestra that is incredibly skilled at creating vivid mental scenarios of the worst possible outcomes, featuring occasional solos of worry, doubt, and self-criticism.

Take Sarah, for instance. Her DMN tends to follow a theme of rumination, dwelling on past mistakes and worrying about future uncertainties. One of the songs on Sarah's DMN soundtrack was composed a few years ago, during a civil lawsuit she was handling for a client's dispute over a property boundary. As always, Sarah was meticulous in her preparation of the case, but when one of her children got sick, she took a much-needed day off. Exhausted from a night awake with her little one, she didn't even think to check her schedule for the day and overlooked the deadline to file a crucial piece of evidence that would have strongly supported her client's claim. The judge ended up ruling in favor of the other party. Naturally, Sarah attributes this outcome to her mistake.

While it's important to own our mistakes, the influence of this one has gone well beyond utility for Sarah. While her office learned from the situation and built new safeguards around it—a shared calendar policy, a new system to ensure deadline coverage, better communication with the courts when a staff member is unexpectedly absent—Sarah still ruminates about the ruling and lives in terror of making such a serious error in the future.

Her sleepless nights are filled with haunting songs of missed deadlines, parenting mistakes, and her relationship crumbling. All of this amplifies the intensity of her anxiety, which naturally decreases the likelihood of sleep. While she can distract herself from these foundational worries during the day, a composition of self-consciousness accompanies her every move, backed by the rhythm of her racing heartbeat and shallow breath:

This outfit is horrendous. What will people think?

Don't suggest that café—nobody will like it.

Ugh, stop talking, you idiot. You sound foolish.

Does any of this sound familiar? Chances are that you, too, have noticed that the music of your mind is composed mainly of your mistakes, both real and imagined. Fortunately, you have the power to teach your brain a new tune.

Neuroplasticity

I grew up in Canada and therefore spent my winters tobogganing, a classic pastime that starts with slogging up to the top of a hill with a snowsuit on and a crazy carpet in hand. (For the non-Canadians, a crazy carpet is a rectangle of bright-colored plastic with two handles cut in the front.) Once at the top, you sit down on the slippery carpet, grip the handles, and prepare for an exhilarating ride.

Well, *eventually* exhilarating. The first ride down the slope would usually feature a bit of resistance, especially if it was newly fallen snow. The upside was that you could carve out your desired path through the fluffy powder by using your body weight to steer left and right. If yours was the second run, you might have some luck steering, but you'd be more likely to fall into that first track. The third, fourth, fifth, and following runs would more and more predictably follow that path, packing the snow down harder and making the journey quicker and quicker, until eventually the snow became as slick as an ice rink, sending each rider rocketing down into a powdery wipeout.

The patterns in your brain work in much the same way. The more you travel a certain mental "pathway" by thinking a specific thought or engaging in a specific behavior, the more likely you will default to that path again. This means when you actively reflect on that incredibly uncomfortable conversation with your coworker again, you'll be even more likely to think of it every time you see them. This could be useful if you were still brainstorming potential ways to repair the relationship or were considering what you might do differently in a similar situation next time. However, if you keep going over it repeatedly, your mood will be impacted and the insights you gain will be limited by keeping the pain of that experience active in your mind. You may even find the pathway widening, so to speak—the painful memories and self-criticism begin to arise not just from the sight of that one coworker, but from all your coworkers: *There was that one time when I told a joke in a meeting and Carl didn't laugh. Maybe everyone else was just laughing politely. Oh, no . . . do they* all *think I'm awkward? Does my boss think so too?*

For another example, you might have an intrusive thought that is super upsetting—vivid images of making a major mistake at work, perhaps, or hurting folks you care about. The clinical descriptor for these experiences is *egodystonic*, meaning that your brain has created a thought that is different from the way you truly feel or want to act.

When a thought like this appears in your brain, you probably try your best to push the thought away, yet it keeps resurfacing, causing worse distress and anxiety. There's a neurological explanation behind this paradox: Every time you try *not* to think of something, you activate the same neural network as when you *do* think that thought. It's the principle behind the game that starts with someone telling you, "Do *not* think of a purple elephant." If you haven't played it before, try it now—take a minute and do everything in your power *not* to think of a purple elephant.

You get it: this is a near-impossible exercise. What makes it so difficult is that the very neurological path you use to suppress the image of the purple elephant is the same one that evokes it. So, the harder you try not to think of the purple elephant, the more you do think of it. You may find that having tried not to think of the purple elephant in this moment makes you more likely to think of the purple elephant in the days ahead.

The point is that you don't get to choose where the DMN takes you. However, you can control how gently you hold that thought or what other thoughts you might choose to focus on. Going back to the music metaphor, it's like choosing to focus on the trumpet in the orchestra. The other instruments continue in the background, but as you intently focus on the one instrument you've chosen to hear, your awareness of the others will dim.

EXERCISE: Turn Down the Radio

In this exercise you'll be learning a strategy that you can apply when the thoughts in your mind are unhelpful or painful.

First, I want you to imagine that your mind is a radio. All of your self-critical, defeatist, or otherwise unhelpful and painful thoughts are raucous music playing on the radio of your mind. It's blaring so loud that you actually feel pain in your ears, and you can't concentrate on any of the activities you wanted to get done.

Unlike a real radio, you can't simply turn your mind radio off or change the station. However, you can turn down the volume. This helps the unpleasant music become background noise, rather than the focal point of your attention.

Imagine what it is like to turn the music down. Picture yourself going about your day with the music playing quietly in the background.

This is a tricky radio, and from time to time the volume will get louder again (because no doubt your attention will come back to the painful experience). You might have an inner dialogue about how much you dislike this song or how you wish you could change the station. Simply notice that, and turn down the volume down again, as you turn your attention back to what you're doing.

Now, try this exercise in your daily life. When you notice a stream of unhelpful or painful thoughts, imagine turning their volume down. Don't try to turn the radio off or change the station; let the thoughts play, but turn your attention to something that matters. This is where you get freedom.

EXERCISE: Trains of Thought

Another way to visualize managing your DMN is choosing which train of thought to "board." Imagine you're in an unfamiliar city, using their subway system to go somewhere exciting: a museum, a botanical garden, a shopping district—anything you like. Being unfamiliar with the subway in this city, you hop on the first train that arrives and seems to be going in the direction you want. But after a few stops, you realize it's taking you far afield of where you want to go. The only thing to do, of course, is get off the train, study the transit map, and deliberately choose a different train to take.

In the same way, whenever you notice that your mood is changing for the worse or you're lacking the energy or focus you need, it's a good opportunity to use present-moment awareness to notice what train of thought has carried you to that state. This empowers you to get off that train of thought you've unconsciously boarded and choose a different train that will get you where you want to go.

Give it a try now. First, notice and label the train of thought you're currently on, or recall a train you rode recently that you didn't like. Maybe it's a self-defeating thought ("the little engine that couldn't") or maybe it's self-blame (a real "guilt trip"). Instead of letting that train take you along for the ride, pause and disembark. Let that train continue without you, perhaps even vanishing into the distance.

Then consider what kinds of thoughts you would rather be having, and board that train instead. These might be more positive, realistic thoughts about the situation, such as "I am capable and my goals are worth striving for" or "Making mistakes is part of being human; I can forgive myself for mine." Or you might simply turn your focus back to what you were doing before the negative thought arose (reading this book, working on a project, washing the dishes, etc.).

The more you practice this technique in your mind, the easier it will become.

This is neuroplasticity in action: your brain's capacity to adapt, change, and "rewire" itself in response to your experiences and what you learn from them. Present-moment awareness—the ability to notice what is unfolding as it's unfolding—amplifies your ability to establish patterns and pathways that are conducive to your healing and well-being.

The Freedom to Choose

Dr. Viktor Frankl was an Austrian psychologist whose most famous work came about as a result of what he suffered in a Nazi concentration camp. Observing the horror around him, Frankl noticed that his fellow inmates who could find no sense of purpose or meaning in their suffering were the least likely to survive the experience. In contrast, those who found a sense of purpose—offering compassion and care to others, focusing on completing tasks well, and facing their suffering with dignity—showed greater mental and physical resilience to the torment inflicted by their captors. There is a popular quote from an unknown author that is often attributed to Frankl because it succinctly captures his essential message: "Between stimulus and response, there is a space. In that space lies our freedom and our power to choose our response. In our response lies our growth and our happiness."

Frankl's life and work show that meaning can be found in every moment of life, even in the most extreme suffering, by exercising our freedom of choice—will we respond to circumstances in a way driven by despair, or in a way that supports our healing and growth? Present-moment awareness brings us to this crossroads. When we nonjudgmentally experience events inside the brain and in our external environment as they unfold, moment by moment, we can create the conditions to choose exactly how we want to respond to an experience, rather than defaulting to the unconscious patterns of our past and the perceptual hook of our brain's negativity bias.

Present-Moment Awareness Versus Mindful Attention

If presence is a skill, how do we practice it? The answer is through mindfulness.

While they're often thought of as synonyms, present-moment awareness and mindfulness are different. Think of young children—they are masters of connecting to the present moment, captivated by any little thing that grabs their attention. However, they are rarely conscious of what they're thinking, feeling, and experiencing inside their skin. As a result, their big emotions can arise quickly and, often, blow over with the next distraction. Mindfulness allows us to notice what is unfolding outside the body while also being aware of what is happening inside the body.

This dual awareness helps us remain flexible in how we maintain attention. Just as a violin will be out of tune if its strings are too tight or too loose, having your attention too rigid or too distractible hinders you from accessing the information you need to respond in healthy ways and grow in positive directions throughout your life.

Rigidity Versus Distractibility

Perhaps you've heard of folks getting so absorbed in something—playing a video game, studying for an exam, working on an important project—that they continue for hours without a break to eat, drink, or sleep, not even noticing that they are hungry, thirsty, and tired. You might have experienced this yourself. This state of hyperfocus is an example of rigid attention, wherein you are very present but not very flexible.

Maintaining such a high degree of focus requires a lot of energy. If you've been so focused that you've delayed eating, hydrating, and sleeping, your glucose reserves are likely depleted, resulting in a general sense of unpleasantness in your body.

This isn't necessarily problematic if it's an occasional thing. If you've got a huge deadline approaching, the state of hyperfocus could be what gets your project across the finish line. The trade-off, though, is that you'll likely crash on the other side of it and need to spend some time rebalancing through reengagement with the therapeutic lifestyle habits we talked about in chapter 5. It should go without saying that operating from a state of rigid attention on a regular basis is not something your body can healthily sustain.

On the other side of rigidity is distractibility, the experience of not being able to maintain your focus on one thing. In this state, you are incredibly flexible but not particularly present. Every sensation seems to capture your attention, from the car passing outside the window to the wrinkle in your sock. Constantly following different "rabbit trails" makes it difficult to finish anything, from a task to a conversation. Often, this state can follow periods of hyperfocus, as your mind tries to rebalance from the cognitive load, though it can also arise following periods of general stress.

Mindfulness

Mindfulness bridges rigidity and distractibility to cultivate a state of compassionate, deliberate, flexible attention. Famously defined by Dr. Jon Kabat-Zinn as "the awareness that arises by paying attention on purpose, in the present moment, and non-judgmentally" (Kabat-Zinn, 2013, p. xxxv), mindfulness requires noticing and accepting exactly what is showing up inside and outside your skin, here and now. Developing mindfulness is like cross-training for your brain, empowering you to pull yourself out of the DMN's unhelpful patterns by reconnecting with your felt sense. This is why mindfulness is a cornerstone of somatic psychology.

There are both formal and informal ways you can practice mindfulness. The most well-known of these is meditation, to the extent that many people are under the impression that mindfulness is simply another word for meditation. To be clear, mindfulness and meditation are not the same, though they are very much related! Mindfulness is a quality, a state of being in nonjudgmental awareness. Meditation is a formal mindfulness practice. Absolutely, mindfulness can be cultivated through formal meditation practices (like the ones you'll explore later in this chapter). But you can also practice mindfulness informally, as you go about your daily life. This tends to be an easier entry point, so it's where we'll begin.

Informal Mindfulness

The informal ways to practice mindfulness involve taking advantage of the many seemingly mundane moments in your life that offer a sacred opportunity for paying attention. When you are washing the dishes, for example, you can focus your attention on really feeling the temperature of the water, noticing the sensation of the bubbles, and witnessing the shine of the cutlery. This transformative practice can be applied to any activity.

EXERCISE: Informal Mindfulness

An easy way to bring more mindfulness to your day is to practice present-moment awareness during an activity you're already doing. The following are just a few ideas. Choose one or two from the list to start with, then build up your practice over the coming days:

- Brushing your teeth
- Drinking your coffee or tea
- Walking
- Eating
- Washing dishes
- Sweeping the floor
- Cuddling a loved one
- Washing your face
- Watering the garden
- Taking a shower

As you do the activity, follow this process:

1. Pay attention to the sensations of the activity, noticing from the inside out. You might notice sounds, smells, flavors, colors, shapes, textures, and so on.
2. When a thought, image, judgment, or urge arises, note it, and then gently let it go by coming back to awareness of the present moment. Tune back into what is unfolding inside your skin and outside of you.
3. When you notice your mind is stuck on a sensation or wanders off entirely, congratulate yourself for noticing—this means your brain has returned to the present moment. Return again to observing each sensation as it arises.

It is important for me to highlight that you may or may not feel relaxed or "better" after your practice. If you don't, it doesn't mean that you're doing anything wrong or that the practice isn't benefiting you. Mindfulness is about feeling whatever it is that you are feeling simply because you're feeling it. It's also not about perfection—it is a practice. Your mind will wander. Just as lifting weights involves reaching a point where your muscles need a break before doing another rep, the whole point of mindfulness practice is noticing when your mind has wandered and bringing it back to a state of deliberate attention, over and over.

EXERCISE: Noticing and Naming (Your Felt Sense)

In a gentle step toward more formal meditation practices, you can use this exercise to enhance your felt-sense awareness. This increasing awareness will support your nonjudgmental observation in the formal practices ahead. Use the body map on the next page to note where in your body you experience the sensations, and describe these sensations using the following qualities as a guide.

Size	Shape	Texture	Temperature	Pressure	Movement
• Small	• Round	• Smooth	• Warm	• Light	• Tingling
• Large	• Oval	• Rough	• Hot	• Heavy	• Buzzing
• Tiny	• Square	• Grainy	• Cold	• Pressing	• Vibrating
• Vast	• Rectangular	• Silky	• Cool	• Squeezing	• Throbbing
• Minuscule	• Triangular	• Velvety	• Chilly	• Compressing	• Pulsing
• Gigantic	• Irregular	• Gritty	• Icy	• Constricting	• Fluttering
• Microscopic	• Blob-like	• Slimy	• Lukewarm	• Pinching	• Trembling
• Enormous	• Sharp-edged	• Sticky	• Scorching	• Gripping	• Quivering
• Petite	• Circular	• Slippery	• Freezing	• Bearing down	• Shaking
• Massive	• Angular	• Bumpy	• Tepid	• Crushing	• Wobbling

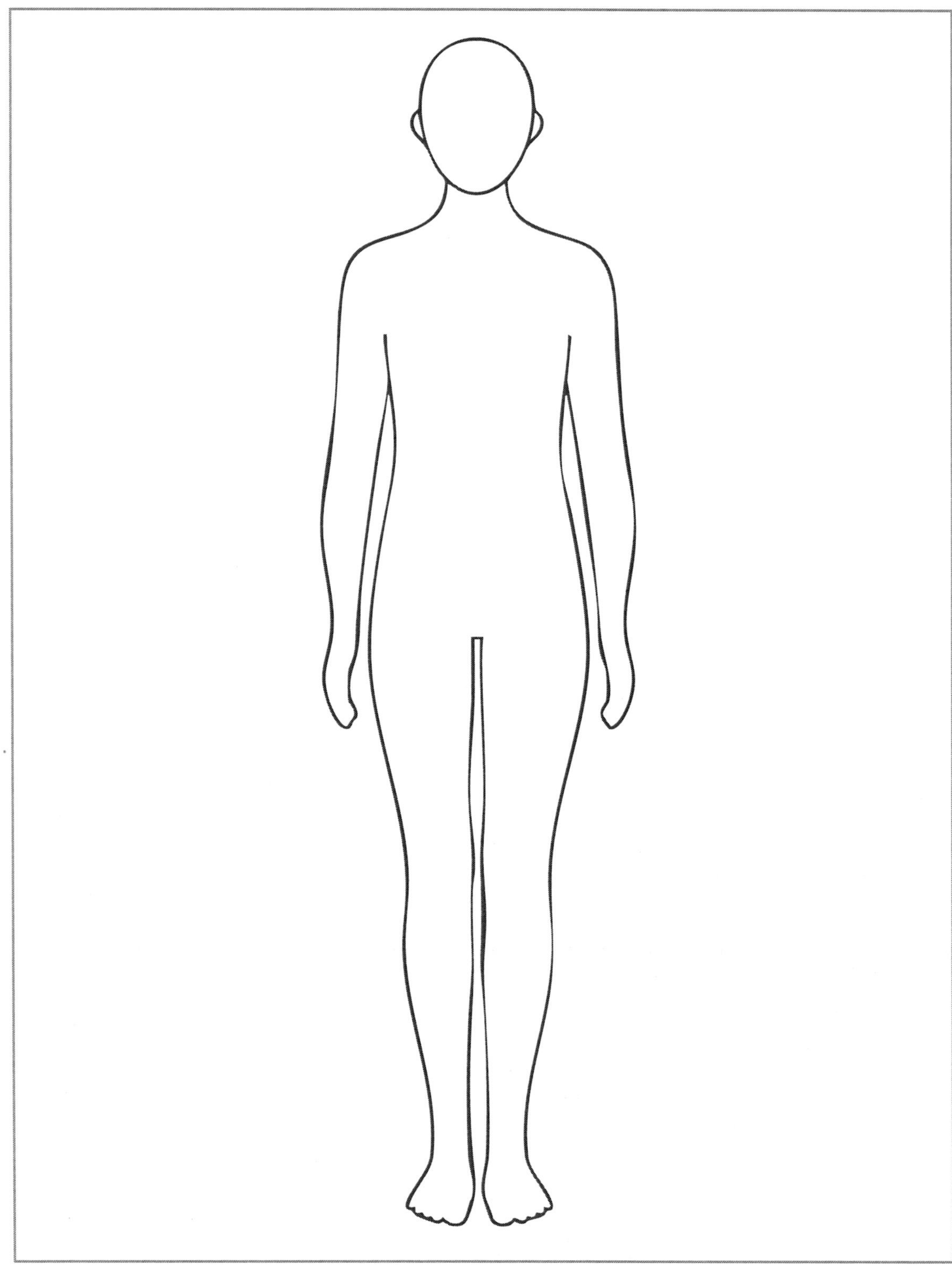

Even in the presence of painful feelings, emotions, thoughts, and the like, a ventral vagal state (social engagement) can be found. This connected experience is found by gently holding your felt sense and the experience unfolding, meeting it with kindness, compassion, and curiosity. In such a state, you can more effectively meet your needs and move forward with clarity.

Formal Mindfulness Practices

Formal mindfulness practices are a bit more structured than the informal activities you've just tried. Most formal practices are designed to promote a state of mindfulness, while other types of meditation can focus on fostering other qualities, such as compassion or peace; such a focus is likely to result in more prosocial behavior, while a focus on mindfulness is more conducive to present-moment awareness (Roca et al., 2021). Similarly, focused attention meditation practices have different psychological benefits than open awareness practices. I'll unpack these styles in the paragraphs ahead. You can choose the ones that align with your lifestyle and cultivate the mental skills that sound most beneficial for you, then search for that type of practice online or in a meditation app.

Open Awareness

This approach involves holding your thoughts, feelings, and bodily sensations in nonjudgmental awareness. Whenever you notice your mind has wandered, you deliberately come back to nonjudgmentally watching your private experiences come and go again.

Open awareness practices support creative thinking, concentration, and memory. When you experience less mind-wandering, you'll be less likely to find your mind caught in worry or rumination, and you'll become more aware of where your attention gets hooked.

Focused Attention

This style involves anchoring your attention on a single point, such as a sensation, sound, or sight. For instance, you might focus on your breath, a mantra (a repeated phrase), or a candle. Whenever you notice your attention has wandered away from your focus point, you deliberately come back to it, again and again.

Given the one-pointed nature of this practice, it improves attention and focus. This makes focused attention a particularly useful style to practice if you have a mind that often wanders and is easily distracted. Interestingly, while mindfulness should never be practiced specifically for relaxation (that is where relaxation or self-soothing strategies come in), one-pointed focus on your breath specifically often does offer a sense of calm and relaxation.

Of course, just because something is helpful on average doesn't mean it will necessarily be helpful for you—certainly not all of the time, anyhow. There are times when being with your inner experience is far from advisable, particularly if you find that practice leaves you feeling overwhelmed and distressed. At these times, it's important to move—you can benefit from the diverted attention, as much as the physical movement can benefit your health.

Mindful Movement

Essentially, this is a more formalized version of the mindful movement you've already learned about in this book. In this form of meditation, you coordinate a specific physical movement with sensorimotor feedback while engaging in a mindful exploration of the physical experience. Its unique benefit lies in blending two attentional styles: open awareness and focused attention.

Mindful movement cultivates executive function, attention, and skilled behavior control. Additionally, it provides physiological benefits—from mobility to cardio and strength. Depending on the style and intensity of the practice, these benefits can carry their own anxiolytic and antidepressant effects.

Compassion Focused

Most, if not all, mindfulness practices include compassion to some degree, but this style is designed specifically to cultivate it. While there are a range of definitions from Buddhist and Western psychological perspectives, compassion-focused meditation typically includes five components (Strauss et al., 2016):

1. Recognition of suffering
2. An appreciation of its universality
3. Emotional resonance with the person suffering (as opposed to a "look on the bright side" attitude)
4. Tolerance of uncomfortable feelings that come with experiencing suffering
5. Motivation to alleviate the suffering

There are also practices designed to cultivate self-compassion specifically (like the one in chapter 3 of this book). Self-compassion is often a good place to begin, especially if you are feeling anxious or depressed.

Loving-Kindness

This variation of compassion-focused meditation involves silently repeating the intention of safety and ease for yourself, loved ones, neutral people, and those you find difficult. For example, you might say, "May I be safe," "May I be happy," or "May I be free from suffering," then "May you be safe" and so on.

Loving-kindness cultivates a positive mood state and the ability to hold space for others' suffering in a way that does not result in your own neural circuits lighting up such that you are experiencing the pain yourself. This results in protection from the compassion fatigue many sensitive and caring individuals are at risk of.

It is worth noting that this practice is less likely to cultivate a sense of relaxation, given the cognitive demands. However, it does reduce distress and increase well-being, while enhancing one's sense of social connection.

The Ultimate Dose-Response Ratio

How do you get the most bang for your mindfulness buck? To say it another way, what is the shortest amount of time you need to practice for the biggest impact?

The ultimate mindfulness dose is somewhere between 8 and 12 minutes. In this relatively brief time frame, neurological changes will unfold that start to reduce your perception of stress, anxiety, and distress.

Naturally, we can't live our entire day in a state of intentional mindfulness. There are times when we have to consider the past or plan for the future. The goal with mindfulness practice is to lessen our brain's tendency to follow the patterns of the DMN. The more we develop our ability to counteract the anxiety and overwhelm that these patterns encourage, the easier it becomes to make room for painful inner experiences when they happen, manage them in a healthy way, and let go of them once they've passed—all things you'll explore in the next chapter.

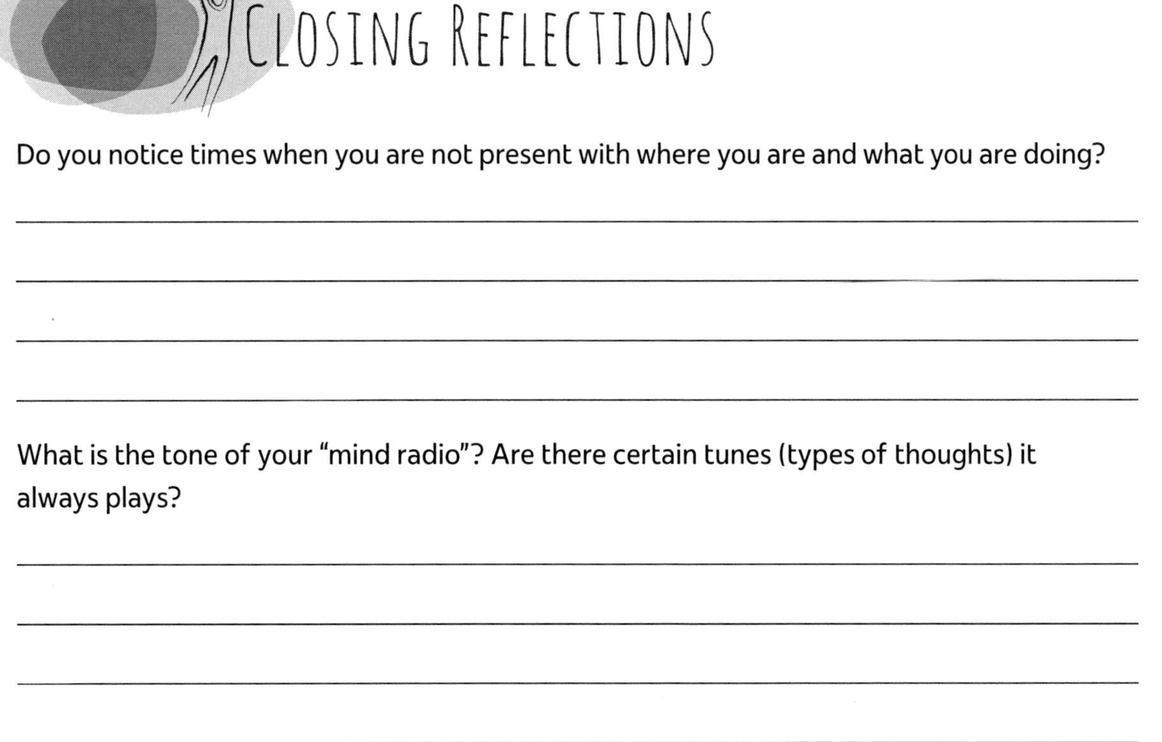

Closing Reflections

Do you notice times when you are not present with where you are and what you are doing?

____

____

____

____

What is the tone of your "mind radio"? Are there certain tunes (types of thoughts) it always plays?

____

____

____

____

How will you ensure you regularly practice neuroplasticity-building exercises?

Do you struggle more with rigidity or chaos in your mind or life?

What would be the things that might get in the way of practicing a form of meditation for 10 minutes each day? Can you plan around these obstacles?

Takeaway Messages

- The default mode network (DMN) has your brain always engaged in thought if you don't have your attention focused on something else.
- On average, you are scarcely present for 50 percent of your day.
- The mind has a negativity bias that evolved to ensure that survival-related information is prioritized.
- Through the process of neuroplasticity, you can shift unhelpful thought patterns.
- You can practice formal or informal mindfulness exercises to enhance your present-moment awareness.

CHAPTER 8

Opening to Home: Cultivating Acceptance in Your Body

"Let go of the battle. Breathe quietly and let it be. . . . Let your body relax and your heart soften. Open to whatever you experience without fighting."

—Jack Kornfield, *A Path with Heart*

Without question, you have done the best you could in every situation you've encountered to this point, using whatever resources you had (which are likely quite different from those you are building now). In this chapter, you'll be working on developing a new resource called *openness*. Few skills will allow you to transform your life as much as this will.

From a psychological perspective, openness is your capacity to experience emotional pain or distressing inner experiences without judgment or struggle. Without this resource, you aren't willing to experience painful thoughts, feelings, urges, or somatic sensations; instead, you try to avoid or control them, which ultimately creates more suffering in your life. When you are in a state of openness, you free up all that time and attention you would have spent avoiding or controlling and can instead channel it into aligning your behavior with your deepest intentions and values. Moreover, by releasing old patterns of emotional tension that have been held in your body, you free up energy to support you in making these shifts.

Key Elements of Openness

By now, you've built your somatic and emotional awareness, cultivated a sense of interoception, and enhanced your compassionate mindfulness. This grounding offers the anchor you need to practice the two key elements of openness:

- **Acceptance:** A nonjudgmental and compassionate stance you hold in acknowledging and creating space for the thoughts, emotions, sensations, and urges you are experiencing. The active part of the acceptance process is willingness—your choice to engage with your life fully, regardless of the presence of pain or challenges.

- **Defusion:** The ability to create a sense of space from the literal content or impact of your thoughts, feelings, and bodily sensations. This allows you to recognize them as passing experiences, which are not absolute truths or commands requiring immediate action. This is in contrast to resistance and avoidance of pain, which are recognized as contributing to anxiety, stress, depression, and general suffering over the long term.

Acceptance

Acceptance is embedded in seminal philosophies of the East and West, as well as modern psychology and somatic therapy. It starts with recognizing the reality that life is unpredictable and that, at times, you experience situations and feelings you don't want—difficult thoughts, emotions, bodily sensations, and the like. Acceptance asks that you be willing to experience these painful aspects of your life without trying to avoid, suppress, or control them. In other words, acceptance is an active, ongoing practice.

Acceptance is sometimes best understood by describing what it is not. It is not liking, wanting, or choosing something. It is not approval or forgiveness. Acceptance is also not resignation. Resignation is passive—it removes your agency to make a change, to release, or to grow. In contrast, acceptance is the first step in taking effective action. For instance, if someone finds themselves in an abusive relationship, no change can be made until they accept that they are in an abusive relationship—in this instance, that means letting go of what the relationship used to be and how they thought it would be, seeing the situation as harmful and untenable, and being willing to fully experience the heartache of that realization. Anytime you find yourself in a situation that is not supportive of your well-being, acceptance is what allows you to clearly see that situation for what it is and decide how best to move forward toward safety and comfort.

To further explore acceptance, let's revisit Sarah's situation. One of her major triggers is feeling like she's being disapproved of. This feeling came up in full force when she was passed over for a promotion at work. Having diligently put in extra hours over many years while sacrificing such activities as her kids' sports games and weekends away with her partner, Sarah felt she had demonstrated her commitment to the company. These sacrifices made it even harder to see the promotion awarded to another colleague—so hard, in fact, that Sarah was convinced that the decision had been made unfairly. She felt bitter and started resenting her boss. She constantly replayed the interview in her mind, dwelling on what could have been. Without accepting the situation, she was stuck.

EXERCISE: Embodying Openness

Reflect for a moment: What does acceptance mean to you?

When you integrate acceptance with defusion, you create a state of openness. The following exercise will support you in integrating these two components: willingness to experience inner events without trying to resist or change them (acceptance) and an ability to recognize your inner experiences as words, images, and sensations (defusion). Often these processes of acceptance and defusion are practiced through metaphors, and that is exactly what we are going to do here to help you have a felt experience of openness.

Take a moment now and hold this workbook with one hand. With the other hand, open your fingers and turn your palm open to the sky. Perhaps sigh or make a *hmm* sound as you do so.

Notice that your fingers may start curling back in. If so, gently open your palm back up. Notice the urge to make this experience be anything different from what it is. Perhaps you feel a pull to hurry things up or to experience something else. Continually practice accepting this resistance and being willing to open your hand again.

Reflect on what it was like to open your palm as an act of acceptance.

How did you relate to any resistance?

Consider the areas in your life where you might practice acceptance.

EXERCISE: Navigating Efforts to Suppress, Control, and Avoid

Acceptance of pain in life isn't intuitive. You might instead find yourself attempting to suppress, control, or avoid it. I'll show you: Put both hands on this workbook. This workbook represents the difficult things in your life—those painful thoughts, feelings, memories, and bodily sensations.

Bring the workbook right up to your face, so close you cannot see anything beyond the workbook itself . . . perhaps so close that you can no longer even read the words. But try to see the room beyond this book, those things you love. This represents those times when you are entirely focused on the pain and difficulty you experience, stuck in the "would have, could have, should have" space.

Consider what it is like when you're holding these painful experiences so tight. Can you engage with all of the beautiful people, experiences, and opportunities that surround you?

Next, push this workbook away with all your might. Hold it out firmly, as far away from you as possible. Whatever you do, don't lose your grip on the workbook, and try not to look at it. After all, you don't like it.

How much energy does it take to keep the workbook—your pain—away?

Does this effort to avoid the pain bring you relief, or a different form of suffering?

____

____

____

____

Finally, pick the workbook back up. See if you can drop it down into your lap rather than trying to push it away. Your hands become free to open back up to everything around you. Sit this way for a moment, noticing how it feels. You may still experience some discomfort, of course, but also openness.

What was it like to sit with the workbook in your lap and to be open?

____

____

____

____

Reflect on what it is like to have pain and acceptance exist simultaneously.

____

____

____

____

Note that just as you can't half-drop the workbook, you can't be half accepting. You've got to be all in. However, like any skill, you can practice with smaller steps first. You can drop the workbook from one inch above your lap, or you can drop it from a foot above your lap. Both are practices of acceptance, of being willing to drop your battle against your experience, seeing the inner experiences for what they are, and turning your attention toward revitalizing your life. You start with the micro and build to the macro.

Defusion

Openness requires you to create a sense of separation from unhelpful thoughts, feelings, and bodily sensations you experience. The ability to step back from a painful experience and see it as something separate from you is called *defusion*. When you held the workbook right up close to you, it might have seemed like it was your entire reality. You could describe this as the experience of fusion, being entangled in the content of your mind.

The easiest way to practice defusing is in the form of your language. Thoughts can have excessive influence over your behavior, and language influences how you experience the world (Satpute & Lindquist, 2021). For instance, some languages have more words for specific emotions or concepts than other languages. These nuances have impacts on your sense of self (Zhou et al., 2022). There is even research to suggest that bilingual individuals score differently on personality tests depending on the language in which they take the test (Veltkamp et al., 2013).

In Sanskrit, the language of ancient India, we see a richer vocabulary for love, with different words evoking specific connotations and context (Hara, 2007). How brilliant and beautiful to be actively guided to differentiate between the romantic feeling state of attraction, desire, and passion (*shringara*); the practice of goodwill, kindness, empathy, and mutual respect we see as foundational to healthy relationships of all types (*maitri*); and the spiritual surrender and sense of oneness with the divine evoked in a devotional form of love (*bhakti*). There are several other "loves" in this wise language as well.

Love is a powerful human driver, a place of connection, companionship, purpose, and self-worth. The other side of the coin is that love is the source of our deepest wounds and pain. Given that it touches nearly every aspect of our lives, I can think of no other emotion that we would want to be more precise in describing. Yet it is a place where we continually get stuck and confused. I spend a lot of time with folks unpacking how *love* can be both a feeling and an action.

For instance, if you only define love as the felt experience of hormone-rich chemistry, you might not see love as clearly in the form of actions—such as behaving with kindness, respect, and consideration—that can be demonstrated regardless of the biophysiological feeling. In fact, this lack of language specificity and understanding about the different forms of love contributes to many healthy relationships ending (Harris, 2009), while other folks battle hard to stay in toxic relationships with high levels of chemistry. This is just one example of why precision matters and how it can transform your experience.

Of course, just as you don't get to choose your feelings, you don't get to choose your thoughts. Like feelings, thoughts can be managed but they cannot be controlled. What you can control are your words, and this can grant you transformative power over your experience. As a popular saying goes, "Watch your thoughts, they become your words; watch your words, they become your actions; watch your actions, they become your habits; watch your habits, they become your character; watch your character, it becomes your destiny." If you state, "I am anxious," you are linguistically defining yourself by the experience of anxiety—you *are* anxious. It seems to say something about your essence. It constricts your ability to shape a different form of embodiment in the moment you are holding it as a belief. It's a state of fusion.

When you believe something about yourself to be true, you'll make behavioral decisions based on that belief. For instance, you might not go to a party because you're anxious, or you might not submit an application for an interesting job or training because you're a failure. Whereas if you are able to practice defusion skills, you can see the thoughts as simply thoughts. Their believability then decreases, which frees you up to choose behaviors based on what you value in life.

My client Cole often avoided experiences. "I'm too anxious," he would say. These situations could range from practicing at a new yoga studio to catching up with friends. He was acutely aware of his anxiety symptoms—his rapid heartbeat and racing thoughts about how awkward he would come across and everything that would go wrong. He often made excuses about why he couldn't catch up with his friends so that he could stay home, but after a moment of relief, he'd start to feel guilty, chastising himself for lying. Over time, Cole started to feel incredibly lonely as invitations to catch up came less frequently, perpetuating his belief that nobody really cared about him. Being able to shift to saying "I'm *feeling* anxious" helped Cole defuse from the experience. It was his stepping stone to acceptance; he learned that feelings pass. Now it's time to explore your language so you can start this journey too.

EXERCISE: Notice, Name, and Neutralize

All the practice you've had accessing your felt sense and becoming aware of your emotions will now be integrated with developing language specificity. It is your ability to specifically name your inner experience and the process (e.g., a thought, feeling, or memory) that allows you to start neutralizing it—decreasing the intensity of painful inner experiences. So, let's get started.

First, describe your present-moment experience.

____

____

____

____

Next, think back to a recent situation in which you felt uncomfortable inside your own skin—a moment when your inner critic came in hot, saying something like "I'm such an embarrassment," "I'm too much," or "I look ugly." To safely practice this, choose a situation that brings up only mild or moderate distress when you think about it—a 5 or less on a scale of 0 to 10, where 10 is the most distressing.

What would you rate your distress right now as you recall this experience, on a scale of 0 to 10?

____

Use the following prompts to describe what you were experiencing at the time when you spoke those words about yourself:

- I am noticing the feeling of ______________________________.
- I am noticing the thought that ______________________________.
- I am noticing the urge to ______________________________.

- I'm noticing the memory of ______________________________.
- I am noticing the sensation of ______________________________ in my ______________________________ (area of your body).

Take a moment to review your responses to those prompts. Do you notice any connection between the specific experience you're describing and other experiences in your life? For example, when you feel the way you felt in that moment, do you typically have the same kinds of thoughts or memories that occurred in that moment?

____

____

____

____

Next, you will write a description of the situation using nonjudgmental language. This means simply articulating what you experienced in your mind and with your senses, without judging those experiences as positive or negative. Remember to keep your description focused on what you visually see outside yourself or what you are experiencing internally—resist the urge to describe what someone else might be thinking or feeling, no matter how much you believe you're right about it. The goal of this exercise isn't to access another person's inner landscape; it's to see your own more clearly.

To help you understand the difference, consider the two examples that follow. Example A is full of judgmental language, assumptions about someone else, and fusion with inner experiences. Example B shows how to describe the same situation with nonjudgmental language and a focus on your own experience.

> **Example A:** *My house is a total mess. The kitchen counter is packed with dirty dishes, and there's laundry on the furniture. I am so ashamed and anxious! Now my dinner guests will think I'm a total loser who can't get it together. I'm never going to be able to cope with this.*

> **Example B:** *My house is a mess. The kitchen counter is full of dirty dishes, and there's laundry on the furniture. I am feeling ashamed and anxious. My whole body is feeling tense. I'm imagining my dinner guests looking around my house and possibly thinking I'm a total loser who can't get it together. This thought feels triggering—my mind is going back to the challenges I've had with friendships in the past.*

Yes, it takes a lot longer. Hence, we all use language shortcuts to support quicker decision-making and day-to-day communication. The cost is that accuracy is lost, and biases, errors, and oversimplifications occur. So for now, practice being deliberately descriptive to see how it might reduce the believability and unconscious influence of your inner experiences. This is defusion in action.

You might also notice that it supports you in practicing acceptance of uncomfortable inner events, so that you can shift your focus back to the life you're experiencing. For example, you might have the thought that you're socially awkward, but in labeling it as a thought, you may be able to focus more on exactly what the person in front of you is saying.

Now it's your turn. Come back to that recent experience you chose at the beginning of this exercise and describe it in detail, using nonjudgmental language and focusing on your own experience.

____

____

____

____

How would you rate your distress now, on a scale of 0 to 10? ______________

Compare this distress rating to that which you had at the beginning of the exercise. Has it changed? What about this exercise did you find helpful, surprising, or interesting?

____

____

____

____

Rules and Reasons

Rules are rigid beliefs about how you should be behaving or feeling, while *reasons* are justifications or explanations to support these beliefs and the behaviors they demand. Like the judgments we examined in the last exercise, rules and reasons are major fusion factors—keep an eye out for them in your language!

Typically, we unconsciously adopt rules and reasons in a context or time when they are helpful to us, allowing us to fit in with a group or succeed in something important to us. As a result, we may find ourselves fused with them even in other times or domains of life where they are not helpful. If you can dis-identify with the believability of the rule or reason, you'll find the freedom to evaluate whether it is currently serving your highest good. Remember, all these rules and reasons are mental events, not ultimate truths.

Tick any of the following rules that you recognize in yourself, and add any more to the list:

- ❒ I should always be in control of my emotions.
- ❒ I should never make mistakes.
- ❒ I should always put others' needs before my own.
- ❒ I must always be productive and accomplish something.
- ❒ I should never show vulnerability.
- ❒ I must always be happy and positive.
- ❒ I should never feel anxious or depressed.
- ❒ I must always be liked by others.
- ❒ I should never take risks.
- ❒ ____________________
- ❒ ____________________
- ❒ ____________________
- ❒ ____________________

Tick any of the following reasons that you regularly consider, and add your own to the list:

- ❒ I don't have the time.
- ❒ I might look like a fool.
- ❒ I don't have the money.
- ❒ I'm too busy.
- ❒ I'm too old.
- ❒ I don't have the talent or skill.
- ❒ I'm too overwhelmed.
- ❒ I don't know where to start.
- ❒ I don't want to be uncomfortable.
- ❒ ____________________
- ❒ ____________________
- ❒ ____________________
- ❒ ____________________

EXERCISE: Get Back in Your Body

We've been talking about language as defusion strategy with a focus on thoughts. This next exercise will bring your defusion skills into your body as you cultivate awareness and attunement to your somatic sensations without becoming overwhelmed by them. Your mind extends into your body, and experiencing defusion viscerally is a crucial step on your journey to experiencing openness in mind and body.

> **Note:** If exploring the sensation you notice does not feel manageable for you right now, you can titrate your felt experiences by pairing your reflection with an attention modifier, such as walking around or tapping your foot.

Review each rule and reason you identified with in the previous section and ask yourself the magic question: "Where do I feel that?" Notice what comes up in your body and write it down beside the statement. If you do not notice any bodily sensations, write that down too. Perhaps even ask yourself, "What would be the consequence of breaking this rule or challenging this reason?" and see if any bodily sensations or any insights around the mind-body disconnect arise.

You might notice your mind and body start to communicate, that the rules and reasons evoke something in your body, and as you tune into that sensation another thought or feeling comes up, which you could then follow back into your body. Maybe a different sensation will be present. Evoking curiosity in this process will support you in cultivating openness to your painful inner experiences.

The Suffering Equation

You may have heard the saying "Pain is inevitable; suffering is optional." Let's explore the nuance behind these words.

In the last chapter, we reaffirmed that pain and suffering are an unavoidable part of life. This truth can easily lead us to feel like victims, at the mercy of every hard experience that comes our way. But there's a qualifier to this truth. While painful events can't be entirely avoided or controlled, the degree of suffering you experience from them depends on what you tell yourself about them.

An old Buddhist fable captures this truth with a metaphor: Experiencing physical or emotional discomfort is like being struck by an arrow. Suffering—through our resistance to the discomfort ("This shouldn't be happening! I have to stop this now!") and the stories we tell ourselves about the pain we experience ("I'm so unlucky," "Everyone is laughing at me," "I'll never get over this")—is like being struck by a second arrow, one that we shoot at ourselves.

To put it more simply, pain comes from the experience, while suffering comes from how we meet the experience. We can minimize our suffering by opening ourselves to what we experience from the first arrow. Rather than attempting to repress or correct our painful thoughts and feelings, we intentionally notice their ebb and flow, observing them without judgment of ourselves or the experience.

Struggling against the reality of your painful experience tends to increase your suffering. Opening yourself to your reality allows you to ultimately release the tension unconsciously stored in your body and mind. For example, have you ever found yourself fuming at a parking ticket, feeling your body tense with outrage at the injustice of it and anxiety about having to contest it, only to later pay it and find yourself sighing with full-body relief? This doesn't mean you like having to pay or that you agree with the ticket; the relief comes from no longer being in battle with the reality that you did receive a ticket. It's the same with things that feel bigger, from distressing events in childhood to a relationship breaking down. A letting go can occur with acceptance of what is, even if this also means making space for the grief and processing that might come along with it.

Let's say you have a painful memory come up. Perhaps it's about a time that you really dropped the ball on being there for a friend you care deeply for. Maybe this memory comes rushing in with a flow of judgments—*I'm a bad person. I'm selfish. I can never get anything right*—along with the feelings of guilt, shame, and sadness.

Next, resistance kicks in. You might tell yourself to stop thinking about this, that you can't change the past and it's not worth feeling so upset, that you just don't have time for regret right now, that it isn't fair you should feel so much guilt about this when you're constantly doing things for other people, and so on. If those arguments don't work, you might reach for a bottle of wine or flick on the television to distract yourself from the suffering.

Of course, the memory hasn't been resolved—it's simply been pushed aside for now. But pain is only intensified by resistance. The willingness to be with painful feelings and do difficult things will ultimately create more ease and vitality in your mind and body. If you can notice an experience and just let it be there, without needing it to be different than it is, you can simultaneously focus your attention back to a task or experience of your choosing. Both can coexist.

EXERCISE: Understanding Your Pain and Suffering

This exercise will help you consider the pain you experience in your body, mind, and heart, as well as the ways in which you resist your pain.

Think about a recent triggering situation. (In interest of keeping yourself safe, pick a situation that registers no higher than 5 on a scale of 0 to 10, with 10 being the most painful.)

What was the original pain you experienced? Write this in the "pain" circle in the diagram that follows.

How did you resist the painful experience? Write this in the "suffering" circle.

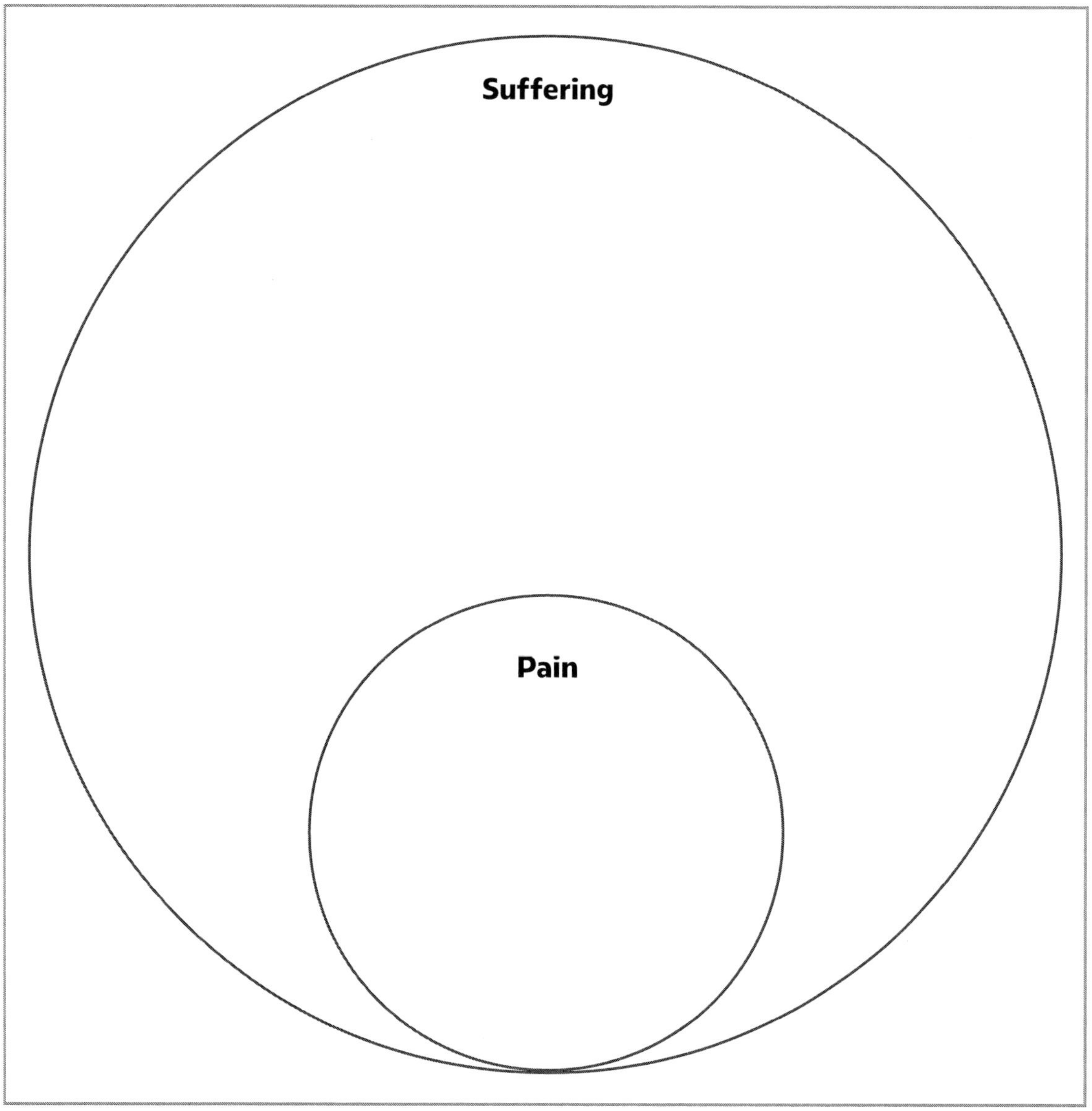

Suffering

Pain

Elements of Emotional Avoidance

Since we can't avoid painful situations in life, many of us instead develop strategies to avoid the emotions they bring up. But given the integral connection between your mind and body, avoiding or suppressing your emotions negatively influences your health. It can lead to cardiovascular disease, cancer, and even early death (Chapman et al., 2013). Understanding any emotional avoidance patterns you might have is an important aspect of willingness, and an important part of healing in general. As you set aside your avoidance strategies, you release the accumulation of unresolved emotional energy and are empowered to engage more compassionately with your emotional experiences.

Avoidance Strategy #1: Emotional Bypassing

Emotional bypassing is a pattern of avoiding difficult emotions through defense mechanisms designed to minimize the emotions' intensity. These mechanisms include the following:

- **Denial/suppression:** Trying not to think about or feel something
- **Overanalyzing/intellectualizing:** Thinking about something beyond utility, speaking about emotional experiences in a detached way
- **Distraction:** Focusing intently on something else, such as excessive work, entertainment, socializing, or sensory indulgence
- **Substance abuse:** Misusing alcohol or drugs
- **Isolation:** Withdrawing from others

As you likely know from experience, these options are ultimately exhausting—they require a perpetual fight against the feelings behind these mechanisms.

For instance, Sarah's workaholism offered her a distraction from the overwhelm and insecurity she felt. She thought if she could constantly keep busy, she wouldn't have mental or emotional space to feel any painful emotions. Her evening glasses of wine also provided a way to suppress her feelings. But as she soon learned, distracting herself from her emotions was not the same as discharging those emotions. Suppressing her feelings soon led to missing other somatic cues, which in turn caused buildup of emotional tension. Over the course of one such day, she failed to notice her jaw tensing up when she received corrections for a work project, the tightness that arose in her shoulders when she got stuck in traffic, and her face flushing when dinner burned. When she walked into her daughter's playroom to find the entire contents of the dress-up box on the floor, the pent-up emotional energy could no longer be contained. Suddenly, Sarah found herself standing back in shame after screaming in frustration at her six-year-old daughter.

This is the problem with emotional bypass. We may think that we are transcending the emotional dysregulation or keeping it at bay, but all we are really doing is tuning out our felt sense. The dysregulation is still present in the body, unprocessed and unresolved, building up until it inevitably results in a harmful consequence. Whether it comes out as an overreaction to an event, a disconnect in relationships (ultimately, closeness is built through emotional vulnerability), physical illness, or even early death, there are lots of reasons to practice being with our emotions rather than bypassing them.

Avoidance Strategy #2: Toxic Positivity

Toxic positivity refers to the exclusive focus on positive emotional experiences as a way of avoiding difficult or complex ones. It centers the belief that if you always maintain a positive mindset, regardless of the circumstances, you can override any painful or uncomfortable feelings.

Cole has struggled with this. There were many years where he depended on a near-daily meditation practice to cultivate that calm state he idolized. Whenever his meditation session didn't end with his feeling relaxed and calm, he found himself descending into panic. The unrealistic expectation that he should only experience the narrow range of "good" feelings limited Cole's capacity to grow in his meditation practice; after a day when it didn't leave him feeling good, he would abandon it for several days or weeks.

Cole's yoga practice was similarly compromised by his quest to experience constant happiness and optimism. While he generally felt more energized after he attended a class, his practice wasn't necessarily about embodied mindfulness. Instead, throughout the class he would focus on anything but what he was experiencing—the music, the person in front of him, what he would get from the supermarket afterward. He had even had a few injuries because he was disconnected from the interoceptive signals warning him that he was at the edge of his capacity. Moreover, his rigid devotion to his practice schedule caused him to miss his best friend's mother's funeral. Cole later reflected that he felt that he couldn't cope with all the sadness and grief people would be expressing at the funeral. He had internalized the idea that "negative" emotions are unhealthy and that he should not experience them if he wanted to feel his best.

To be clear, there is no inherent risk in thinking positively or in pursuing activities that bring relief when you are feeling overwhelmed. As we discussed in chapter 3, there are many circumstances where it's a good idea to disengage (intentionally and temporarily) from an experience to regulate your emotions and protect your psychological well-being. In that case, you are practicing self-soothing or self-care in order to replenish your energy or cultivate a better mental state. The toxicity comes when guilt, shame, and fear arise from experiencing anything other than positive emotions. In other words, you feel guilty about feeling guilty, or scared about feeling scared.

Affirmations of Acceptance

Affirmations focus and center your attention on a deliberate intention or path forward. They cultivate the quality of acceptance in your mind and support your capacity for openness. When you notice pain, you might recite an affirmation to yourself as you practice gently holding the pain and re-engaging in your life. The purpose of an affirmation is not to bypass your experience or interpret it as anything other than what it is. Rather, the affirmation should remind you that you can open to the experience and be with all of the emotions it brings up, that it is natural to experience pain and suffering at times, and that you have the power to choose how to respond to this experience.

Here are some helpful affirmations of acceptance—what else can you add to the list?

- I release resistance and invite acceptance into my heart.
- I acknowledge and honor my emotions without judgment or resistance.
- I can hold this experience and return to this moment.
- I open to this moment and everything arising and passing in it.
- I can have this thought [*or feeling, urge, sensation, etc.*] and connect to my true self.
- I am infinitely expansive.
- This hurts because I care, and I can hold that.
- I let go of resistance and open myself to the flow of life.
- Other: ____

The Power of Your Complexity

Life is complex. You are complex. You can be happy and sad. Excited and nervous. Heartbroken and in love. You can have the urge to smash a plate, and you can serve up a nourishing meal. You can feel comfortable under your covers, and you can get up to go to the gym. You can value hard work and you can actively relax. You can feel tense in your stomach and be able to relax your shoulders. You might feel strong in your legs and shaky in your arms.

A vital part of your healing journey is learning to hold seemingly contradictory thoughts and emotions simultaneously. In therapy terms, we can describe this as a "both/and" experience. The more you realize that difficult painful experiences are as much a part of being human as easy and joyful ones, and that one type of experience does not negate the other, the less you will be governed by the intensity of your emotional pain. This frees you to act in alignment with your values and intentions, opening you to your purpose and your power to choose what comes next.

EXERCISE: Opening to Your Power

Power posing has been found to influence your physiology and psychology. Adopting an expansive posture can lead to increased confidence, reduced stress, and improved body awareness.

Body Scan Pre-Power Pose

What is your internal experience right now? Notice any emotions, thoughts, and so on.

____

____

____

____

How is your body positioned? Describe each part (e.g., shoulders rounded, head down, spine straight).

____

____

____

____

Superhero Posing

1. Stand with your feet about hip distance apart, pressing down into the earth to ground yourself.
2. Gently lift your chest up. Notice the sensation of your chest opening. Roll your shoulders back and down, and lengthen the crown of your head up to the sky. Keep your chin up and look straight in front of you.
3. Bring your hands to your hips and take a few breaths, channeling your inner superhero.
4. For the next stage, extend your arms out in front of you with the palms facing forward.
5. Gently inhale, feeling a sense of energy and strength empower your body. With the exhale, press more deeply into the ground, perhaps allowing your elbows to bend and retract slightly back, so that they can extend farther with the next inhale.
6. Anchor by shifting your attention to your feet, ensuring they remain grounded, to your sternum area, ensuring it is lifted, and to your chin, ensuring your head is tilted up.
7. Hold this pose for 60 to 120 seconds (about six breath cycles). Allow yourself the time you need to embody a sense of gentle strength, a sense that you can open to hold the entirety of your experience.

Open Arm Pose

1. Stand with your feet about hip distance apart, pressing down into the earth to ground yourself.
2. Gently lift your chest up. Notice the sensation of your chest opening. Roll your shoulders back and down, and lengthen the crown of your head up to the sky. Keep your chin up and look straight in front of you.
3. Extend your arms out to your sides at shoulder height. Relax your shoulders down, away from your ears. Gently open your palms up to the sky.
4. Inhale, feeling a sense of energy and strength empower your body. With the exhale, press more deeply into the ground, perhaps ever so gently letting your fingers curl in, so that they can open farther with the next inhale.
5. Anchor by shifting your attention to your feet, ensuring they remain grounded, to your sternum area, ensuring it is lifted, and to your chin, ensuring your head is tilted up.
6. Hold this pose for 60 to 120 seconds (about six breath cycles). Allow yourself the time you need to embody a sense of gentle strength, a sense that you can open to hold the entirety of your experience.

Body Scan Post-Power Pose

What is your internal experience right now? Notice any emotions, thoughts, and so on.

____

____

____

____

How is your body positioned? Describe each part (e.g., shoulders rounded, head down, spine straight).

____

____

____

____

Reflections

Reflect on how you could incorporate power poses into your daily rituals, such as before you head out the door in the morning.

____

____

Consider how you might use these poses, or certain elements of them, before important events or during moments of stress. (For example, you could drop your arms down by your sides during a presentation but ensure your chin stays lifted and your chest is open. Or you might take a few moments to practice in private beforehand.)

Consider how you can deepen your practice. How might you integrate these power poses with your acceptance affirmations, heartfelt intentions, visualizations, or other somatic practices?

EXERCISE: The Altar of Acceptance

In this exercise, you'll introduce acceptance elements into an altar that offers you a grounding space. Start by adding elements to the altar that bring you a sense of connection and joy. Then, create a replica of a painful experience you regularly witness showing up for you. You might simply write out an unhelpful thought (e.g., *I can't cope*, *I'm worthless*) or feeling (e.g., anxiety, shame). Alternatively, you might find a visual representation that feels powerful, such as a stone to represent the pressure you feel on your chest or a knot of rope to represent the pain in your stomach.

Place this icon on a table or other surface in a space that feels safe and potentially even sacred to you, to acknowledge that this pain can exist embedded within elements of your life that offer you connection and joy. You can practice your power poses near your altar. This metaphor of acceptance can support your compassionate opening to the whole range of your emotions and experiences, countering any internalized beliefs that you should suppress or deny your experience. Opening to your authentic experiences will scaffold the release of the self-censoring that will be needed in the chapters ahead. Your acceptance icon will explicitly serve as a reminder to disentangle from your private experiences so that you can willingly witness them as you go about living your life.

While opening to your emotions may sound vulnerable, it is actually empowering. Openness comes from letting go of your fear about feeling scared, your anxiety about feeling anxious, and your anger about feeling angry. You can also let go of the resistance you might have to feelings of joy and delight. Yes, there is always the possibility that your joy will pass—all emotions do, sooner or later. But part of being human is the capacity to experience fear and joy simultaneously—you can open enough for that!

Closing Reflections

In what ways do you see resistance and avoidance negatively impacting your quality of life and health?

____

____

____

____

What transformations might unfold in your life if you were willing to feel uncomfortable?

____

____

____

____

How can you build defusion into more of a habit so you can gain a clearer perspective on your painful thoughts and experiences?

____

____

____

____

What compassionate and nurturing practices might you offer yourself when you notice you're experiencing emotional pain or suffering?

____

____

____

____

Reflect on how awareness and openness could help you to release old patterns of tension.

____

____

____

____

Takeaway Messages

- Suffering comes from resistance to the pain you experience. While you can't avoid pain, you can choose how you respond to it.
- Developing openness through acceptance and defusion can reduce the suffering arising from difficult thoughts and emotions.
- Acceptance does not mean you like, condone, or agree with something, nor is it resignation. It is the willingness to make space for difficult experiences so that you can respond to the reality of your situation.
- Your nonjudgmental use of language can support you in defusing your beliefs, feelings, and the like so that you are not influenced by assumptions and can see experiences as passing events.
- You can experience distressing experiences and cultivate a feeling of grounded power when you open and ground your body in power poses.

CHAPTER 9

Your Sacred Self: Unraveling the Patterns of Your Mind

"You are the sky. Everything else—it's just the weather."

—Attributed to Pema Chödrön

Spend time outside daily for a year, and you'll experience many different weather patterns. You'll witness so-called bluebird days featuring stunning sunshine without a cloud in the sky. On other days, there will be clouds. You might wait for shapes to unfold as you delight in the light and fluffy ones, wait for raindrops with the gray ones, and witness the thrilling bolt of lightning when a thundershower sets in. Depending on where you live, you'll witness snowfalls and maybe even a blizzard, tornado, or cyclone.

One thing you'll never question is the sky's capacity to hold the unfolding weather. Its seemingly infinite expanse makes space for any condition, no matter the intensity. I have yet to hear someone worrying that the sky would cave in with the lightning or melt in the rain. We know that the clouds eventually always part and that clear sky will be revealed again.

Your thoughts, feelings, memories, and sensations are like the weather, held in the sky of your transcendent experience of being—we can simply call it your Self (with a capital S). This part of you is timeless, ever present, and spacious. When you are connected to your Self, you'll find an expansive, stable, nonjudgmental refuge from which you can witness the transient nature of your thoughts and feelings. Such ephemeral internal events do not define you or control you any more than a weather pattern controls the sky.

EXERCISE: Who Is Noticing?

I know—shifting from awareness of your thoughts to awareness of yourself having the thoughts is a tricky concept, and practice. We call this experience of tapping into different types of awareness *perspective shifting*, and that is exactly what you'll be practicing in the exercise ahead.

1. Take a moment to tune into yourself. You might choose to lie down or sit in a comfortable, relaxed posture. Take a few breath cycles, inhaling gently and exhaling slowly. Come to center yourself and bring your attention to the present moment.
2. Notice something that arises in your immediate experience. It might be a thought, a feeling, or anything you perceive with your senses. Allow your attention to sit on this focal point. *Notice "X" [e.g., your breath, a thought, a feeling, a sensation].*
3. Next, shift your awareness to the part who is noticing. See that there is an observing Self, a part of you that is aware and present of the internal experience you were noticing. *There is X, and there you are noticing X.*
4. Reflect on your observing Self. Notice who is noticing—you are cultivating awareness of the part of you that observes without judgment. *If you notice X, you cannot* be *X.*
5. Acknowledge that while the content of your inner experiences may change, the observing Self remains constant. This awareness is not subject to the fluctuations of inner experiences, like thoughts or sensations. *X changes continually, but the part of you who notices X does not change. It has been here throughout time . . . and when you notice who is noticing, you can deliberately connect to it.*
6. As you conclude this meditation, bring your attention back to your surroundings. Take a couple of conscious breath cycles, slowly opening your eyes if you closed them.

Reflection

What was it like to watch your inner experience?

____

____

____

____

____

____

____

So, Who Are You?

You are born into this world with the distinct entity of Self inside you. It is an energy of deep wisdom and authenticity that travels with you as a silent witness throughout your lifespan. This Self can also be considered the neural equipment needed to act in a fundamentally caring, compassionate, and curious manner, all of which is inbuilt, yet requires you to expand out and to connect with the world around you.

Unlike your Self, your mind is not an entity, but rather the collective experience arising from information processed by your brain. Constantly generating thoughts, interpretations, memories, and urges, the mind is masterful at weaving a narrative about yourself and the world that is anchored in your cultural conditioning and shaped by the themes of your past experiences. Sometimes that narrative might be helpful, sometimes unhelpful, but it isn't inherently problematic. Rather, problems arise because of our tendency to confuse the content of the mind for the Self. Taking the passing events of your mind as literal truths erodes your freedom to choose what you'll focus on and how you'll behave.

Take a thought like this: *I'm such a loser. I'm so awkward. Nobody at this party is even going to talk to me.* If I believe that thought to be a truth, I'll either ditch the party or just sit at a table by myself playing on my phone. Then, when nobody talks to me, I'll consider it further evidence that I really am a loser. If someone does come up and talk to me, my menacing mind will likely create another story: that they just felt sorry for me . . . because I'm such a loser. It's a no-win situation.

Now, if I have the exact same thought and consider it just a thought, I have different options. I might choose to focus on the reason I'm attending the party to begin with. If I'm going to celebrate the birthday of a dear friend, I can focus my attention on helpful thoughts, like how I can show my value for the relationship (*My presence at this party will make my friend feel loved and appreciated*) or a sense of curiosity about the other people attending (*Because my friend is a good person, they must have other good people in their life*). Along with reflecting on these thoughts as I enter the party, I can practice present-moment awareness—listening to the music, noticing the people around me, observing if anyone is smiling and letting my face soften in response. At no point do I have to consciously rid myself of the thought *I'm a loser*. Instead, I can experience it as just an inner "event" passing through me, the way a cloud may drop some rain as it passes over my house. As I consciously focus my attention on more helpful thoughts, I eventually hear it only in the background, until it fades away.

Now, I know that sounds way too simple. It is true that some thoughts are just stickier or more triggering. The mental events that evoke an intense biophysiological response don't feel like mere thoughts; they feel more like beliefs. We'll explore this more in the pages ahead. For now, I just want to make it clear that having a cruel thought does not make you a cruel person, nor does having an unhelpful urge mean that you must act on it. You can choose to act with integrity and come closer to connecting with your values. To better understand this idea, let's map out your inner landscape.

Mapping Your Mind

In the previous exercise, you practiced perspective shifting from the content of your mind (such as thoughts, emotions, and memories) to a state of awareness—your observing Self. Hopefully, you felt the shift. Now it is time to *see* it.

Take a moment to think of thoughts, memories, urges, and emotions that you often experience. Write them down in the corresponding circles on the map that follows.

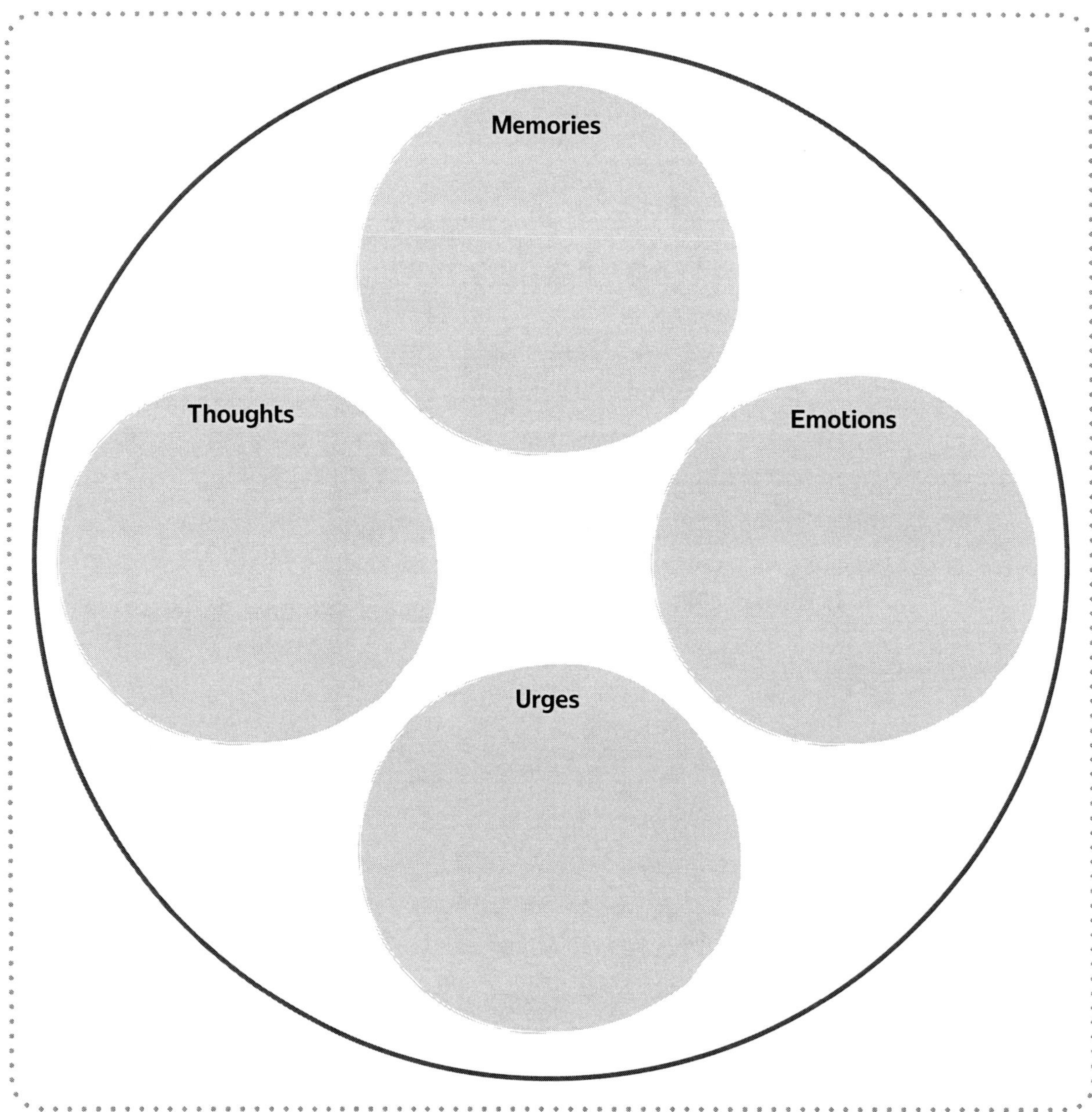

Everything in this circle—all your thoughts, memories, urges, emotions, and so on—is a product of your thinking mind. Sometimes you might be fused with these experiences, which is to say you cannot separate from these experiences. This results in your behavior being directed by these cognitive experiences rather than your values.

In the previous exercise you tapped into your observing Self, the part of you that can witness these inner experiences unfolding while staying connected to the outer world of direct experiences. You can picture it like this:

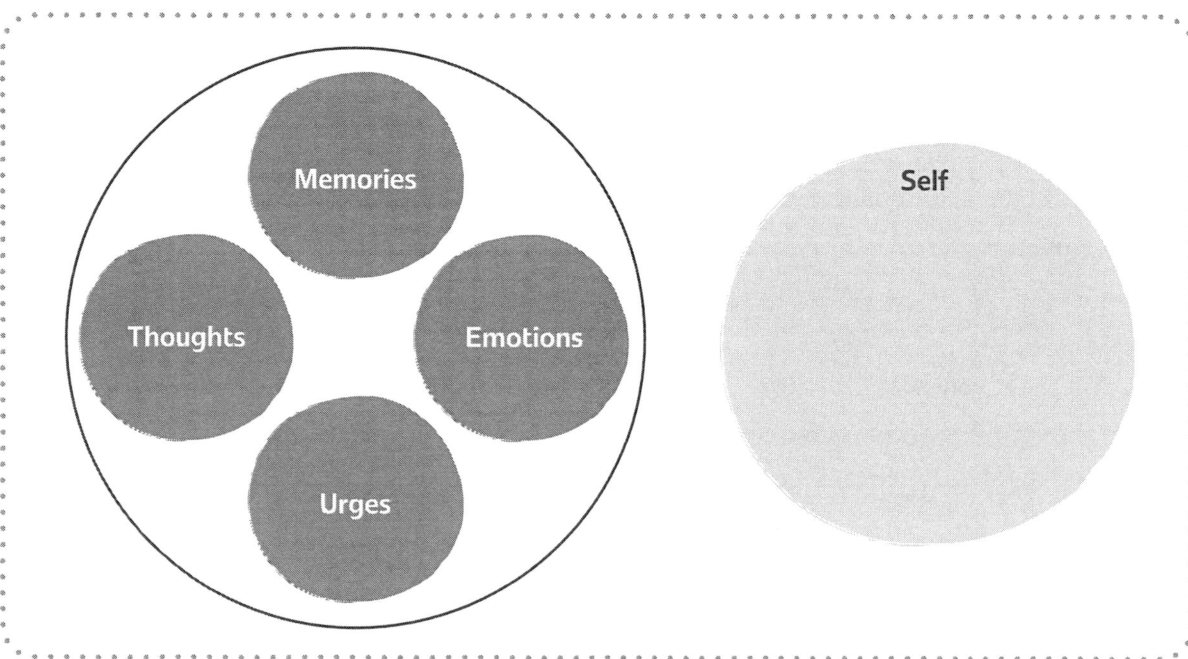

You can even go ahead and write in the "Self" circle any descriptors of this observing Self that you find helpful. (I find the word "transcendence" captures the feeling of it best for me.)

This isn't the end of your map. The fact is, you can hold your thinking mind in awareness as you tap into your observing Self. This is through the process of *self-awareness*. Let's look at a final map that captures the expansive nature of your observing Self and the self-awareness that allows you to experience the processes of your thinking mind in a defused state. Make any notes you need to help you remember the felt sense of these processes.

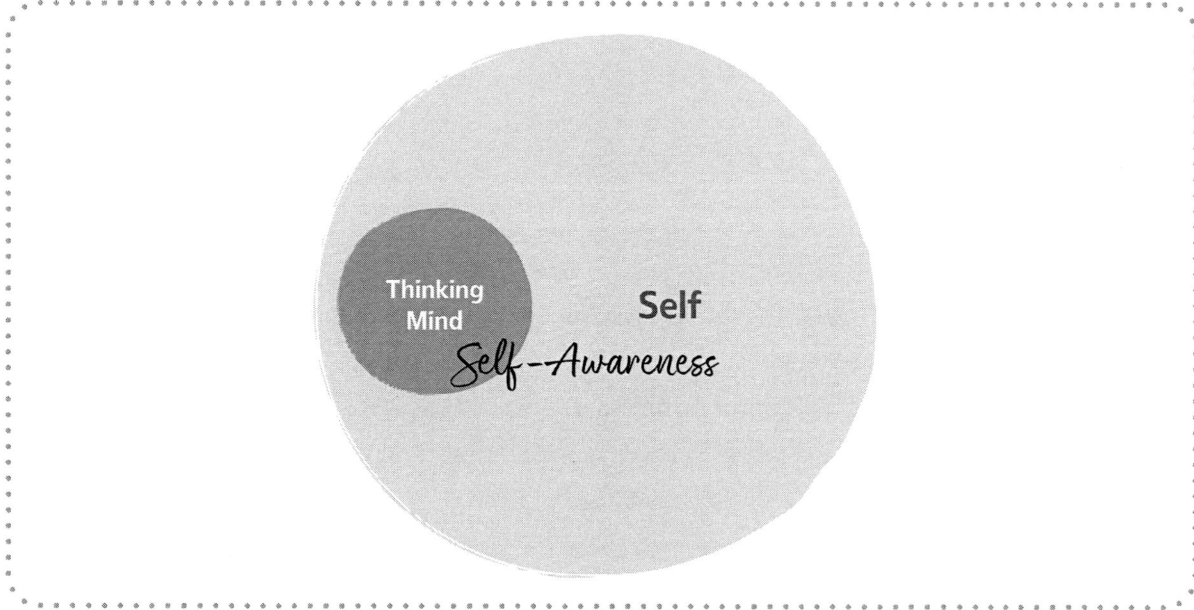

We cannot escape our inner experiences—they have messages they want heard. But when all your attention and awareness is focused on the content of your thinking mind, you tend not to notice your somatic sensations, ignoring these signs of needs that must be met. Eventually, the body increases the intensity of sensation to the point that it feels overpowering. This is how we go from panic and anger to illness and chronic pain.

Self-awareness includes the physical information provided by interoception (which you were introduced to in chapter 2), such as hunger cues, muscle tension, and fatigue, as well as thoughts and emotions. We develop self-awareness through mindfulness practices, which, as you learned in the last chapter, support you in noticing what is happening in and around you without judgment. Self-awareness allows us to distinguish bodily sensations from Self, so that we can understand the messages within these sensations.

Let me show you how I picture it. Cognitive experiences and somatic experiences are both observed through the process of self-awareness.

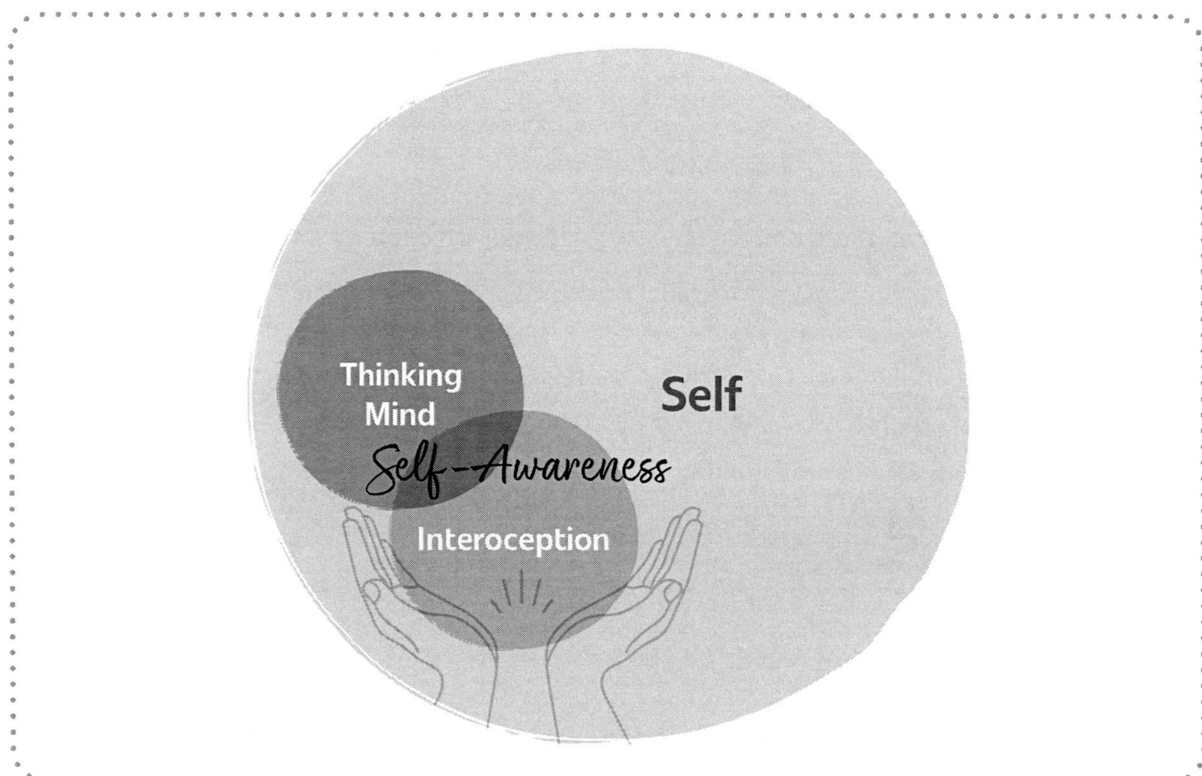

Now it's your turn! Use the "Bodily Sensations" circle in the diagram that follows to jot down what you're sensationally experiencing within your own skin now. Then, go ahead and fill in any other categories of experiences you're noticing. (For instance, I notice a tension in my jaw and a dryness in my eyes right now. Building from that, I notice the urge to blink and rub my eyes, alongside an urge to yawn and release the jaw tension. Emotionally, I notice a sense of being unfocused, and thoughts about afternoon activities swirl.)

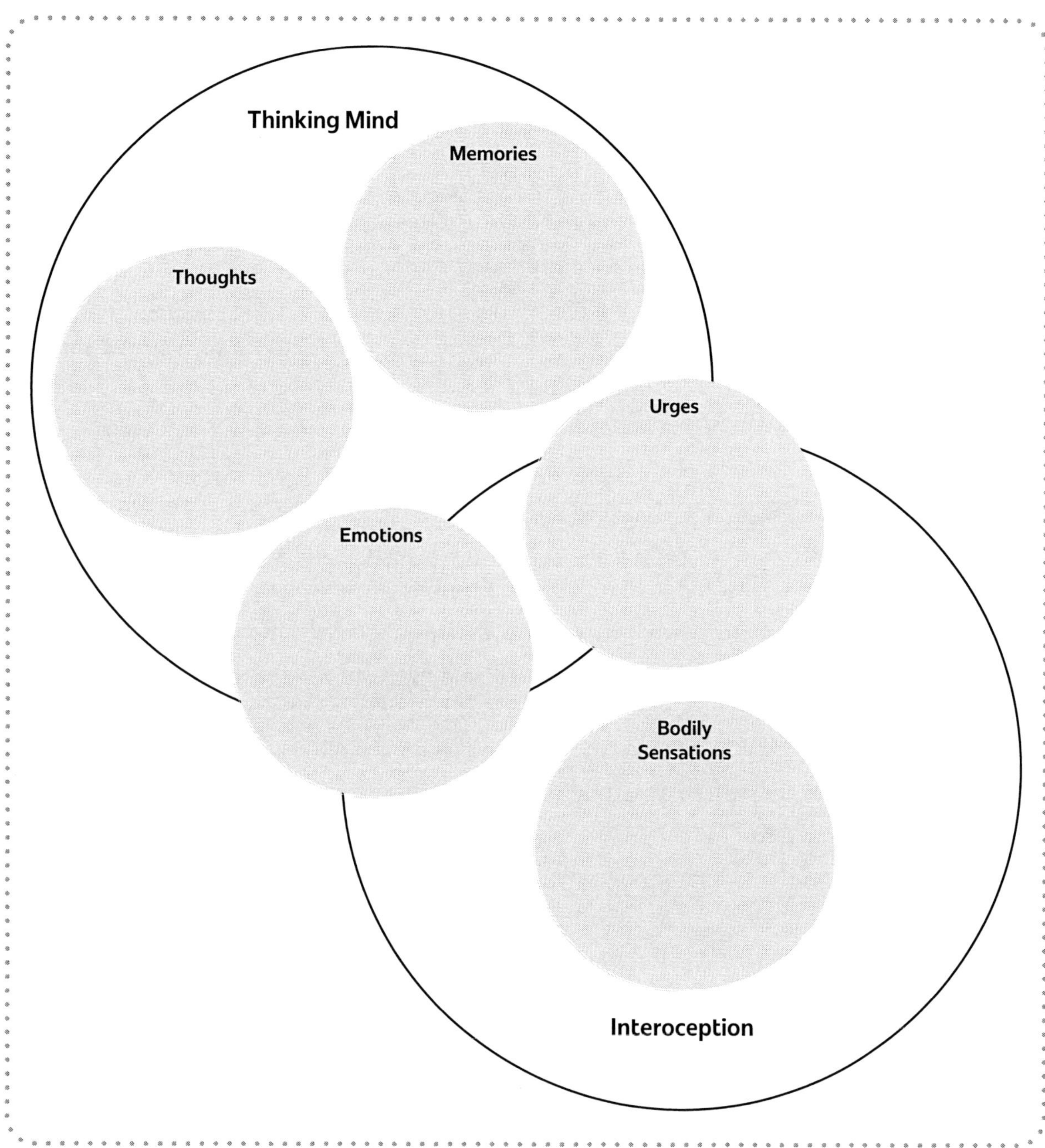

Why is this helpful? In chapter 6, you practiced labeling emotions and thoughts. Labeling plays an important role in developing self-awareness around physical sensations as well. Naming feelings, whether they come from the body or the mind, ensures you remain defused from the feeling and are able to cultivate the distance needed to experience it as a passing event.

For example, saying "I am anxious" has a very different quality from saying "I'm feeling anxious." When you label yourself as the feeling, the feeling is construed as something fixed and innate in your character—it's who you are, and you can't choose to be or do anything different. When you label the feeling as a feeling, you maintain freedom for your Self to choose what you will do with the feeling. It works the same way with sensations in the body. When you can describe a physical experience—"I'm feeling a tightening in my throat and a churning in my stomach"—you contain the experience instead of getting overwhelmed by it.

Tuning Into Your Self

From an early age, most of us are taught "mind over matter": that we are our thoughts, and that our body's sensations and urges are a hindrance, a distraction. That our body has little function apart from meeting others' expectations and desires. Hence, most body awareness is about how the body looks and how it can please other people. From jamming your feet into high-heeled torture, to working through exhaustion, to pushing yourself too hard at the gym, to finishing all the food on the plate (or not having another serving when you're hungry), you have likely been taught to see your body as an object to be controlled, rather than as a source of embodied wisdom.

In chapter 8, we talked about the danger of toxic positivity. Our culture is currently leaning hard into body positivity, a swing to the other extreme from body negativity. The challenge here is that both mindsets position the body as an object. In fact, body positivity can actually loop us back into body negativity—if we don't truly believe what we are deliberately affirming about our body, our mind will call us out, and then we feel like we failed at our efforts to be positive.

A better approach is to practice body neutrality. You don't need to like or love what your body looks like to appreciate its function. Of course, there are cognitive ways of doing this, like reflecting on the fact that our bodies are vessels to hug loved ones or how our legs can be used to carry us up a mountain into the bliss of nature. However, a healthy sense of body image is also fostered by increasing your capacity to experience your body from the inside—namely, interoception.

You see, a healthy sense of self-awareness grows from the inside out. Reduced interoceptive awareness (body disconnect) can predispose you to a greater level of body dissatisfaction (Badoud & Tsakiris, 2017), which is to say a negative body image—even if you're trying to be positive! As you shift your focus from your appearance and thinking mind to increasing awareness of your somatic experience, you're less likely to be driven by painful emotive states and unconscious reactions. You're better able to recognize your inner urges, clarify your emotional state, and nurture your body. You can choose conscious behavior responses that align with your deeper Self. This is why cultivating awareness of your body's felt sense matters so much. This energetic experience of awareness in your body is the space where healing happens.

EXERCISE: Perspective Taking

In this exercise, you'll experience embodiment by spreading conscious awareness through your nervous system while you engage cognitively in a perspective-taking practice—in other words, intentionally integrating mind and body.

Bring to mind a recent experience that has been causing you distress. For example, maybe you stuttered when you went to speak at a recent meeting, and you had the thought, *I'm a loser.* Choose an experience that you would rate as a 5 or lower on a scale of 0 to 10, where 10 is totally distressing.

Lie down or sit in a comfortable position. Close your eyes or soften your gaze. Imagine observing yourself from a distance—across the room or with a bit of space from wherever you are now. See yourself, sitting or lying here as you read this. As you look toward this person who is suffering, trying so hard, actively engaged in a somatic healing journey, all the while being a deeply feeling human, can you offer some loving-kindness, some compassion, for this person?

What warm feelings, words, or gestures can you offer to yourself in this moment?

____

____

____

____

Now imagine an older, wiser version of yourself sitting here with you now. Perhaps you are 10 or 20 years older, having gone through a journey of healing, integration, and connection. Let your wise older Self hold you in loving-kindness and compassion. How does this feel? What advice and perspective does your wise older Self have to offer to you in this moment?

____

____

____

____

Finally, travel back to when you first experienced this feeling—to meet your inner child. Notice when this belief developed, how young this inner child is. Can you evoke a sense of compassion for that young child experiencing this thought, these feelings?

____

____

____

____

If you'd like, you can expand on your inner child work here, starting the process of modifying unhelpful beliefs and coping strategies that might have developed about yourself and the world from these past experiences. This is done through imagery rescripting, which is the focus of the next exercise. Rescripting the image changes the emotional experience and memory. Given that our memories and perceptions are constructed, reimagining an experience can support you to enhance your self-worth and value.

EXERCISE: Imagery Rescripting

This exercise asks you to transcend time, place, and person to explore your perspective on a given moment or situation, utilizing your own self-awareness of your inner needs and capacity to meet them.

Close your eyes or soften your gaze. Bring the recent experience that has been causing you distress to mind again and notice what you are feeling in your body. Really attune to the bodily sensations you're experiencing, as uncomfortable as they may be.

Next, intensify those bodily sensations. Let them get stronger and stronger.

Stay with those intense bodily sensations and let yourself travel back in time, back to an earlier situation in your life where you experienced the same thing. Notice what image comes up.

What is going on for little you in this image? What are you feeling in your body? What emotions are here? What are you thinking? What do you need? (You can write down your responses to these questions if you like, or you can remain immersed in the image. Remember, if at any point this experience becomes overwhelming, you can use your skills of titration and pendulation—for example, focusing on pressing your feet into the ground while spreading your toes, and then coming back into the image.)

____

____

____

____

Take yourself as you are now, with the life wisdom and experiences you've had—particularly those you drew out in the positive events timeline in chapter 5—and really see this little person, suffering.

Walk into this memory, this image, and take care of this little person as a wise, compassionate, parent-like figure. Act with loving-kindness—be the gentle but strong person little you needs to protect and guide them. If you don't feel able to do this alone, take your resourcing figure or your older, wiser self with you, and notice how they attend to this little you. You can meet the needs of your inner child by validating, holding, and encouraging them. Make sure little you feels safe and soothed.

If there is another individual who is behaving poorly toward little you in the situation, you can call them out. For example, you could say, "That is a terrible thing to say (or do) to a small child. It needs to stop—right now!" You can also change the image to make sure you have the full power to successfully shift the offending behavior. You might put the antagonist in a bubble or grow yourself taller, for example.

Then, check in with little you. Make sure they feel secure with the outcome of the confrontation (if one was needed). Ensure that your inner child feels totally protected and supported by you.

From here, it is always nice to affirm little you. For instance, if little you experienced a sense of rejection, you can see how it feels to speak to the person little you felt rejected by. You might say something along the lines of "This is a precious little kid who is trying their best, and you are missing out on getting to know them. I cannot wait to go spend some time with them."

Then, while you're in the inner image, you can embrace your inner child by doing an activity they would find soothing, delightful, and special. Or you can take them to your safe space and spend time together there. Finally, attune to what your inner child is now experiencing emotionally. Perhaps they have found a sense of security, love, and connection.

When you're settled, let go of the image and travel back on your body's felt sense to this current place and time.

Reflection

What did you learn about little you from that image?

____

____

____

How did it feel to protect little you and meet their needs?

____

____

____

Has anything shifted in how you perceive that past experience? What about your current experience?

____

____

____

Experiencing Your Self-Energy

We've been talking about the transcendent and expansive nature of your Self and the sense of wisdom that can come with it. But the real magic of self-awareness is that it's not just about connecting to these different aspects of yourself. When you connect to the expansive presence of your Self, you'll find that you become more open and able to connect with others in a state of consciousness. This is the nature of transcendence, inherent belonging, and connection. When you touch this space, you'll feel it. Perhaps you even got a feeling of its essence when you looked at yourself, connected to your older wiser self, or nurtured little you. But how do you actually know when you are connected to your authentic Self?

Your Self is a state that aligns with your social engagement (ventral vagal) nervous system branch. It is the place where you access compassion, curiosity, and an openness. Self-energy is the feeling of being in a safe state of connection (as opposed to following or avoiding the urges of your survival responses). I appreciate this all sounds like an abstract concept, and we can get stuck in language and intellectually trying to explain it when the easiest path is to feel into it. After all, Self-energy is an embodied experience.

Take a moment now to see if you can gently relax into Self. It might mean lengthening your spine and allowing a sigh sound to flow. It could mean rolling your shoulders back and reaching through your fingertips. Just take a moment to see if you can access a glimmer of this energy.

For instance, you might feel:

- A gentle expansion in your chest
- A lighter feeling in your body
- A quieter mind with clear and calm thinking patterns
- Smoother and deeper breathing
- Relaxed facial muscles
- Rejuvenating tiredness (when there is significant stress in your life)

When you access Self-energy, you'll find you have a great capacity to experience passing thoughts and emotions as the "weather," rather than getting stuck in an unhelpful story about yourself and the world. You can practice tapping into this embodied state by literally tapping points on your body, as shown in the next exercise.

EXERCISE: Butterfly Hug

The butterfly hug supports you evoking your parasympathetic nervous system—a sense of calm. You can use it to pair a soothing tapping with the calm, connected energy of your Self. This is also a form of bilateral stimulation, which is incredibly beneficial for reducing emotional distress.

Put your arms across your chest so that your left hand lands on your right shoulder, and your right hand lands on your left shoulder. Then, slowly tap your fingertips against your shoulder, one hand at a time, alternating from left to right. Find a steady rhythm with this.

Next, call to mind your resourcing figure or your wise Self. Keep tapping as you allow yourself to expand this sense of Self, with the intention of offering yourself soothing, wisdom, and trust.

Ultimately, the opposite of the uncertainty that comes with anxiety isn't a certainty; it's trust. Trust in your Self. You will never get to fully control the future. But if you can cultivate a sense of trust in your Self and your ability to cope with whatever happens, you no longer need certainty about what the future holds. Instead, you can rest in the faith that you'll always be okay.

To aid your practice of tapping into this felt sense of security, you might consider using what's known as a transitional object. When you were a child, you may have had a stuffed animal or a blanket that you would cuddle through the night and carry with you throughout the day. As you came to feel more comfortable and confident in your environment, you may have set aside that object more often, but picked it up again when you needed special comfort or felt nostalgic. Adults also benefit from the transitional support from meaningful objects. For example, in the early days of my yoga journey, I wore certain rings and necklaces that gave me a sense of security through their history or sacred imagery. Part of my pre-practice ritual involved taking off each item and arranging it in an altar style at the front of my yoga mat. Looking at these items connected me to my intentions for practice, as well as to my family, friends, and a clear sense of purpose. At the end of the practice, I put the items back on again with the intention of taking the embodied state I felt from the practice out into the world with me. In tougher times or painful moments, I would rub or twist these pieces of jewelry as a way of resourcing myself.

Today, I keep a few special objects at home and in my workspace, including a preserved four-leaf clover my grandmother found, a pair of knitted socks that belonged to my grandparents (delightful to cuddle into for physical and emotional warmth), and a little laminated image of Ganesh that a mentor gave me. The latter also represents the yoga community in which I first really started to find my sense of connection. All of these transitional objects help me in tough times by realigning my thoughts and emotions with my people, my heartfelt purpose, and that felt sense of Self-energy.

EXERCISE: Transitional Objects

While transitional objects are things outside the body, they are considered body-based practices because you're using the object to embody the felt sense from one environment as you move into another environment. Whether it's a photo of your family in your workplace, a rock you carry home from a nature walk where you felt really peaceful, or a shell from a lovely day at the beach with your loved ones, transitional objects offer comfort and support that help you embody a state in which you felt aligned with your authentic self.

1. Choose an object related to a place or person with whom you experience feelings of safety and calm. This can be any item that can come with you and elicit that sense of safety and calm when you touch it or look at it.
2. Recognize the situations or emotions that trigger your need for comfort and bring your object with you at these times.
3. Hold or interact with your transitional object in a comforting way. Let it evoke positive memories and emotions. Let the object anchor you to better open into unconditional acceptance of whatever other feelings arise.

Reflect on your feelings, challenges, or sources of stress. Allow your transitional object to provide emotional support and healing.

Just as a transitional object can evoke a memory network that supportively influences your perception, attitude, behavior, and somatic and emotional response, previously stored memories influence how you interpret and experience new situations. In this way, memories shape who we are right now, for better and for worse. But, as you'll remember from the rescripting exercise earlier in this chapter, we can make shifts in how we hold and interpret our memories.

EXERCISE: Tricky Times Timeline

Now that you've established your ability to resource yourself, you can look more directly at the tricky moments in your life. While this exercise can be more difficult than many we've practiced thus far, it is important to try because it will help you explore your sense of self more deeply. We cannot disentangle how you view yourself and the world from your history. Ideally, you will add the content from this timeline to the other side of your positive events timeline from chapter 5 so that you can see them together.

Note: This could be a trauma timeline at points, so please go very gently and use your resourcing and regulating exercises.

On the timeline that follows, write down major events and memories you have that feel painful or stressful. As much as possible, start from when you were in utero—if your mother was under significant stress during pregnancy, or had a tricky birth or postpartum period, this will have an impact on you even though you cannot remember it.

Birth

Negative Events:

Like the positive events in your life, you're shaped by your negative experiences. These timelines—your life history—will have shaped how you see yourself and the world and prompted your psyche to develop various patterns and parts to help you survive. We'll explore this further in the next chapter.

Closing Reflections

Are there specific painful thoughts that you notice regularly cross your mind? Does viewing them as passing events decrease their intensity?

What bodily cues and needs do you struggle to meet? Have you noticed any changes in your relationship with your body by engaging in body neutrality?

Consider the moments when you feel most connected to your Self. What is it about those times that opens a sense of transcendence?

Have you noticed you are connecting to your wise self and inner child more regularly in your day? If not, consider ways you can remind yourself to check in with them (perhaps using your transitional object as a cue or putting up pictures or prompts on your bathroom mirror or on your altar).

When you completed your timeline, were there any events that you had previously taken little notice of that started to seem more relevant? Make sure you add any other events that come up over the next couple of days, as once you start looking at your history you may find more things come to mind.

____

____

____

____

Takeaway Messages

- Your Self is a timeless part of you that is always present and that you can connect to for a sense of spaciousness, peace, and wisdom.
- Your thinking mind is the part of you from which cognitions arise, like thoughts and memories. (It might help to consider that your default mode network is part of the thinking mind.)
- Attuning to your felt sense and bringing awareness into your body is vital for deeper healing and experiencing.
- Perspective-taking exercises offer you different ways to experience yourself, while imagery rescripting offers a corrective experience for painful events in your past. This embodied experience can then shift your embodied belief structures.
- Creating a timeline of the tricky events in your life provides clarity on how unhelpful belief structures developed.

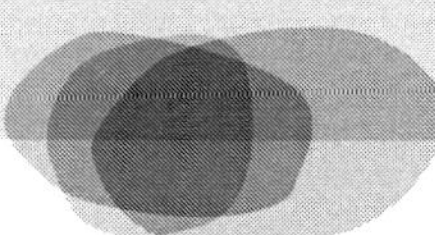

CHAPTER 10

Mapping Your Inner Landscape: The Pattern of Parts

"We do not see things as they are, we see them as we are."

—Anaïs Nin, *Seduction of the Minotaur*

When you entered this world, you were entirely interconnected with your primary caregiver. You had no sense of self, just a relationship. You were completely dependent upon your caregiver for your basic needs to be met, from nourishment and diaper changes to the profound emotional need to feel loved, secure, and valued. By about three years old, you had a sense of self-awareness emerging. Here, with the gentle and clear guidance of caregivers, you could learn how to manage your emotions and navigate intense feelings effectively. This is known as *co-regulation*, the process through which one person, by remaining calm, grounded, and compassionate, supports another person in regulating their emotions as well.

Your early experiences set up your blueprint of the world, essentially teaching you what to expect and tolerate. Of course, life is never simple, and receiving perfect co-regulation isn't possible. Your caregivers struggled along the way, as their own nervous systems became dysregulated. At times, it was hard for them to access Self-energy and parent from a place of availability, sensitivity, and supportiveness. While it just isn't possible for any person or parent to be perfect, a "good enough" caregiver meets your needs enough of the time to support you in developing a secure attachment, social competence, and a generally positive sense of yourself and the world around you. Not having important needs met enough of the time can result in you developing an unhelpful sense of yourself and the world around you.

You might be thinking, *But my parents were great—they did the best they could.* That may absolutely be true. At the same time, it can also be true that you still had needs they were unable to meet. Or you may have experienced painful events outside of your relationship with your parents that led to similar issues. After all, other relationships and experiences impact our sense of self, too—for instance, in childcare settings or at school.

I also want to acknowledge that it is possible that your parents were not good enough, and that is not your fault. You are and always were worthy, even if you don't believe it yet.

Why is it that these early life experiences are so impactful, affecting our lives even decades later? You see, as a kid, you were totally egocentric. Your prefrontal cortex was not fully developed, and you naturally believed everything was about you. If, at four years old, I spill the milk and my mum yells at me, I am not cognitively developed enough to recognize that my mum's fuse is short because she had a long day at work and had planned to use the milk for dinner. Nor could I recognize that, given the time of night, Mum already felt like she didn't have enough time to get a meal on the table. I couldn't know that her own mother insisted on things always being done perfectly, that an intense sense of failure overpowered her when I spilled the milk and her nervous system went into fight mode. Without a repair from Mum—perhaps an apology for her losing her temper, a reminder that it was just milk and nothing to worry about, and an offer of a hug to reconnect and soothe—I might interpret this whole situation as evidence that I am somehow deeply flawed, leading to a sense of overwhelming anxiety that my mother will no longer love me because I am so bad.

The same effect can occur from missed opportunities to meet our childhood needs—for instance, not having lunches and warm clothing packed for you, not having your important people show up for school concerts or sporting events, or not having your emotions noticed and treated with care, like cuddles when you were sad or reassurance when you were scared.

In light of our human need to be connected, to be part of the clan, to be safe, this is a massive threat for a developing brain. Remember, when we are under threat, our survival responses kick in: fight, flight, freeze, or fawn. These responses instigate the development of behavioral patterns and beliefs for protecting ourselves in relationships.

Seeing Your Schemas

Co-regulation is important, even vital, because the way you learn to self-regulate is through the co-regulation you experience with your caregiver.

Let's say your sibling snatched your toy and you screamed and hit them. Co-regulation might be your parent stepping in and saying something like, "Oh, I wonder if you're feeling angry right now. That makes sense. It wasn't okay for them to take your toy; that wasn't fair. Let's stomp our feet, because we don't hit other people. I'm here with you. I'll help you." Much of what makes this effective is what's happening behind the words—if your parent can be calm and present with you while you're feeling anger, you not only learn acceptable ways of expressing it, but you also learn that intense feelings don't make you a bad person, nor are the feelings themselves bad or scary. You learn that you can have those feelings safely, without hurting yourself or others.

However, things do not always go perfectly. Inevitably, in some situations, we won't get the co-regulation we need, and our nervous system will experience extreme charge. (This is often where that shark music develops.) As a consequence, the intense emotional state will develop alongside a particular mental attitude linked to and learned through the experience. This is how beliefs about ourselves and the world develop. We experience bodily sensations and emotions in the context of an event, our minds interpret those sensations and emotions and condense them into a belief, and later, when a similar event brings up similar inner experiences, that belief will show up.

As we grow, this collection of emotions, sensations, beliefs, behaviors, and the like is reinforced through repeated experience. Eventually, it becomes what is known as a *schema*—a mental framework that allows you to understand and respond to the complexities of the world.

In chapter 6, we talked about the blueprints developed by past experiences that influence your emotions. Schemas are like a blueprint that shapes how we perceive and interpret new information and experiences. To illustrate what I mean, imagine I'm wearing glasses with blue lenses, and you're wearing glasses with green lenses. We see the world differently. The color of the grass might be more intense for you, while the color of the sky will be accentuated with my lens. Neither of us are seeing the world as it truly is. But if we don't know we're wearing glasses, we'll see evidence that the world is greener or bluer everywhere, and we'll believe it.

Where your needs were consistently met, you're more likely to develop positive, helpful schemas. Looking back at your positive events timeline, you can probably notice some helpful schemas that developed from them. Schemas can also be negative and unhelpful, arising from the painful experiences in your life, from being bullied to missed moments of comfort from a caregiver. In either case, your schemas color your interpretation of memories, emotions, cognitions, and bodily sensations. Essentially, they are subconscious beliefs that you don't think to question because they come with a felt emotional charge. When an unhelpful schema is activated, you experience intensely painful emotions, such as anxiety, sadness, or loneliness. Interestingly, this emotional charge creates a sort of "schema chemistry" that pulls us into similar relationships over and over again. This is why so many of us find ourselves in romantic relationships that mirror our parents' struggles to fulfill our core childhood needs—essentially, we are following a familiar feeling. In this way, schemas are self-perpetuating, drawing you repeatedly into internal and external environments similar to the environment where they developed, embedding their message more and more deeply, until you start to see it everywhere.

For example, Cole's last relationship started when he swapped numbers with Mike, a handsome nurse whom he met at a coffee shop one evening. From the get-go, the chemistry felt intense, and Cole was infatuated. However, Mike was unpredictable: floods of messages and flowers were interspersed with extended periods of unavailability. While Mike certainly worked long hours, he also seemed randomly withdrawn. At these times, Cole would experience intense waves of anxiety, panic, and insecurity. He felt overwhelmed by a deep sense that he was unlovable and unworthy of Mike's attention, and he'd seek reassurance by calling and texting him, compulsively. Mike would generally not respond, or if he did, it was only to tell Cole, "Chill out! You're just too much."

Looking back, Cole can see that his clinging and demanding behavior unconsciously contributed to the exact outcome he feared: Mike ending the relationship. "You're too much! I can't stand how clingy you are," Mike shouted as he hung up the phone for the last time.

Cole sobs while telling the story to me, three years later. It is yet another confirmation of his deeply embedded schema that anyone he cares about will eventually abandon him. Terrified that he'll feel this level of pain again, Cole has avoided dating since. After all, everyone leaves, and it all hurts too much.

When I ask him when he first remembers feeling this way, he answers, "When I was eight years old." This was Cole's age when his dad left the family home and also not long after he'd started to experience rejection and bullying from his peers at school. Though Cole is close with both his parents today and has built an incredibly loyal and caring group of friends around him from high school onward, it feels impossible for him to move past the schema that everyone leaves him. Even in his late twenties, he still finds himself consumed by the intense grief of his need for stability, predictability, and belonging not being met.

EXERCISE: Schema Tracking

Going back to the Tricky Times Timeline you created at the end of the last chapter, identify all the events that relate to formative moments where you felt intense emotions and your needs were not met. Write these down in the space that follows, then make a note of what you needed in that moment (if you can identify it), along with the belief that might have developed about yourself and the world as a result of that situation. If this belief still feels true now, it's a schema.

Here are some examples of dysregulating events to guide you (though this is by no means an exhaustive list):

- Bullying
- Neglect
- Hospitalization
- Accidents
- Death of a loved one
- Emotional invalidations
- Abuse
- Difficult parental separation
- Rejection
- Witnessing violence
- Chronic illness
- Parentification
- Poverty
- Natural disasters
- War
- Excessive pressure to achieve
- Discrimination

____

____

____

____

____

____

Schema Survival

Your schemas will pull you into unconscious survival patterns like the following:

- **Disconnection:** Staying socially and emotionally separate from others. You might fear rejection or abandonment, feel unworthy of love or belonging, or struggle to trust others in your life.
- **Impaired autonomy and performance:** Difficulty asserting your needs, desires, and boundaries, along with feelings of inadequacy or failure. You might struggle with feelings of incompetence, perfectionism, or self-doubt that can negatively impact your sense of self or your ability to achieve your goals.
- **Impaired limits:** Difficulty in setting and maintaining healthy boundaries, as well as a tendency to feel overwhelmed by your impulses or emotions. You might have difficulty saying no or experience feelings of being out of control.
- **Other-directedness:** Focusing excessively on meeting the needs and expectations of others, at the expense of your own needs and desires. You might prioritize others' opinions over your own, have difficulty asserting yourself, or struggle with feelings of guilt or inadequacy when you prioritize your own needs.

Now, I promise we wouldn't be exploring these painful patterns if there weren't a path to healing and transforming them. You've already taken the first step in this journey: cultivating the self-awareness to notice your schemas and understand them as internalized messages and patterns rather than as truths about yourself and the world. Awareness moves you from your mind into the body, allowing you to feel your unmet core needs so that you can find healthy ways to meet them. The ongoing practice of engaging in heartfelt values–aligned behaviors helps you to resist the pull of schema survival patterns.

Your healing steps are:

1. **Awareness** of your schemas as internalized messages and emotional patterning (rather than truths)
2. **Healing** at the emotional level by meeting your core needs in a felt, embodied way
3. **Engagement** in action that aligns with your values and Self-energy (rather than patterns of the past)

Parts Develop to Protect You

Schemas show up in your life as what we call *parts*—groups of thoughts, feelings, memories, and desires that assemble and operate together, depending on the interaction between your felt sense and the situational triggers you encounter. While this understanding of parts comes from different forms of therapeutic approaches, including schema mode therapy and internal family systems (IFS), most of us already talk and think about our parts in daily life. For instance, after dinner with a friend, you might say, "A part of me wants to go out for a drink, and another part just wants to go home and snuggle up in bed." Or, when you feel hurt by a text message, one part of you might want to fire off a brutal reply, while another part might want to hold off on a response until you can talk in person. Our parts are what cause us to want and experience different things simultaneously.

In a situation with low emotional stakes, like deciding whether or not to go out for drinks after dinner, arbitrating between our parts isn't an issue. However, challenges arise when we haven't cultivated the self-awareness to facilitate connection between our different parts and our true Self. Self-awareness is what allows us to effectively communicate with and lead our parts in a way that supports deep healing and alignment with our values and purpose.

Understanding Your Parts

We develop parts for a variety of functions. Some parts fight back against your schemas or overcompensate for them; for example, a feeling of loneliness could be underpinning a part that is constantly trying to get attention and approval in unhealthy ways. Perhaps you might see this part bragging or behaving very competitively. Some parts find ways to escape from your schema and block your pain, such as an addictive behavior that is an attempt to self-soothe or numb yourself from an underlying feeling of defectiveness. Some parts try to repress other parts of you that feel like a burden or a liability; for example, a feeling of failure could underpin a part that is constantly striving for perfection and status. All of your parts are trying to help you cope with experiences your nervous system finds threatening.

Each part is associated with its own painful emotions as well as behavioral patterns intended to protect you from feeling those emotions. A given part is activated when your unhelpful schemas determine it is needed—for example, when an unhealed emotional wound is triggered or you are reminded of this past pain in some way. In this way, parts are the "soldiers" of our schema-driven survival patterns.

Parts are not inherently problematic. Some of them are even deeply infused with Self-energy, offering you vitality and wisdom. We can call this type of part your "healthy adult" or "Wise Mind." However, parts can often show up in situations where they are no longer beneficial to your well-being—in fact, they might even be detrimental.

Your Inner Child Part

Like all of us, children experience the full range of emotions. They are joyful, angry, impulsive, sad, and scared. And they are incredibly vulnerable. This vulnerability remains at the core of our being, regardless of our age. Your vulnerable child part is a repository of distressing experiences, overwhelming emotions, and often intense physical sensations. It arises in neuroceptively similar situations to those dysregulating moments in your life where your needs were unmet. You might recognize it in feelings of extreme shame, dependency, neediness, loneliness, worthlessness, fear, grief, failure, and loss.

In the imagery rescripting exercise last chapter, you started the process of nurturing your inner child, and we'll come back to doing this more in depth after we work through your protective parts. The reason for this is that sometimes it's hard to go directly to your inner child because your protective parts have been pushing it back for years!

Protective Parts

Protective parts are the ones that exist to help you cope with threats and overwhelm. A classic presentation of a protective part is the "inner critic," characterized by perfectionism and punitive self-talk. For instance, you might have had the experience of hearing an inner voice telling you that you're going to be seen as lazy and unreliable if you don't get a project handed in. Scared into action, you get to work but then find yourself frozen—now the inner critic is telling you that what you're writing is terrible and you'll get awful feedback. You ruminate on your own worthlessness as a writer for a while until suddenly, you hear the same voice criticizing you for not speaking more compassionately to yourself—after all, you're trying to heal. Dealing with this voice can be so difficult! But believe it or not, the inner critic has a positive intent: It is trying to protect you from the judgment of others.

The inner critic is just one of many parts that are trying to help you cope with unhelpful schemas. There are many more we can identify, each of them falling under a category of survival reactions. Let's examine them now.

Overcompensation

Overcompensation is a way of trying to overpower the unhelpful schemas associated with your vulnerable child. If you feel like a failure, you might overcompensate by going above and beyond what is required of you, so that no one can question your success. If you feel frightened you will be abandoned, you might overcompensate by playing it cool in your relationship, so that your partner will feel compelled to keep pursuing you.

These patterns can sometimes look helpful from the outside. For instance, approval seeking can leave folks feeling positively toward you, though it may come at the cost of your own integrity or authentic self-expression. Being perfectionistic and overcontrolling at work could result in higher achievement, but it will likely come alongside burnout and an imbalanced life.

Let me introduce you to some common overcompensating parts I see showing up. You can go through them and consider which ones you relate to, if any.

The Overcontroller

An overcontrolling part is characterized by an excessive need for preparation and control, regarding both external circumstances and your own emotions and vulnerabilities. This part tends to catastrophize situations and imagine worst-case scenarios; it finds it difficult to relax and let its guard down, even in safe environments. This includes when you're curled up in bed, meaning that constant vigilance may disrupt your sleep. Not only that, but significant physical tension is also often experienced, alongside shallow breathing. As the body gets more uncomfortable, this part disconnects from sensory and emotional awareness further, hindering your capacity for self-awareness. Believing that relying on others is risky, this part insists on handling situations independently rather than risking the vulnerability of asking others for support.

An overcontrolling part likely developed in response to past experiences of betrayal, deception, or exposed vulnerability. The work you need to do will involve learning when it's appropriate to be cautious and when it's safe to let go of excessive control. Along with building a sense of trust in yourself and others, you can reconnect with emotions and sensory experiences for better self-awareness and healing.

The Overachiever

An overachieving part is characterized by an extreme internal pressure to achieve and gain recognition for success. This part fears the experience of guilt when goals are not met and often focuses on "shoulds" and "musts."

If you have a strong overachieving part, you may experience constant muscle tension, shallow breathing, and high anxiety. This results in blocking out sensory and emotional information, hindering healing.

An overachieving part likely developed in an environment where your achievements were praised more intensely than your efforts. Your caregivers might have been perfectionistic in their expectations, offering more limited emotional support.

Healing this part requires learning to value rest, play, and mindfulness. Overachievers must understand that relaxing and lessening pressure doesn't threaten their long-term success and well-being.

The Intellectualizer

When navigating an emotional challenge or personal issue, an intellectualizer will analyze and dissect the situation from a purely logical, detached perspective, rather than feeling emotions. Its emphasis on rationality can leave it feeling cold to others (both your other parts and people in your life).

The benefits of embracing the body's felt sense will have to be logically presented to this part. From here, your attention needs to move to somatic therapies and embodied awareness instead of pure talk.

EXERCISE: Reflect on Your Overcompensating Parts

Do you identify with any of the overcompensating parts that were just described? Why or why not?

Do you have other patterns of overcompensation that you notice show up in your life? What are the pros and cons of these patterns?

Avoidance

Where patterns of overcompensation focus on trying to control the feelings of an unhelpful schema, avoidance focuses on trying to suppress them. These patterns use activities like workaholism, exercise, social media scrolling, extreme fandom, daydreaming, or the abuse of substances like food, drugs, and alcohol to push away the negative thoughts and feelings.

The Dreamer

A dreamer part is characterized by engaging in imaginative thinking or envisioning positive scenarios as a way to escape overwhelming emotions. The ability to dream, visualize, and think creatively is a valuable trait, but it is less beneficial when it makes us prone to escapism and disconnects us from our bodily sensations or values-based action.

Working with this part involves noticing when real-world needs are being avoided and practicing moving into the feeling body. To heal, the dreamer must increase embodiment and emotional tolerance, spend time in healthy relationships, and learn to co-regulate emotions. From here, it is important to make a practical action plan for achieving goals.

The Lone Wolf

When this part feels threatened, it uses hostile angry behavior to keep people away. It can even be violent at times, though more sullen forms of behavior, such as sulking or stonewalling, can also be engaged. Often the behavior has the desired consequence of creating distance, but this will likely reinforce unhelpful schemas.

Attachment styles, which we explored in chapter 5, can help you make sense of this relational pattern. Healing starts with developing felt-sense awareness of what it feels like when the anger kicks in, along with engaging in self-soothing strategies. As you build a relationship with this part, you can use your Self-energy to support it stepping back so that you can be more vulnerable to build connections with others.

The Fog

The fog is a sense of disconnection from your thoughts, feelings, and body, or from the place and people around you. It may feel like you're watching yourself from a distance or like the world is artificial. In this mode, you may struggle to concentrate and find that images, sounds, and sensations are distorted.

Working with this part involves enhancing your awareness of your physical sensations, actions, and thoughts, as well as using grounding strategies that stimulate your senses. This will support a felt connection and allow you to move through the fog rather than being pulled back into it.

The Shadow Stuffer

This part relies on stuffing feelings down, with behaviors that range from procrastinating, to distracting yourself with social media or a streaming binge, to using food, exercise, alcohol, drugs, or self-harm to banish intense feelings.

Healing this part happens through work on noticing and naming thoughts, feelings, memories, and urges as a way of slowing down harmful behavioral responses. This said, choosing more helpful forms of distraction is often a useful first step as you work on learning to connect with your parts. This can involve self-soothing practices like those introduced in chapter 3. A dynamic form of mindfulness (one that involves body movement) might be helpful as you learn to experience this part, as opposed to a seated mindfulness practice where you would be left with potentially dysregulating thoughts and emotions you have not yet learned to effectively nurture.

EXERCISE: Reflect on Your Avoidance-Based Parts

Do you identify with any of the avoidance-based parts that were just described? Why or why not?

____

____

____

____

Do you have other patterns of avoidance that you notice show up in your life? What are the pros and cons of these patterns?

____

____

____

____

Surrender

If overcompensation or avoidance doesn't work, we tend to surrender to our schemas, behaving as if our beliefs, emotions, feelings, and behaviors are true.

Informed by the freeze and fawn responses, this state encourages passive, submissive, self-deprecating behavior and reassurance seeking, because of the deep fear of rejection. People driven by this part may seem like they are not taking care of their needs or are allowing themselves to be mistreated. This tendency is unfortunately self-perpetuating, as this part will pull you toward relationships and behaviors that strengthen the established patterns, such as investing in a relationship with someone who is emotionally unavailable.

The People Pleaser

The people-pleasing part is characterized by prioritizing others' needs and desires over one's own. When acting from this part, people sacrifice their own needs and desires in hopes of receiving approval and avoiding conflict or rejection. They go to great lengths to accommodate others, even at the expense of their own well-being.

Healing of this part happens when you learn to connect to your true felt sense. This allows you to discern the authentic values, wants, and needs of your Self from the urge to act in a way that prioritizes others' expectations for fear of disappointing them. Fostering self-compassion and cultivating a sense of clarity in your purpose will support you in tolerating your fears of rejection.

The Self-Care Neglecter

This part is marked by a relentless focus on external responsibilities, whether related to work, family, or other obligations. Self-care neglecters constantly put the needs of others before their own, sacrificing personal time and the activities that nourish and recharge them.

When acting from this part, people find it challenging to set boundaries or express their needs, often feeling a sense of guilt or inadequacy about prioritizing themselves. As a result, they can experience increased fatigue, stress-related symptoms, and a decline in overall health.

Healing this part starts with deepening your connection to Self and learning to navigate the experience of guilt. This often involves fostering self-compassion and cultivating a sense of worthiness that will help you gradually integrate healthier self-care habits.

EXERCISE: Reflect on Your Surrender-Based Parts

Do you identify with any of the surrender-based parts that were just described? Why or why not?

____

____

____

____

Do you have other patterns of surrender that you notice show up in your life? What are the pros and cons of these patterns?

____

____

____

____

Healing Your Parts

Healing comes as you infuse Self-energy into your various parts, cultivating a sense of connection and clarity between them. This trains your parts not to hijack your mind, body, and behavior, but instead to work together in a way that serves your highest good. You're essentially transforming your familiar self-protective patterns by supporting your parts in experiencing something unfamiliar in a way that feels safe to them. This expands their flexibility and moves your unconscious patterning into alignment with your conscious desires.

The first step in this healing process is identifying your parts and learning to consciously engage with them. You need to know your parts well enough to recognize when they are activated and be able to communicate with them in a way that softens their determination to protect you through maladaptive patterns.

One way to engage with your parts is to imagine them personified—their face, their voice, even their wardrobe. You can then visualize sitting them down for a cup of tea and a conversation. Another way is to look at where each part exists internally. As an example, my inner child seems to live in my throat—when it's activated, my chin tucks down and I curl inward with a tearful feeling.

My overcompensating protector part doesn't live too far away—I feel it most keenly in my tightly clenched jaw and the neck pain that often comes with this state. Meanwhile, my avoidant dreamer part seems to float above me in the clouds as my mind wanders, or sometimes in the pages of a book, where I lose track of time and of my body altogether.

The next exercise will help you start building your parts profile so that you can identify when each part is activated, learn its needs, and establish a connection to it.

EXERCISE: Building Your Parts Profile

In this exercise you'll build a parts profile for each of the protective parts you identified in your system. Before you begin, grab some extra paper and make a few copies of the body outline on the next page (or you can draw your own if you're so inclined). Use one of the body outlines to map out each part you explore and record any insights you uncover. You can organize these notes into the categories of beliefs, sensations, emotions, and memories.

I'll provide an example first—a map of my own people-pleasing part—to help you get started.

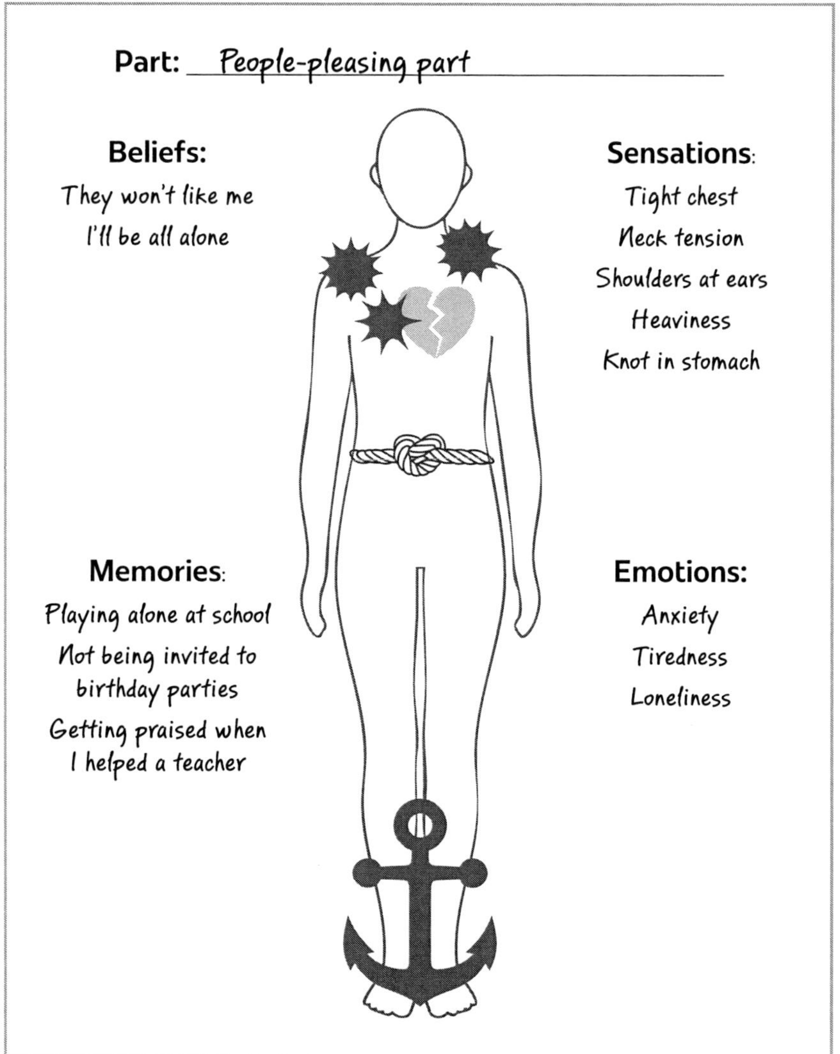

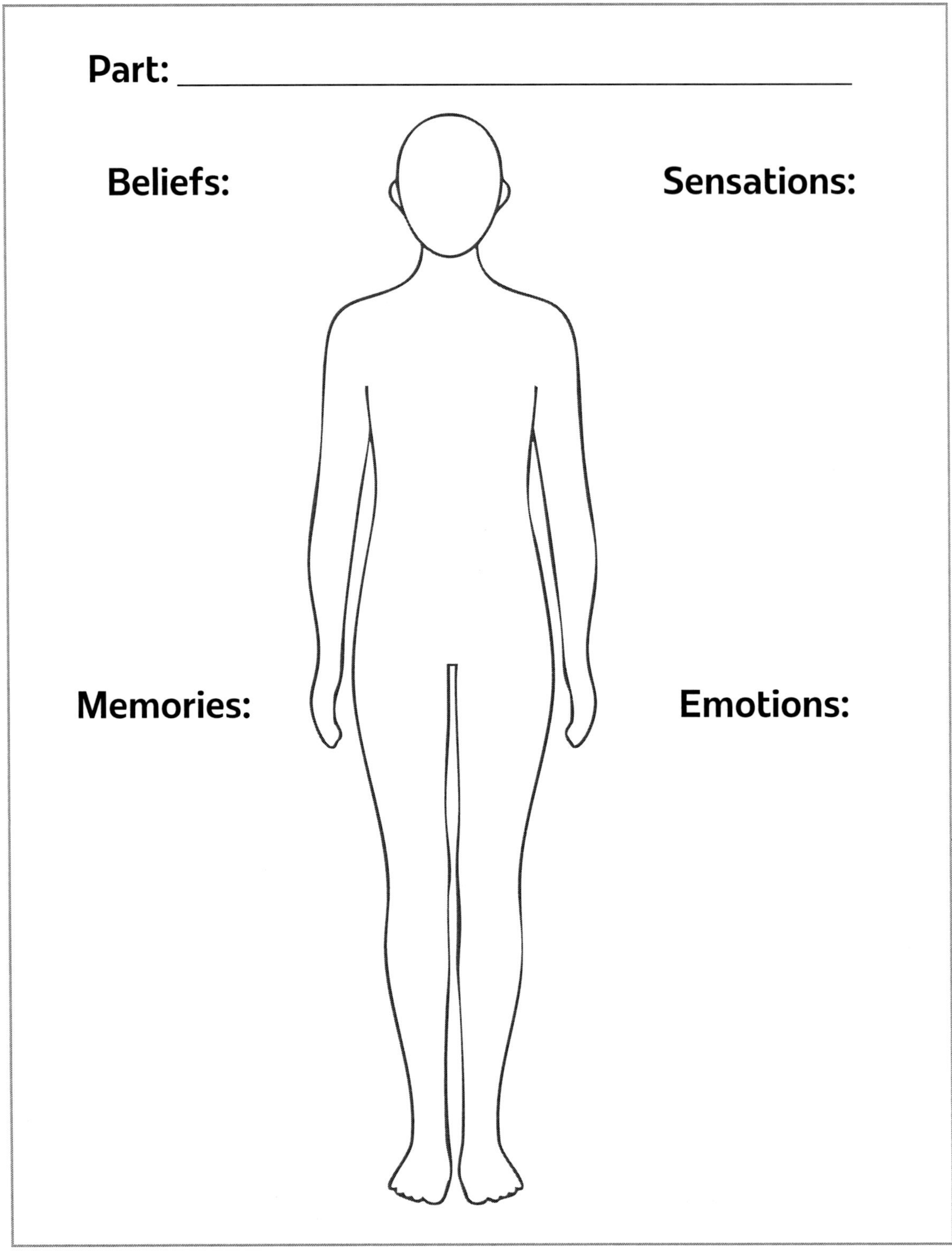

By developing a respectful relationship with your protective parts, you'll find more success in asking them to step back as you turn your healing attention toward your inner child. Remember, your parts have always wanted what was best for you—they developed to help you survive at a time when you had an emotional problem, and they are still seeking safety. The familiar is safe, and their familiar pattern is to repress the inner child and engage in what they see as protective behavior. Your job is to heal them by holding them in loving-kindness and compassion. After all, they are exhausted! They have put in so much effort and energy yet are constantly stuck in the negative schemas and unfulfilling behaviors. These parts deserve to be treated kindly as much as anyone.

The Retirement or Reassignment of Protective Parts

We learned earlier that the protective parts suppress the inner child as a way of keeping it safe. It's important to know that as you begin to heal your protective parts, all the big emotions of your inner child will likely come to the surface. Your main responsibility here will be to assure your protective part that you can now meet your unmet emotional needs. You've already spent time developing your self-soothing skills, but please go back to them if you need a refresher. Keep coming back to anchor in your healthy adult so that you can hold space for the emotions.

As you learn that you can safely feel your feelings, those protective parts will become less and less activated. This gives you an opportunity to reflect on whether each part can be reassigned to a new, healthy role or if it should be retired from service. Maintaining a connection to your Self-energy (your ventral vagal state) will allow you to engage in the reflection needed to explore if the unhelpful part would like to end its career, as it were, or if it would like to use its energy in another way by developing supportive patterns that are Self-energy infused.

Take Sarah and her overachieving part, which constantly pushed her to take on too much work and punished her for making even the smallest mistake. Through a process of inquiry with this part, Sarah realized that it was driven by a deep need to feel significant—an unmet need from her childhood. Rather than trying to reject or suppress the part, which had only led to heighted anxiety and a low mood in the past, she worked on trying to understand it better and appreciate the times it had helped her. Sarah worked with her overachieving part to find a new role for it that would acknowledge its good intentions but channel them in a healthier way. It is now tasked with promoting self-compassionate excellence. It encourages high-quality work while equally honoring rest, play, and the other important areas of Sarah's life.

Not all parts want to be reassigned. Sarah's self-care neglecter—a part that had criticized her for taking any time or care for herself—opted for retirement. After exploring this part and looking at the healthy ways she can now meet her core need to belong and feel connected, Sarah imagined this self-neglecting part sitting with a pina colada on a blue-and-white sunchair, feeling relieved and happy to be let go.

Meanwhile, Cole worked with his people-pleasing part and reassigned it to being a boundary guardian. In this new capacity, it focuses on aligning his energy with his values. It supports him to behave in a kind way, but without sacrificing his authenticity out of fear of rejection. Cole finally gets say yes with joy and no with confidence.

EXERCISE: Reassigning or Retiring Your Protective Parts

While your protective parts once served you, you may find that they are now exhausting, restricting, and harmful. A process of gentle inquiry can help you explore whether your protective parts are ready to take on healthier roles or consider a restful retirement.

Start by taking a few moments to engage in some deep breathing and connect to your Self. See if you can find the space where your Self-energy sits in your body.

Next, focus on one of your protective parts, this part that has been working so hard to try to keep you safe. Imagine where this part sits in your body.

From here, you can work through the questions here to guide an inquiry from your Self into your part. Remember, treat the part with respect and seek for understanding. As painful as the part may be in your life now, it developed to protect you as best it could.

What were you trying to protect me from when you developed?

____

____

____

____

How are you feeling about how your role has progressed over the years?

____

____

____

____

If you didn't have to work so hard in this role, what would you like to be doing?

____

____

____

____

What are you afraid will happen if you were to step back from your role? What need are you meeting?

____

____

____

____

How can you guide me in meeting that need in way that supports my well-being too?

____

____

____

____

What do you need from me to feel safe enough to let go of your old role?

____

____

____

____

If you were to support me in a healthier way and take on a new role, what would you like it to look like?

____

____

____

____

If you were to retire, where would you like to go and what would you need to feel comfortable there?

____

____

____

____

Remember, these parts developed to protect your inner child. As you connect them to the wisdom of your Self-energy and your capacity to nurture and protect your inner child as a healthy adult, they will feel more comfortable with reassignment or retirement. Let's explore that vulnerable inner child in more depth now.

EXERCISE: Understanding Your Inner Child

To soothe a vulnerable inner child part, you need to recognize when it is present. However, this awareness can be challenging because you are likely to resist the intense feelings that come with it, and other parts work to detach you from it. So start building your relationship with this part in a calm moment using the points of reflection that follow.

What typically evokes this vulnerable part? (For example, people, remarks, circumstances, emotions)

____

____

____

____

What emotions arise when you are in this part? (For example, fear, isolation, sadness, self-doubt, rejection, anxiety)

____

____

____

____

What are the felt-sense sensations when you are in this part? (Bodily sensations, such as a racing heart rate, rolled shoulders, a sinking stomach)

____

____

____

____

What challenges tend to emerge when this part is present? (For example, impulsiveness, feeling overwhelmed, escapism)

____

____

____

____

EXERCISE: Building Your Inner Child Profile

In this exercise you'll build a parts profile for your inner child. Many people find that they have a number of different inner child parts. For example, you might have a vulnerable child part, a playful child part, an angry child part, and an impulsive child part. Therefore, I suggest you start by making several copies of this page. Use the child-shaped body outline to map out each part that fits within your inner child and explore any insights you uncover. Like you did with your protective parts, you can organize these insights into the categories of beliefs, sensations, emotions, and memories.

Part: ______________________________

Beliefs:

Sensations:

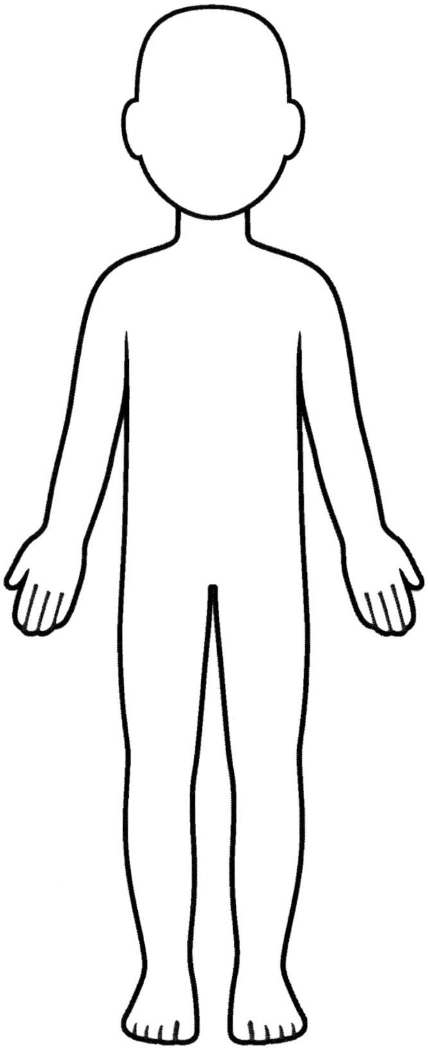

Memories:

Emotions:

Nurturing Your Inner Child

Let's explore now how you can ensure your inner child feels heard, seen, valued, accepted, loved, and safe. Your inner child needs nurturing, compassionate boundaries, and firm but fair discipline. Like a good parent, you can hold your inner child accountable for unhelpful behavior and coach them through their big feelings. This is how your inner child learns to self-regulate.

Nurturing means establishing a secure connection with your inner child. This is done by anchoring to the felt sense of Self-energy. This will allow you to attune to moments when your inner child is activated by a perception of needs going unmet. In these moments, you can turn to the practice of self-soothing, offering solace to your inner child on a somatic level. You might already have experienced a felt sense of security when practicing the self-soothing techniques you've learned so far in this book. What is unique in this part of the work is maintaining a connection with both your vulnerable part and your healthy adult, applying your mindfulness practices to ensure you are responding rather than reacting.

The first step is to listen to what your inner child has to say, exactly like you did in the *Understanding Your Inner Child* exercise. You might notice a sense of vulnerability, shame, guilt, anxiety, fear, anger, sadness, insecurity, abandonment, rejection, failure, or loneliness. Once you're able to recognize what your inner child is experiencing, you can take steps to meet its needs, soothe its feelings, and practice responding to your vulnerability in a new and transformative manner. Doing this repeatedly over time will decrease the intensity of your negative schemas and that felt sense of distress that comes with them.

This said, the relationship with your inner child isn't just about navigating the painful feelings and unhelpful schemas. Investing energy in connecting to your joyful child through play and delight is also important. This is something we often forget about when we are in survival mode, so let's dive in now!

EXERCISE: Encouraging Your Inner Child to Experience Joy and Play

Doing activities for pure delight is an essential ingredient of well-being. Try engaging in activities that bring joy to your inner child—for example, chewing bubble gum or rolling down a hill. Pairing this with supportive inner dialogue allows you to nurture your inner child. Read through the following affirmations, and let your Self determine if any of them will be helpful in healing your parts.

- You are allowed to have fun and play.
- Let's go on an adventure together and explore the world around us.
- It's okay to laugh and be silly.
- I believe in your creativity and imagination; let's create something wonderful.

- We can dance like nobody's watching and sing our favorite songs.
- Remember those moments when you felt pure happiness? Let's relive them.
- I love the way you see the world with wonder and curiosity.
- Your delight matters to me, and I'm here to nurture it.
- Every day is a new opportunity for joy; let's make the most of it together.

If you sense resistance coming up here, it's likely because your protective parts are online. Remember, healing is not a linear process—it is not unusual to shift between nurturing your inner child and reassuring your protective parts that you can take care of this vulnerable part. These protective parts, too, need to learn that it is safe to play and experience delight.

Closing Reflections

Which of your schemas most negatively impact your life? How did these negative schemas develop?

____

____

____

____

What positive self-schemas do you have? How did these develop?

____

____

____

____

Do you find it easier to conceptualize your protective parts individually or to group them? For instance, your inner critic might comprise multiple fight, flight, or freeze parts.

____

____

____

____

What circumstances, activities, or foods connect you to your inner child?

____

____

____

____

Can you envision a family portrait of all your parts? You might even draw it out. How do you feel looking at it? What changes might you need to make in the seating to make sure all your parts feel safe and supported?

____

____

____

____

Takeaway Messages

- Beliefs coupled with felt-sense shifts and patterns of behavior are called schemas.
- Unhelpful schemas develop when your needs are not met and your nervous system is dysregulated.
- Your psyche is trying to protect you from psychological injury in the same way your body is trying to protect you from physical injury; this results in protective parts developing.
- Protective parts come in the form of patterns that correspond to fight, flight, and freeze or fawn: overcompensate, avoid, and surrender.
- Your inner child part experiences the core emotional wound and the sense of dysregulation. Often this part is called the vulnerable child, though you also have other forms of the inner child, like the playful part.

PART 3

Integrate and Engage

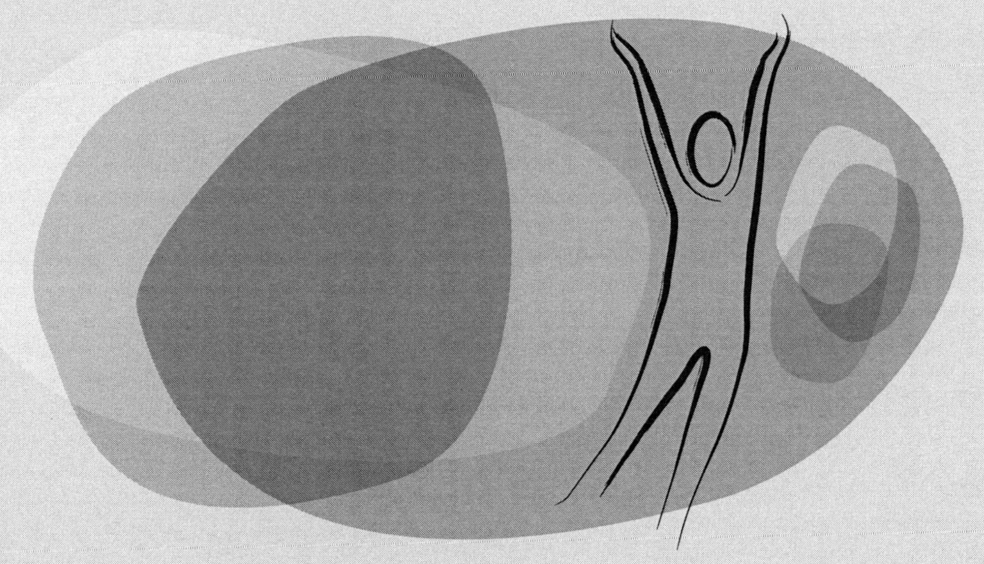

CHAPTER 11

Memory Network Transformation: The Power of Bilateral Practices

"You can outrun the lion chasing you, but you cannot outrun the lion in your head."

—African proverb

Throwing open the door and pulling her spelling test out of her backpack, seven-year-old Sarah raced down the hallway to find her mom in the kitchen. "Mom, Mom! I got 8 out of 10!"

Sarah's little face was beaming. The spelling list had been the toughest one yet and she'd struggled with four of the words, practicing them over and over in the week leading up to today's test. Her mother, however, had the phone to her ear—only half-hearing what Sarah said and not thinking about the effort Sarah had put in throughout the week, she barely glanced at the waving piece of paper. "Oh. That's disappointing, dear," she said absentmindedly. "You can study harder this week." She turned her back to Sarah and continued her conversation.

Sarah's face dropped. So did her heart. She didn't realize her mom was in the middle of an upsetting conversation with her father about finances. As a result, she took the distracted engagement as evidence that her mother was disappointed by her, that her achievements didn't mean anything if they were not perfect.

Sarah still remembers this day. She was seeking connection and validation, and her mother's distracted response felt like rejection. The memory, constructed by her feelings, was then encoded with a sinking feeling, an urge to curl up into the fetal position, and a belief that she was ultimately unworthy. This belief was more deeply encoded every time Sarah felt like a failure or undervalued and dismissed by others. Before long, the belief made up her internal narrative. Many weeks later, when her father found a spelling test when taking out the recycling, he commented to Sarah about how he hadn't seen it and added, "Well done." But Sarah felt certain that this was evidence he just felt sorry for her, not that he really saw her as good enough.

As Sarah's story shows, memories are meaningful, but that doesn't mean they are exact—otherwise her memory would have focused on her mom's struggle with attention, not her own perceived failure. If your nervous system was dysregulated at the time of the original event, as in the case of traumatic memories, the sensory elements will be stored in a fragmented way—some elements might be vivid, while others will be lacking detail. For example, Cole clearly remembers the car lights fading down the driveway when his dad left the family home, but he does not remember what his dad whispered in his ear as he hugged him goodbye.

A memory is not a static recording of an image or event that happens in your life. Your memories are constantly being reconstructed and updated. Whenever you remember something, you're pulling together the image, sensory elements, thoughts, and beliefs. The process is influenced by new associations, experiences, and the context in which you're recalling the memory. Additionally, traumatic memories can feel like they're being relived through flashbacks. When a friend says goodbye and goes to head out the door, Cole often feels a nauseating stomach-dropping feeling, while Sarah reports a full panic response whenever a new email comes through, as that was how she learned of her mistake with the court submission.

Hence, no memory exists alone. You're always responding to the present in the context of the past. Essentially, your memories exist in a network that integrates them all. This network is a way for your brain to organize and access the incredible amounts of information gathered through your life: images, thoughts, sounds, physical sensations, emotions, and beliefs. Recalling a single event brings up all the related memories with their emotions, sensations, and beliefs. For example, for Sarah, the sound of an email arriving not only brings up the memory of the court submission but also that discarded spelling test, along with every instance of failure in between. But this network also encourages connections among positive memories. When Sarah sees a soccer ball, she feels a sense of specialness, connection, and belonging, all derived from the many Saturday mornings when she and her parents would head out to kick the soccer ball in the cool fall weather, with hot chocolate following. Positive memories like these offer a refuge from our unhelpful schemas. Better still, they can be consciously harnessed to develop helpful schemas that support our healing.

Bilateral Healing

Healing the memory network begins with integrating the sensory elements from dysregulating, traumatic, and schema-evoking memories into a coherent memory that is less charged. From there, you can go on to experience the painful memory in a different way that bolsters your positive beliefs. This integration is accomplished with a method called *bilateral stimulation*.

As the name suggests, bilateral stimulation involves stimulating both the right and left sides of the body with rhythmic sensory input, such as moving your eyes from side to side, tapping your hands on your upper chest (like in the butterfly hug you learned in chapter 9), marching your feet up and down, or using headphones to listen to sounds that alternate from one ear to the other. Engaging in bilateral stimulation when remembering a painful situation can decrease the emotional intensity of the memory, enhance your accurate recall of the memory, decrease the negative schematic beliefs, enhance positive self-beliefs, and increase heart rate variability (which, as you might remember from chapter 2, indicates increased vagal activity of your social engagement system).

To be clear, this transformation isn't about changing or erasing a hurtful memory. You will still recall the event as awful or sad. The difference is in how the memory "sticks" with you. By dislodging the memory's connection to other events, beliefs, emotions, and so forth in the memory network, bilateral stimulation empowers you to move past the negative associations of that memory and build new positive associations and integrated adaptive beliefs about yourself.

While the exact mechanism of this method isn't completely understood, there are a few theories about how this transformation happens. There are two hemispheres in our brain, the right and the left, joined by the corpus collosum, a part of the brain that sends messages back and forward. Another part of your brain, the motor cortex, runs down the middle of your brain on either side, controlling your physical body. The left side of your body is connected to the motor cortex on your right hemisphere, while the right side of your body is connected to the left hemisphere's motor cortex. As sensation moves from your left side to your right, messages from your left and right motor cortex are being sent back and forward across the corpus collosum. This activates both hemispheres simultaneously, which fosters communication between the left and right brain.

When your nervous system is overwhelmed, survival mode shifts your brain's focus to just getting through the experience. In this state, your brain fails to effectively integrate information into a cohesive narrative. Sense data is stored separately from language, and images, sounds, sensations, and feelings get locked away in different brain networks. The way this information is encoded is generally more inaccessible than it would be for normal events, due to the changes in your brain's chemistry during survival responses (Quaedflieg & Schwabe, 2018). As a result, the experience has no sense of cohesiveness. But by using different forms of auditory and tactile stimulation to evoke bilateral communication in your brain, both sides of your brain are activated; this increases communication between different regions and structures (Hill, 2020), helping your brain locate all the parts of your memory. This activation is coupled with the focus on a particular emotional memory, which allows you to integrate language with visual data, along with adaptive information about yourself and the world. All of this supports decreasing the associated distress. Essentially, healing happens by reprocessing, reintegrating, and reinterpreting the memory pieces.

Another theory on how bilateral stimulation works is that with the eye movements, you evoke a change in consciousness. Have you ever seen someone sleeping with their eyelids not quite closed, so that you can actually see their eyes moving back and forth? Rapid eye movement (REM) is important for memory consolidation, one of the important tasks our bodies accomplish while we're sleeping. Since bilateral stimulation provokes similar eye movements, it's suggested that this stimulation activates the same kind of neurobiological state that allows us to process painful memories into normal networks (Jeffries & Davis, 2013).

It's worth noting that since eye movements have been found to be the most effective in this technique, bilateral stimulation is usually associated with a form of therapy known as eye movement desensitization and reprocessing (EMDR). However, eye movements may not suit folks who have a seizure disorder, an eye condition, or frequent headaches. This is something you'll want to bear in mind as you move into practicing bilaterial stimulation yourself.

Bilateral Stimulation Practice

The first step in practicing bilateral stimulation is to resource yourself for the work and the memories and emotions it may bring up. The safe space imagery and protective figure you have established in previous exercises are important to keep ready. This is what you'll use if you need to nurture yourself at any point in the practices ahead.

The Risks of Practicing EMDR Solo

EMDR can be a powerful tool for processing trauma; however, engaging in this practice without a trained professional does come with risks. These risks include retraumatization, where the distressing memories, emotions, and sensations from the original traumatic experience are reactivated.

If you are experiencing any of the following, I advise you to seek professional support for your EMDR processing, as self-guided EMDR may increase your symptoms:

- Severe emotional distress (overwhelming anxiety and/or panic and a sense of losing or being out of control)
- Feeling disconnected from your body, foggy, numb, like you're watching yourself from outside your body, or like the world is unreal
- Unresolved complex trauma (which comes from a history of repeated and/or prolonged traumas, such as childhood abuse)
- Thoughts of suicide or self-harm

If you are in doubt, seek professional guidance from a trained EMDR therapist. They will ensure that you can safely process without additional distress.

While you're waiting to access professional support for processing trauma, you can use the bilateral stimulation techniques for grounding. Skip the step of focusing on a traumatic memory and consider using the strategies as emotional regulation tools (like the butterfly hug you learned in chapter 9).

Next, you'll review the painful events that have impacted how you see yourself and the world, one at a time, particularly those that are related to any current triggers you experience. The following exercise will help you get clear on the events that might be targets in this work.

EXERCISE: Float Back

Take a large piece of paper. In a corner, draw a circle diagram with three equal sections labeled "Situation," "Emotions/Sensations," and "Beliefs," like this:

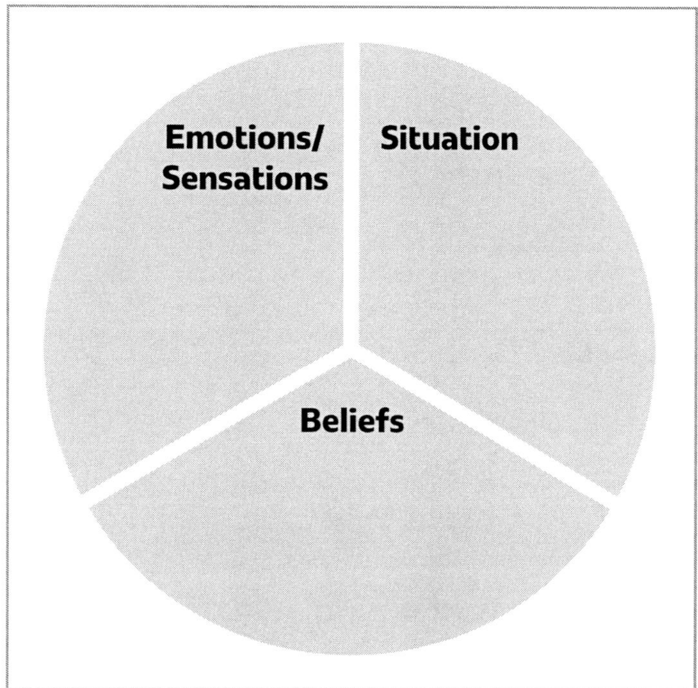

Consider a recent moment where you noticed yourself getting triggered into a dysregulated state—maybe a moment where you noticed one of your protective parts or experienced the vulnerability underneath. Write it down in the Situation section of your diagram.

When you bring the situation to mind now, what sensations do you feel in your physical body? What emotions do you notice? Write them down in the Emotions/Sensations section of your diagram.

What is the unhelpful belief that shows up? Perhaps this is one of those schemas that underpins one of the parts we unpacked last chapter. Write it down in the Beliefs section of your diagram.

Now, from this situation, "float back" to an earlier time in your life where the same beliefs showed up before. (Alternatively, you can use bodily sensations or symptoms, like the muscle tension of anxiety, to float back. This is similar to how you traveled back on the bodily sensations in the perspective-taking exercise in chapter 9.) Draw another circle to represent this earlier situation and fill out the three sections.

Repeat this process of floating back until you reach the earliest memory or until you have collected about 10 memories that have a similar negative belief. You'll end up with a map of the schematic belief, like the following example showing Sarah's negative schema:

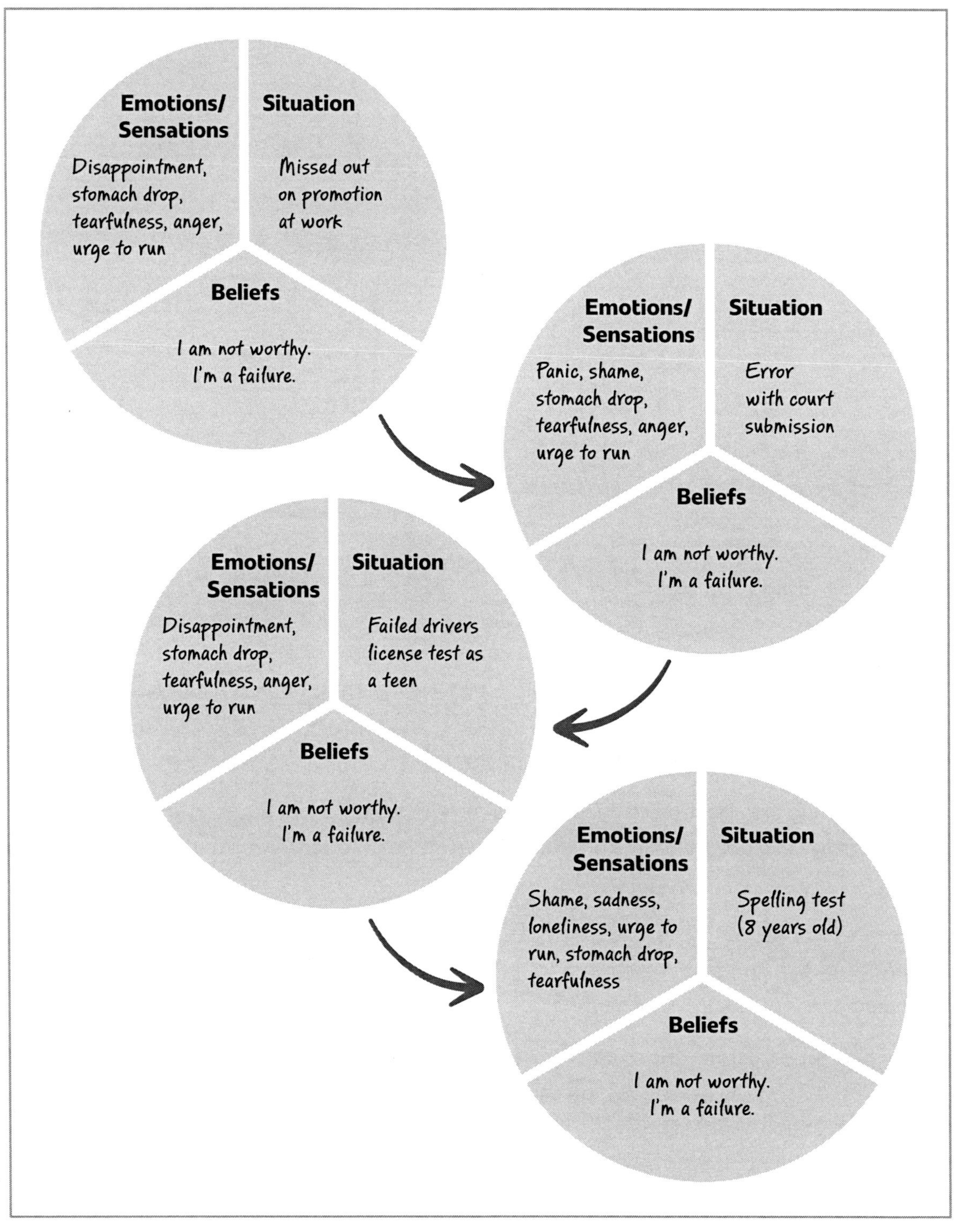

Once you've finished mapping these events, review your diagram and decide which memory you'd like to target first. Generally, you should go with the earliest memory or the one that evokes the most heightened emotions; however, that advice is for when you are in the room with a trained therapist. If you are experiencing distress that is greater than 8 out of 10 with a memory, it is best to target that event when you have a professional to co-regulate with. Choose another memory to work with if you're practicing on your own, and make sure you've got self-soothing and grounding strategies ready to go if needed.

Once you've identified the target memory, it's time to get started.

When you bring the situation to mind now, what is the very worst moment? If you were playing it back on a movie screen and paused it at the instant your distress was at its highest, what image would you see?

____

____

____

____

What emotions do you feel?

____

____

____

____

What do you feel in your body?

____

____

____

____

What is the belief?

____

____

____

____

When you hold this image, emotion, and sensation in mind, coupled with your unhelpful belief, how distressing is the situation on a scale of 0 to 10, where 10 is the most distressing?

What helpful belief would you like to believe about yourself instead?

When you think about the situation, how true does this helpful belief feel, on a scale of 1 to 7?

Bilateral Stimulation Methods

There are a variety of forms that bilateral stimulation can take, including:

- **Eye movements:** Focus on a point in front of you and move your eyes from left to right quickly and repeatedly. You might find it helpful to use an object—such as a pen, a ball on a string, or a necklace—that you can move back and forth in front of you. You can also download EMDR apps, use YouTube videos, or even play Tetris! (Seriously. There is evidence that Tetris can be used in this reprocessing.)
- **Tactile stimulation:** Remember that butterfly hug from chapter 9? It's a fantastic way to self-administer bilateral stimulation. For reprocessing, do the movement more quickly. You can also tap on your knees or shoulders with your hands, stand up and march your feet up and down, or try both at the same time. Ideally, go walking outdoors, because your eyes naturally move from side to side in outdoor environments.
- **Auditory stimulation:** Use headphones and listen to alternating sounds in each ear. Certain electronic music tracks offer this; otherwise there are lots of bilateral beats that can be found on YouTube or other streaming services.

You can also pair up the stimulation forms. For example, you might do the butterfly hug with eye movements or listen to bilateral beats while marching in place. Consider which forms of bilateral stimulation might work best for you, and practice them a few times to get comfortable with the techniques. Once you've settled on your bilateral stimulation style, you're ready to move on to the reprocessing exercise described next.

Important Reminders for Self-Administered EMDR

While in a therapy session you are often guided to keep processing through significant distress, doing these processes on your own means that you don't have someone else to provide regulation. For that reason, you need to make sure you're honoring yourself by moving through the practice slowly and with awareness of your limitations.

- **Start small:** Begin with less distressing memories to become comfortable with the process, and use self-soothing as needed.
- **Be gentle:** If you feel overwhelmed or your distress increases significantly, please just stop the process and use your self-soothing techniques.
- **Keep a log:** Document your sessions, noting the memories you worked on, the distress ratings, and any changes in your bodily sensations, emotions, and beliefs.
- **Consider professional support:** If you are experiencing severe emotional distress, dissociation or a sense of things feeling "unreal," unresolved complex trauma, or thoughts of suicide or self-harm, or if you are in doubt, it is advised that you seek professional guidance from an EMDR therapist.

EXERCISE: Reprocessing Through Bilateral Stimulation

Step 1: Attending to the Situation

- Bring the image to mind, attending to the emotions, body sensations, thoughts, and beliefs.
- Start your chosen bilateral stimulation method while focusing on the situation. The side-to-side stimulation you use here should be fairly quick.

Step 2: Processing

- Continue the bilateral stimulation for 30 to 60 seconds.
- Notice whatever thoughts, images, emotions, or sensations arise without judgment. Just notice.
- Pause the bilateral stimulation and take a deep breath in and out.

Step 3: Track the Distress

- Go back to recall the original situation. Note what, if anything, has changed about the memory. Re-evaluate the current level of distress associated with the situation and the unhelpful belief (from 0 to 10).
- Notice any changes in your thoughts, feelings, or physical sensations and write them down as well. Remember, a lot of the pain we experience in our lives is the result of a disconnect with the body. So, when you make note of what has arisen, ask yourself, "Where am I feeling that in my body?"

Step 4: Repeat the Process

- Repeat this process for four sets or until the level of distress associated with the memory decreases significantly (ideally to 0 or 1).

Troubleshooting

If you find that you are getting stuck on the same negative thought, emotion or sensation, try change your eye movement direction (vertically or on a diagonal) or your speed. If the distress from the memory does not decrease all the way to zero in the time you have available, that's okay! Take the memory and imagine locking it up in a box that you can keep stored somewhere safe, perhaps somewhere far away from you. Add locks, chains, or whatever else you need to make sure it is secure.

Then, it's time to self-soothe. You might evoke your safe space imagery, your protective figure, or your older and wiser future version of yourself. Let yourself be held and let your nervous system settle. You may need to be flexible and bring in some of your other self-soothing practices as well. This is exactly why we started this book by building those practices.

Then, later, you can come back to unbox the memory and start processing again. Or you can choose a different belief. Sometimes we need to process other beliefs before really stuck ones will shift. I'll also note that you're not expecting your emotional experience associated with a painful memory to become positive, you're just looking for the intense distress to decrease. It is not healthy to not have a feeling of sadness, grief, or anger when you recall situations or losses where these emotions fit. The goal is simply to feel these feelings without them overwhelming your nervous system or being associated with unhelpful beliefs about yourself.

If you do find the distress has decreased, now is the time to instill your positive belief, as described next.

EXERCISE: Positive Installation

Step 1: Identify a Positive Belief

Once your distress has reduced, return to the positive belief you identified in the setup. Is this still the belief that best fits? (Sometimes it changes due to what came up through your process.) Once you've established the best fit for your positive belief installation, consider the original situation and how true the positive belief feels on a scale of 1 to 7.

Step 2: Install

Use bilateral stimulation while focusing on this positive belief for 30 seconds. You'll go much slower with the bilateral movements than you did when processing the negative belief, about one-third of the speed.

Step 3: Track the Change

Note whether the positive belief is getting stronger, weaker, or about the same. Keep repeating until the positive belief is a 7 out of 7.

If you don't get to a 7, ask yourself, "What is the worst thing that would happen if I fully believed this?" Then do another set and notice what comes up. If you're still at a 6 or less, it could be the case that a protective part has stepped in and blocked you. Consider identifying it and chatting with it about what it believes and all the times it has shown up in your life. That may be a map to the other memories that will need additional reprocessing to successfully integrate the positive belief.

Step 4: Closing Body Scan

Finally, close your eyes and scan your entire body. Identify if there are any areas of tension or niggles that are related to what you've been processing. If so, do further bilateral stimulation while focusing on the sensation until it wanes. You might ask yourself:

- "What does this feeling want to say?"
- "Is there a movement or gesture that my body wants to complete?"
- "What part is present now? What do they need to relax?"

Remember, you don't need to be silent or still in this process—in fact, I'd encourage you not to be! It can be particularly effective to finish the positive belief installation by putting bilateral beat music on your headphones and rocking, shaking, or dancing, making sure your feet are going up and down. You can then allow intuitive movement to unfold within the processing sets, as well as between the sets when you notice and track what is unfolding.

For Cole, this meant dancing around in a dynamic way and roaring at his bullies, finding his inner strength. He described it as a release of his sense of freeze and fawn from the past. For Sarah, it helped to sway gently while giving the butterfly hug to herself and saying out loud, "Slow down, darling. Slow down. You don't need to do anything. You're allowed to relax." Between sets she would move her jaw from side to side and do gentle neck stretches. She took this as a reminder to release all the pressure and tension that her high-pressure overachieving protective part had started evoking in its effort to defend her vulnerable inner child.

Step 5: Closure

Complete your session with a few minutes of deep breathing or a resourcing exercise to ground and nourish yourself. Write down any reflections you have and note any processing that happens in the hours afterward. Other memories, images, sensations, emotions, thoughts, or dreams related to what you've been processing may arise. Use your self-soothing skills, like your safe place or resourcing, to calm your system. Then make a note in your phone or journal as to what triggered them and what they were so that you'll be able to come back to them at a more appropriate time.

While we've been working on integrating cogitation and awareness of beliefs with the bilateral stimulation applied in this chapter, there is a benefit to simply engaging in the practice and letting your mind unconsciously process. This is also not the only dynamic body-based exercise that can support your healing.

While you've no doubt enhanced your felt-sense awareness, increased your capacity to connect sensations to survival patterns, and started shifting some of the stuck memories held in your mind and body, you might find that a body shield is still holding strong. This can be noticed in tension in the neck, headaches, or big changes in your emotional or conscious state that arise when you engage in stretching practices. If bilateral stimulation didn't bring you to a full release, let's move onto another body-based practice to further your felt sense of freedom.

Do you have any memories that you have heard others recount differently? What has influenced this difference in recollection?

____

____

____

____

What activities do you already have in your life that provide you with bilateral stimulation (e.g., walking, playing a musical instrument)? Are there any other forms of bilateral stimulation you would like to introduce into your daily life? If so, where would they easily fit? (For example, you might put on bilateral music while waiting at an appointment.)

____

____

____

____

When you did the "float back" exercise, did you find that you were most connected to the emotions/sensations or beliefs that came up?

____

____

____

____

When you look at the unhelpful beliefs you've identified, do they feel true in all domains of your life, or just some? Consider why this might be.

____

____

____

____

How regularly are you reflecting on the positive beliefs you've been working on installing? Is there a way that you can regularly bring your attention to them, such as putting a sticky note on the mirror or in your car?

____

____

____

____

Takeaway Messages

- Your memory is shifting every time you recall an event, as each time you reconnect the various components—the image, sensory input, emotions, and beliefs.
- You can notice patterns between schematic beliefs, emotions, and bodily sensations and situations using the "float back" technique.
- EMDR and other bilateral stimulation practices can positively impact how you recall a painful memory, helping you to shift the felt sense of unhelpful beliefs and install positive ones.

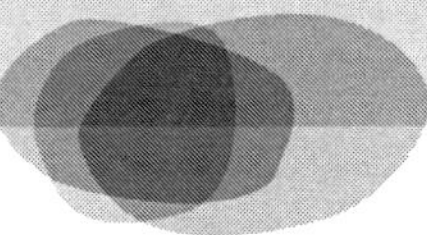

CHAPTER 12

Shake It Out: Tension-Releasing Tremors

> ***"If you get in the water and have nothing to hold on to, but try to behave as you would on dry land, you will drown. But if, on the other hand, you trust yourself to the water and let go, you will float. And this is exactly the situation of faith."***
>
> —Alan Watts, *The Way of Liberation*

Cole remembers watching the red skin on his forearm seem to expand as the cold water ran over it. The sting of the icy sensation hurt so much less than the shame of the snakebite (that awful so-called prank where someone grabs your arm with two hands, twisting one hand forward and the other back). That shame couldn't be washed down the sink and wouldn't vanish after a couple days of wearing long sleeves so his parents wouldn't see the bruises.

He can't describe exactly what had happened. But this is what happens with our memories; certain sensations, smells, images, sounds, and the like stick around, while other parts seem to fade, or perhaps were never even encoded into our memory bank.

In this case, all Cole can recall is being on the schoolyard basketball court, staring at the net. Though he has no memory of the other faces that were surrounding him, he knows who gave him the snakebite out of the faceless crowd—a deep sense of knowing, rather than a clear memory. It was a long-term bully who somehow always mobilized their other classmates with a power no teacher seemed to have.

Then, he was alone. He was always alone. It was desperately lonely, but it was also his reprieve. "I just have this sense of such deep sadness. I used to spend my nights crying so hard into my pillow that I was shaking. This sort of thing happened so often that I don't remember any specifics," he told me.

I explained to Cole that this was certainly reflective of the deep sadness he describes but could also capture how his system was taking the chance to self-soothe in safety. Crying, shaking, trembling—all of these are ways of letting go.

In the introduction, I mentioned the stress-releasing shaking response. Imagine a gazelle racing along with a cheetah in hot pursuit. Suddenly, the gazelle collapses to the ground. The cheetah hasn't touched it yet; instead, the gazelle's nervous system sensed that the sympathetic fight-or-flight response was insufficient and evoked the final survival response. It's frozen, playing dead.

Since predators typically don't like to eat animals they haven't killed themselves, the cheetah wanders off. A few moments later, the gazelle jumps up and flees to safety. But going from a 100-mile-an-hour flight response to the standstill of freeze leaves it with a huge burden of excess energy. The gazelle begins to shake violently, discharging the incredible stress of this near-death experience. Without this response, its system would be left holding all that energy in the form of full-body tension.

Unlike other animals, humans don't tend to release the stress of our nervous system in this efficient way. Instead, we grit our teeth, we hold back tears—and the tension accumulates. That psychological and physical strain needs to be released.

Therapeutic Tremors

When you're in a situation you experience as threatening, your body makes instinctual shifts in posture. For instance, your neck muscles will pull your head forward, while your shoulder muscles will raise your shoulders up and draw them in. Your spine will curve forward while your pelvis pulls up toward your abdomen. This all makes sense—you're protecting yourself from a threat by curling in toward the fetal position. This is a response hardwired into the brain to protect the areas in your body where vital organs sit.

Just like your consciousness holds patterns of experiences and burdens of your parts, your body holds physiological patterns, sensations, and energy. These patterns can become locked into your body like a suit of armor. While this armor may seem to keep you safe, it takes a lot of energy to maintain. Long-held tension can accumulate in your neck, shoulders, pelvis, and lower back. The most significant muscle in this area is the psoas, with tightness here causing everything from pain to bladder and digestive issues. Remember, all of this is unconscious—involuntary. Not only can these long-held patterns of tension result in chronic pain, but they can also reduce your felt-sense awareness and limit your range of motion. It also makes you a lot more sensitive, keeping your nervous system actively looking out for threats.

Thanks to our cultural conditioning—being told to stop crying, being yelled at in the midst of an overwhelming tantrum, and so forth—we often fail to treat ourselves like the instinctive animals we are. This results in a missed opportunity to discharge stress through the body's natural release mechanism.

The scientific name for the shaking response that releases stress and trauma is *neurogenic tremors*. The rhythmic oscillations of your body offer a profound tool for releasing tension and healing from the effects of trauma. They are not simply random muscle contractions but a natural way for your nervous system to restore balance and let your muscles relax. Essentially, these movements release you from the muscular armor your nervous system wears in times of overwhelm. Scientists hypothesize it's because deep-rooted muscular tension is released, regulating the nervous system to support a state of relaxation and calm (Payne et al., 2015).

While these tremors can and do happen organically at times, you can also evoke them. Releasing and accepting involuntary muscle activity supports you in restructuring the body signals and utilizing the experience to enhance your sense of empowerment. Accepting this release shifts the helplessness and fear you've felt in the past, making room for an enhanced sense of trust and safety in your body. Such exercises may allow your nervous system to shift old stories, patterns, and parts even without consciously understanding them. This is particularly useful for the stress our system accumulates before we fully develop language or the capacity to integrate memories, since discharging the survival energy stored from these preverbal experiences cannot be done simply by accessing your logical brain. Cole learned to deliberately evoke shaking in adulthood as he sought to release the somatic armor he'd developed to handle the hurts of the past.

Since it's such a natural process, you might wonder why I've waited until this point in the book to suggest tremors as a means of relaxing and healing the nervous system. It's because having an established set of self-soothing skills is important to support yourself in making space for the intense emotions that can arise with movement release. It's also important to build up your practice of tension release in a slow and steady manner, particularly if you have a history of dissociating in response to psychological or emotional distress. With that in mind, before we move into tremors and shaking, we'll start with the gentler practices of yawning, rocking, and swaying.

EXERCISE: Ahhhhhh, Yawn

Yawning is an evolutionarily old function, one that we don't seem to entirely understand. From making you more alert to reducing anxiety or cooling an overheating brain, there are several theories as to why animals yawn. What is most generally agreed upon is that yawning may leave you feeling more relaxed (Corey et al., 2012; Guggisberg et al., 2010). It's a release that can increase blood flow to the brain as you open the muscles in your skull and jaw, drawing in cool air and potentially stimulating your parasympathetic nervous system (Gupta & Mittal, 2013).

Let your mouth open and take a long breath in with your mouth opened as wide as possible, stretching your jaw. Pause briefly, then release with a sighing exhale out.

How does that feel?

You can then move into neck rolls or anything that feels intuitive.

EXERCISE: Rocking and Swaying

There's a reason little babies love to be rocked—the rhythmic movement stimulates various internal systems such as the tactile, vestibular, and somesthesis systems (Cordero et al., 1986). These same soothing systems are built into every body, and we know that adults, too, sleep better in beds that gently rock (Perrault et al., 2019). Rocking and swaying are ways of gently reconnecting to your felt sense and intuitive movement. If you find a gentle rhythm that offers you comfort and support, you can come back to it at times of overwhelm. Maybe envision rocking your inner child in the way you needed. This exercise is designed to introduce you to the movement practices ahead.

1. Stand with a slight bend in your knees to keep them soft and flexible. Alternatively, you can sit comfortably in a chair.
2. Let your eyes adopt a soft, relaxed focus.
3. Gently begin to sway or rock your body back and forth. Keep your movements smooth and fluid.
4. Let your neck and head remain soft and relaxed. You may even allow your head to bow slightly toward your heart, or move it from side to side.
5. Embrace the soothing, nourishing rhythm of the rocking or swaying motion. Allow yourself to feel supported and comforted by this exercise.
6. Pay attention to the sensations and feelings that arise as you move. Take a moment to acknowledge what it feels like to engage in this calming motion. Notice any changes in your body and mind as you gently rock or sway.

Let's Start Slowly

Tracking internal arousal states using small "micro-movements" is the perfect place to start tuning into the interoceptive feedback needed for tremor-based stress release. Being aware of the sensations of your body will help you titrate the intensity, supporting you in a gradual and controlled release of stress through small, manageable doses of active release, coupled with reset and relaxation. Breaking the process into smaller, less intense experiences ensures the process is more accessible and less intimidating.

The following exercises are designed to release deep muscle tension and stress, integrating practices and wisdom of Dr. Peter Levine's Somatic Experiencing, Dr. David Berceli's Tension and Trauma Releasing Exercises (TRE), and wisdom traditions such as tai chi. We'll work from the outside in, starting with your outer limbs, where there tends to be less emotional memories associated with tension, and gradually moving toward your body's center.

Note: Always make sure you are practicing these exercises safely. This may mean practicing with a professional healthcare provider or a safe person you trust to hold space and support you. It is important to ensure you always maintain clarity in your consciousness. If you feel like you are dissociating, stop the practice and instead use a grounding exercise to settle yourself.

EXERCISE: Ping Shuai Gong (Tai Chi Hand Swinging)

This hand-swinging exercise enhances *chi*, a term from traditional Chinese medicine for the psychophysical energy that moves through all living beings. Chi is said to travel through the body via channels known as meridians. This movement of chi is how health and balance of the body's organs is believed to be fostered.

1. Stand with a slight bend in your knees to keep them soft and flexible.
2. Start shaking your right arm. Back and forward, up and down—whatever feels energizing and energy releasing in your body. You might spend about 30 seconds to a minute on each step.
3. Next, shake your right leg. Like the arm, explore different directions and tempos. If needed, use the wall or a chair to balance.
4. Move on to your left arm, and then your left leg, following the same instructions as before.
5. Now it's time to shake your whole body, while being mindful to relax your jaw and head.

You can perform this exercise anytime you feel tension building in your body. Allow any sounds (sighs, grunts, vocalizations, etc.) to emerge naturally. You can also add intuitive movements like jumping, kicking, and twisting at the waist.

EXERCISE: I Just Want to Shake

It's no coincidence that music and dance exist in every culture around the world as a form of expression and release. Movement gives us a chance to step back from our parts and connect to that transcendent sense of Self.

With that in mind, feel free to add some music to your movement practice. A quick boogie is a lovely way to release the tension associated with anxiety and stress. Just one song is often enough to release and rest your state. One of my favorite pairings is to do the hand-swinging exercise while listening to Taylor Swift's "Shake It Off." The lyrics capture what we intuitively know: the need to joyfully and forcefully release the activation of our schemas and protective parts.

EXERCISE: Isometric Tremors

Isometric tremors occur during voluntary muscle contraction without movement, such as the trembling leg you experience while holding a squat for an extended time. The following series of exercises are designed to evoke spontaneous neuromuscular tremors in the body. These mild tremors can release chronic tension stored deep in your body.

Moving Your Body with Awareness

Start with the following subtle movements to practice balancing and moving with awareness.

1. Stand with your feet positioned comfortably shoulder-width apart.
2. Shift your weight gently to one side of your body, allowing yourself to balance on the outer edge of the foot on the side you are leaning toward, while simultaneously balancing on the inner side of the opposite foot.
3. Take two to three slow, deliberate breaths, focusing on the sensation of your feet connecting with the ground.
4. Gradually return to your starting position, and then repeat the movement by leaning toward the other side of your body.
5. Perform this leaning motion on each side two to three times, allowing the subtle shift in weight to activate and stimulate your nervous system.
6. Try this same exercise again, this time shifting the weight to the front of your feet, and then the back.
7. Conclude the exercise by stretching and gently shaking out your body, releasing any residual tension or stress.

What was this experience like for you? Reflect on how your body responded to your leaning, relaxing and contracting to support you in this somatic motion. What is it like to let your body unconsciously respond to the conscious shifts in weight?

____

____

____

____

Practicing Muscle Fatigue

Next, we'll explore how it feels to induce more significant tremors by practicing muscle fatigue.

We'll start with your lower legs. Remember, you'll be using your witnessing and acceptance skills as tremors are evoked. Tap into your expansive capacity to hold what unfolds, and always know that you can stop if you need to. If you feel any sensation that is less like the release of a tremor and more a sharp sensation that would warn of injury, please stop.

1. To start off, ensure you have a chair or wall nearby for support and stability.
2. Shift your weight onto one foot while bending the opposite knee slightly.
3. Rise up onto your tiptoe, hold the position for a few seconds, and then gradually lower your heel back to the floor.
4. Repeat this motion until you feel your calf muscle is approximately 70 percent fatigued.
5. Switch to the other foot and repeat the exercise.
6. When you've concluded, take some time to stretch and gently shake out your legs to release any remaining tension.

How was that experience for you? Is your tendency to run toward discomfort or away from it? Note any emotions, thoughts, memories, images, urges, or other inner experiences that arose.

____

____

____

____

Engaging the Quadriceps

Next, we'll move to the quadriceps. These are generally the strongest muscle in your body, which means it might take a little more time to fatigue them.

1. Bend your knees to lower your hips into a simple chair-like position until you start to feel a burn in your upper thighs. This can be done with your back against the wall for support.
2. You can explore shifting your weight onto your heels and holding this position.
3. Keep holding this position until you reach approximately 70 percent fatigue. This will likely come with a shaky feeling in your muscles.
4. Once fatigued, slowly return to a standing position.
5. Conclude by taking some time to stretch and shake out your legs to release any residual tension.

Inner Thigh Stretch

It's now time to get into the psoas muscle of your hips. As mentioned earlier, this muscle has far-reaching consequences, from your bladder to your digestive system. Colloquially, it is also called "the muscle of your soul" and is often implicated in the accumulation of tension when you're under stress.

1. Stand with your feet positioned a little wider than shoulder-width apart.
2. Bend forward at the hips, with your knees slightly bent. Allow your head to hang down toward the floor. You can put your hands on your thighs for support if needed, or you can gently take hold of your elbows in a rag doll–like position or reach your hands toward the floor.
3. While in this forward fold, take three full, deep breaths with your head in line with your body's center.
4. Shift your weight to one side, bringing your head into alignment with your knee on that side. Take three more full, deep breaths.
5. Repeat the stretch on the opposite side.
6. Return to center and repeat the stretch once more before slowly coming back to a standing position.
7. Conclude by stretching and shaking out your body to release any lingering tension.

After completing these exercises, you may feel a light tingly sensation. Perhaps you'll feel energized, rejuvenated, relaxed, or tired. Check in on what is showing up—does your nervous system need up-regulating or down-regulating?

____

____

____

____

Taking Tremors into Your Routine

If you're like most of my clients, you're busy. That's why I've designed all the practices and skills in this book to integrate as easily as possible into your day. The tremor techniques we've just learned might fit well into activities you're already doing. Perhaps you can practice the muscle fatiguing exercises during your regular workouts at the gym. Maybe you can do a few minutes of ping shuai gong while you wait for the kettle to boil or sway gently while you brush your teeth. None of this needs to take hours; arguably, it shouldn't. After all, a lifestyle that is entirely focused on these practices would not leave room for you to invest in heartfelt living, building relationships that are meaningful, and pursuing a purposeful vocation.

Those pursuits will be the focus of the next chapter, where we will explore conscious commitment to living a meaningful life, a life of purpose. Remember that in this journey no human is perfectly healed, because no human is perfect. Nevertheless, we all are capable of evolution, of being released and reborn into increasing integrity with every moment.

Closing Reflections

When in your life have you noticed shaking or tremoring occur naturally?

____

____

____

____

Where in your body do you hold tension? What might this armor mean about you?

____

____

____

____

Which muscle fatigue exercise feels most impactful for you?

____

____

____

____

When you consider shaking as therapeutic, are there any other skills you can integrate to support its impact?

____

____

____

____

Takeaway Messages

- We evolved to shake after stressful events as a way of releasing the tension associated with the experience. However, humans tend not to do this.
- If tension isn't released after a stressful event happens, your body stores it as "muscle armor."
- Tension in your body can increase your allostatic load (the wear and tear) on your body and impact your mood.
- You can use movement practices to release the tension buildup and historic patterns. Some practices use conscious movement while others induce unconscious tremors.

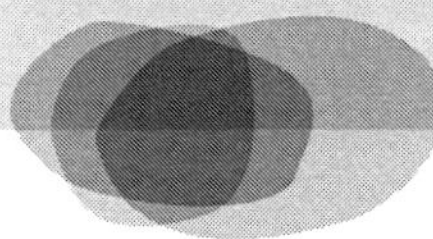

CHAPTER 13

Living with Purpose: Integrating Mind, Body, and Soul

"Friendship is unnecessary, like philosophy, like art. . . . It has no survival value; rather it is one of those things that give value to survival."

—C. S. Lewis, *The Four Loves*

Cole's partner, Luis, is reliable, hardworking, creative, and kind. He manages a small team of carpenters, and Cole knows they all go to him for personal advice because of his listening ear and grounded nature. Cole has frequently described how calm Luis is when he's upset, offering reassurance and never telling him that he is "too much." This is all very different from the relationships of his past.

Cole and Luis were friends for over eight months before Cole agreed to a date. This decision was much more conscious than emotionally driven. When Cole mapped out his values and future on a vision board (a practice you'll learn about later in this chapter), he saw that Luis aligned with it all. Curious, compassionate, oriented toward social justice, delighted by nature, Luis embodied everything Cole was consciously seeking in a partner. Cole had deep respect for him as a person, though he didn't feel "fireworks" between them. However, in his therapeutic work, Cole had begun to recognize that those fireworks he sought in relationships tended to show up when his protective parts were dominating. So, when Luis asked him out, he decided to resist the pull toward emotionally distant, image-focused, hyper-critical men like those he'd dated in the past, and try something different.

Nevertheless, when he gets a text from Luis suggesting they plan a trip to celebrate Cole's thirtieth birthday, which is coming up in a few months, Cole is terrified. While Luis has never demonstrated anything but commitment to him, Cole still struggles to plan that far into the future with him. An old part of him can't let him believe that anyone would actually want to be with him. Historically, his self-protective parts had shown up as clinginess (an attachment-focused behavior). But since it's hard to cling when someone is consistently there, being with Luis has led to his protective parts shifting toward avoidance (fleeing). Confronted by this kind, thoughtful gesture, he feels trapped, disgusted, seized by an urge to run.

Fortunately, Cole is able to identify that he's been activated and that his survival system is online. He knows that he can most effectively soothe his protective parts by creating a little bit of space and perspective while getting his heart rate up through physical activity. So, he grabs his bike and heads up to a local lookout. As Cole pedals, putting distance between himself and the city streets, he starts to experience a similar distance from the turbulence inside his own skin. By the time he reaches the lookout, he feels settled, able to access his true Self again.

Cole has taken himself to his literal safe space, but if he hadn't been able to hop on his bike, he could have transported himself here by closing his eyes and evoking a sense memory of the lookout. When Cole was growing up, his grandfather used to pick him up from school once a week, and then they'd go straight to this same lookout and eat an ice cream cone while pointing out the local landmarks. It was often his favorite part of the week, a time when he felt seen, attended to, valued.

Cole had talked a lot about his grandparents in session. They were his constant—his North Star, as his astronomy-loving grandpa would say. Cole had a personalized compass made with a tiny diamond near the top as a reminder of all the time they spent together looking up at the stars. His grandpa had told him how the Great Bear and Little Bear constellations were said to have been a mother and son transformed by Zeus in such a way that they would be bonded together forever, circling the North Star and guiding lost travelers home. At the bottom of the compass is a little ruby to represent Cole's grandmother's rose garden. In memory of this, Cole has started dabbing rose oil on his wrists or a piece of fabric when he is feeling unsettled—another somatic strategy to help him connect to that felt sense of security, that North Star, that exists within his own heart.

Taking off his bike helmet, Cole sits down and closes his eyes. He takes a deep breath as he runs his fingers along the grass. *What is going on? What do I want?* He thinks about Luis—he really believes that he is a good person. Luis cares about him and has always shown he's open to growing. He supports Cole, he has always been interested in what he's doing, and he holds him in the tough moments, particularly when he's overwhelmed by that childhood burden of feeling like an outcast. Luis makes him tea and rubs his shoulders when he's feeling tense, and he always offers a heartfelt thank-you when he wakes to realize Cole has pulled a blanket over him when he has fallen asleep on the couch.

Sure, a part of him deeply craves fireworks, and recoils at what it sees as the mundanity of this relationship. But, as Cole opens his eyes to look out at the city lights, he knows that this protective part doesn't realize he's now more connected to himself than he's ever been. Cole isn't surprised to feel a yawn coming over him, releasing the tension forming around his jaw. This is how it always is—when he lies to herself or leans on beliefs he knows are false, he notices his muscles tense, but when he feels his truth, his muscles relax. He likens this intuitive reaction to the attraction and repulsion of a compass magnet that guides the arrow north.

Cole has used this truth test a few times recently—once when he signed up for a bookkeeping course he worried he wasn't smart enough for, another time while sticking with a volunteer role even after he made a mistake. In both instances, his inner critic crucified him; however, he discerned that this was his protective parts at work. He took some time to embrace these parts and acknowledge their efforts, then gently informed them that it wasn't going to be helpful to listen to them in this situation. He turned the shark music down, connected into his intrinsic Self, and aligned his behavior with his values.

This evening, as the sun sets and the stars become visible, Cole lies back to look up at the sky. He reflects on how the sky is always there behind every weather pattern and how, in the same way, behind every part exists a state of clarity and freedom. That North Star offers him a path to align his life with his heart. Sure, there is no guarantee that this relationship will last, but right now, Cole decides that saying yes to the possibility is his path north.

Your Map Forward

Life will never be perfect. Difficult feelings and thoughts will arise. Tethers to your past will pull you back into cycles that are not conducive to creating the life you want in the present. This is the experience of being human. My hope is that, as a result of what you're learning and practicing in this book, you can manage the pulls a little more calmly, hold the pain a little more gently, and rest in the assurance that you can keep healing, refining, and moving toward the person you want to be.

Think of your health as a garden. Your well-being habits and healing practices are the weeding, watering, and sunlight needed for growth. But of course, a garden needs something more: seeds, and a plan for where you will plant them. The seeds are your values, and the plan for planting them involves looking at the different domains of your life as the varying garden beds where you want to see them grow and blossom.

Sarah has lately been rearranging her garden beds. She still cares deeply about her career and works incredibly hard, but she has also been investing energy into holding the discomfort of not working late every evening, and instead scheduling time for connection with her family and friends. Her urge is still to work—when she's not answering emails or focusing on a project, her muscles tighten with the instincts of that old protective part. But she recognizes this pattern and, by reflecting on who she wants to be, remembers her value for deeply engaging in important relationships. She takes a big breath, lets out a sigh, and gently asks the overachieving protective part to let go a little more, reminding it that she's okay. Sometimes she puts her hands on her heart and gently sways until she feels her shoulders drop. Then, she hits the power button on her computer. Over time, this response has become easier. The inner landscape of her psyche is shifting, and the tension in her body is relaxing and releasing. She notices herself having a more developed sense of identity outside of what she is producing and achieving, and a greater ease with seeking support from people when she needs it.

In her personal life, Sarah notes that she has laughed and cried more in the past months than in the decades prior. She has also been able to develop some sweet rituals with her family. Every weekend, they all head out for a hike, swim, or outdoor adventure. On Sunday nights, they look at different children's charities and choose one to donate to. These new rituals reconnect her to her passions and her loved ones at the same time.

In the mornings, Sarah puts her hands on her heart as she takes a few moments horizontal in bed to connect to what she envisions as her ancestor's loving wisdom and that embodied feeling of Self-energy, feeling her muscles relax as a result. On Tuesday nights, Sarah does a check-in with all her parts, using a journal to reflect on how she's traveling emotionally and where she's at in her menstrual cycle. Both activities help her expand her window of tolerance—her capacity to hold her feelings in full awareness while maintaining her ventral vagal state (the social engagement system or that expansive Self-energy). Instead of going out for drinks with coworkers on Friday evenings, she uses that time to visit a bath house with an infrared sauna and cold plunge. Sometimes she goes with a friend, while at other times she prefers solitude so she can deliberately evoke a sense of spiritual connection that will carry her through the relentless day-to-day routine.

There are still days and weeks that are hard for Sarah, when her well-being rituals fall off the radar and the creep of anxiety and overwhelm sets in. When this happens, she puts her hands on her heart and reminds herself that she can hold these feelings. When sleeplessness creeps onto her pillow, she calls on her protective figure, the Celtic goddess Branwen, to wrap her compassionate arms around her and reminds herself she'll be fine to cope the next day.

This shows the true transformation in all of Sarah's work: not that she never gets anxious, overwhelmed, irritable, or exhausted, but that she now has a self-belief that she can get through those difficult periods in her life. Consequently, painful feelings and unhelpful thoughts don't scare her the way they have in the past.

I share Sarah's well-being routine to inspire your own journey; however, please remember that Sarah's rituals are underpinned by her values, her neurobiology, her history, and her current circumstances, not yours. There is no universally perfect plan for a purposeful life. From our unique values, parts, and patterns, to our histories, nervous system, relationships, and resources, we're all going to need different soothing strategies, healing practices, and coping skills. Sometimes we need different ones over the course of our lives, as new events cause our variables to shift. This is why I'm so passionate about teaching principles and providing you the resourcing needed to embrace all the parts of yourself, tune into the healing force of love, and evolve into integrity. Key to this process is identifying your unique values so that they can guide your choices and practices.

Values

Let's face it: So much of our effort and energy can be focused on other people's expectations for us, on what we "should" be doing, and letting short-term needs and desires pull us away from the things we genuinely care about. The result: an overwhelming sense of stuckness. Trapped by your mind, your body, and the relentless nature of the day-to-day, responsibilities and obligations can seem to consume every last morsel of your energy, and the harder you work to keep up, the farther away this effort can pull you from your Self. Your values provide the clarity you need for navigating the pull of protective parts and the social pressures of convention and approval. Values are the seeds that bloom into your true nature.

EXERCISE: Values Clarification

Go through the following list and tick the ones that seem to spark something in you. Please keep in mind that this is not an exhaustive list. Different people may hold different values depending on their culture, upbringing, and personal experiences. You can add your own unique values to the list as well.

- ❒ Appreciation
- ❒ Compassion
- ❒ Cooperation
- ❒ Courage
- ❒ Creativity
- ❒ Diligence
- ❒ Diversity
- ❒ Empathy
- ❒ Equality
- ❒ Fairness
- ❒ Forgiveness
- ❒ Freedom
- ❒ Generosity
- ❒ Gratitude
- ❒ Helpfulness
- ❒ Honesty
- ❒ Humility
- ❒ Humor
- ❒ Inclusiveness
- ❒ Integrity
- ❒ Justice
- ❒ Kindness
- ❒ Love
- ❒ Loyalty
- ❒ Nonjudgment
- ❒ Open-mindedness
- ❒ Optimism
- ❒ Patience
- ❒ Perseverance
- ❒ Positive attitude
- ❒ Professionalism
- ❒ Reliability
- ❒ Respect
- ❒ Responsibility
- ❒ Self-control
- ❒ Self-discipline
- ❒ Self-esteem
- ❒ Self-improvement
- ❒ Self-reliance
- ❒ Self-respect
- ❒ Sense of purpose
- ❒ Teamwork
- ❒ Tolerance
- ❒ Transparency
- ❒ Trustworthiness
- ❒ Understanding
- ❒ Unity
- ❒ Wisdom
- ❒ Work ethic
- ❒ ____________________
- ❒ ____________________

Chances are that you have a lot of values! It's a beautiful realization, yet also potentially overwhelming. To make this list easier to work with, we can use something known as the umbrella technique.

Go through your list and group together the values that fall under the same "umbrella." For instance, you might group positive attitude and humor, or fairness and trustworthiness. Write each group of values in an umbrella in the diagram that follows.

Next, let's clarify the domains in your life where you want to apply or live out these values—the garden beds where you want to plant your seeds.

Dr. Kelly Wilson, one of the founders of ACT, identified 10 primary domains of our lives (Wilson & Murrell, 2004). Consider the life domains listed in the following table and rate each one on a scale from 1 to 10, with 1 being not important to you and 10 being very important to you. Then, go back through the domains and rate how consistently you have been living out your values in each of these domains over the past week on a scale from 0 to 10, where 0 represents not showing up and 10 represents showing up fully.

Life Domain	Importance (1–10)	Past Week Embodiment (0–10)
Family		
Intimate relationships		
Parenting		
Friendship		
Work		
Education		
Recreation		
Spirituality		
Citizenship		
Physical self-care		

Pay attention to any areas you rate as very important (between 8 and 10) but where you have low consistency (a 6 or less).

In Sarah's case, she found that while she rated relationships as being a 10 on the importance scale, her consistency in showing up rated a 4, as she was constantly missing dinners and bedtimes, and was regularly prickly with her kids and partner. Meanwhile, she rated her career as a 7 in importance but rated her consistency at showing up as a 9.

Calibrating your consistency in living your values in the domains you consider most important is the key to living in integrity and feeling a sense of fulfillment. You might want to focus on those domains where your rating is mismatched in the next few exercises.

Where Do You Hurt?

The things you care about the most are often the source of your pain and anxiety. There is always a risk of loss in love, betrayal in trust, failure in trying, criticism in creativity, and rejection in connection. The beauty of this pain is that it can support you in clarifying what you care about. In fact, it's likely pain that unsettled you enough to grab this book. Emotional pain is a clear indication of what matters in our lives, of where we find meaning and purpose.

When Sarah started writing about what hurt for her, it became very clear within a few sentences that her relationships were what really mattered. Her workaholism and excessive efforts to avoid making mistakes were ways of trying to protect herself from the belief that she's ultimately unworthy. Ironically, that investment of energy in her image often came at the expense of her relationships.

As Sarah started investing in her relationships, she felt a sense of release. Her protective parts now come online less often, and when they do, she kindly nurtures and holds them while using Self-energy to reorient herself toward how she wants to show up in her life. Sarah's gut-wrenching fear of rejection has softened and her regular headaches have vanished, signs of her reduced allostatic load as she spends more and more time in the ventral vagal state, aligned with that sense of calm and connection she'd always sought.

EXERCISE: Sadness and Sweetness

Take a moment now and write about the place in your life that hurts—the moments that have been particularly painful, perhaps the times when you've cried. What could this mean about what you care about?

____

____

____

____

____

Of course, we don't only shed tears when we're sad. We often cry in the tender moments of life—at weddings and births, while reading good news stories on social media, when seeing a beautiful sunset.

Reflect now on the moments of joy and delight you've experienced today, this week, and this month. Are there people, interactions, or activities that bring you a sense of deep connection, delight, or integrity?

____

____

____

____

____

What could these moments tell you about your values and life domains?

EXERCISE: Who Are Your Heroes?

Another way to clarify your values is to consider people you find inspirational, who help you to connect to your heart, who serve as models for how you want to show up in the world. These are the people who cause you to light up, whether you're around them, watching them in real life or on TV, or reading about them.

Who are these people, and what is it about them that resonates with you?

What could this mean about your own values and life domains?

Some of your values will be consistent across domains, while others will be domain-dependent. For instance, in your family relations you may really value acceptance, while in your career you may value persistence. Moreover, as you consider the domains that you want to focus on right now, you may notice that the ones you care deeply about are the ones where you most struggle to live out your values. It's unlikely that you'll ever find your life perfectly balanced. It's a constant process of adjustment; correction by correction, a path is forged. But you'll find it easier to stay on track when the route is mapped.

EXERCISE: Mandala Life-Living

For this exercise, I like using a mandala. As a symbol of the universe in its ideal form and of the intent to transform suffering into joy, it feels like a good way of envisioning how to take aligned action in your life. You can use the mandala provided at the end of this exercise or create your own. You will also need some coloring utensils of your choosing.

1. First, choose four life domains to focus on exploring. (For instance, Sarah decided to start with intimate relationships, parenting, spirituality, and physical self-care.) Write down one of these domains outside each quadrant of the mandala.
2. Next, identify the important values you hold in each domain. You can go back to the checklist or your written reflections for a little inspiration if needed. Write these values by their domains.
3. Track your valued living each day on a 7-point scale. The template I've included here tracks one week, though you can modify this as you would like. Each day, consider the extent to which you are living your values within each life domain and color in the appropriate number of sections within that "slice" of the mandala, starting from the ring directly beneath the numbered ring (indicating actions that are less in alignment with your values) and working your way toward the center of the mandala (more in alignment). On day 1 you will color in the first slice of each domain you chose, on day 2 you will color in the second slice of each domain, and so on.
4. Reflect on your ratings and any patterns you notice while completing your mandala. If you find you are not making progress toward the center, consider what changes you might make in your daily life to support your living in better alignment with your values.

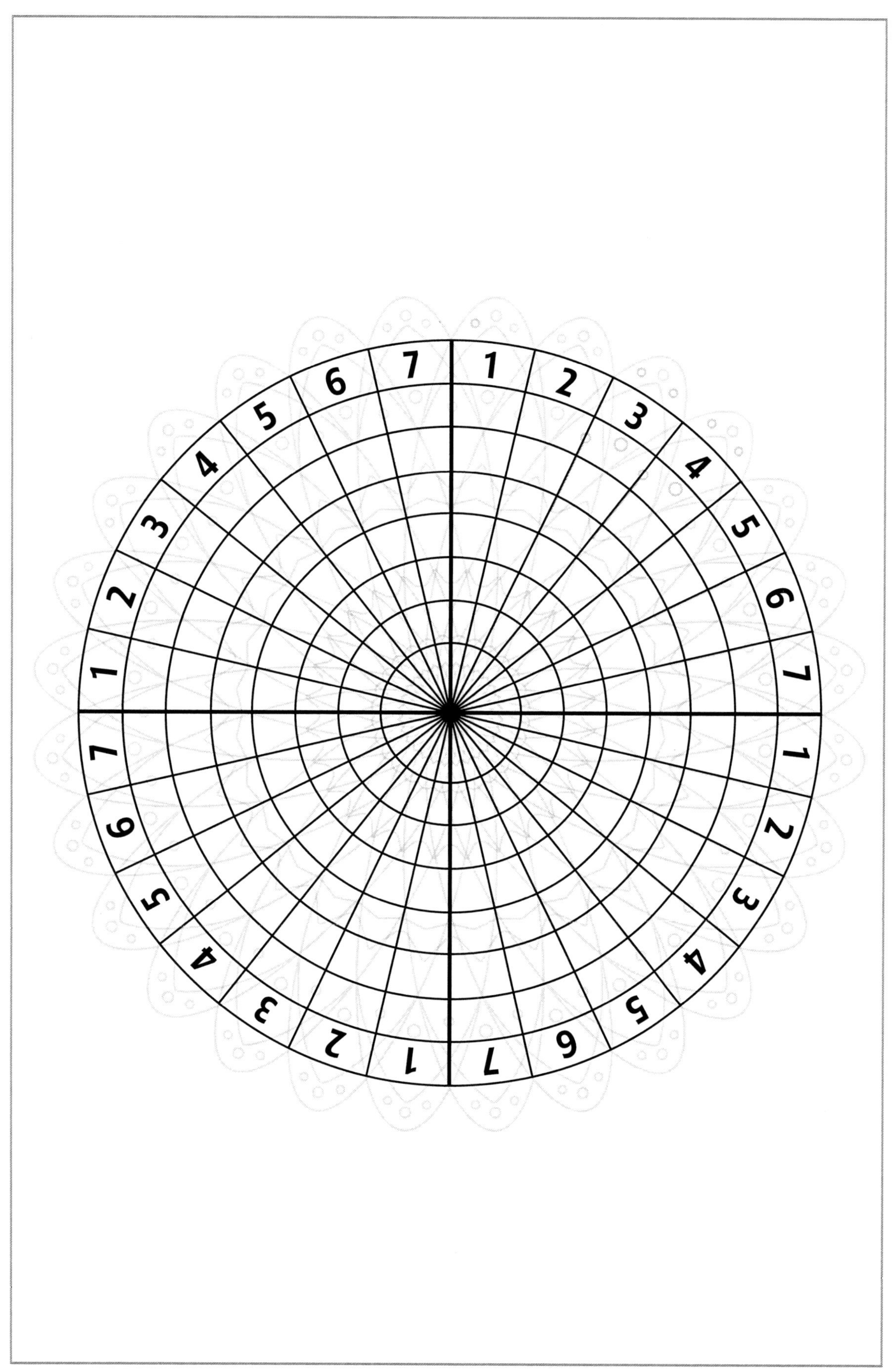

EXERCISE: Your Life Vision

This exercise uses visualization to help you clarify what a purposeful life looks like to you. To be clear, you are not creating a materially focused vision board, cutting out photos of cars, designer bags, or other possessions you might like to manifest into your life. (That type of board became popular in the last decade as a practice of the pseudoscientific "law of attraction.") Instead, you'll collect images that evoke a sense of contentedness in and of themselves, simply because they are aligned with the values you've identified.

1. First, identify your top 5 to 10 values that most resonate with you right now. What do you want to focus on over the next year or two of your life?
2. Next, gather materials for your vision board. You'll want a large piece of paper or poster board and art supplies for collaging: magazines or printed images, scissors, glue, markers, stickers, and so on.
3. Choose a theme for your vision board. Do you want it to represent your life overall or focus on a specific domain (e.g., career values, relationship values)? You can also divide your board into different sections if you have multiple value areas.
4. Cut out, print out, or draw images and symbols that represent your values. For example, if one of your values is adventure, you could include pictures of scenic travel destinations. You can also print or write out words, quotes, or affirmations that inspire you in values-aligned action. Then, arrange the images and words on your board in a way that feels right to you.
5. Hang your vision board somewhere you'll get to connect with it daily. Spend a few minutes each day reflecting on your values and how you can connect to your Self-energy and embody your values in your actions.
6. As you grow and your life changes, your values can evolve too. Allow yourself regular periods to review and update your vision board so it feels current to your life circumstances.

Commitment to Action

Values ought to guide your actions, not be kept secret. In this next section, you'll consider what actions bring you into alignment with your values and create goals around those actions. Goals are specific outcomes or achievements you want to reach in a certain time frame. They support you in cultivating clarity about how you direct your efforts and energy. They take the broad concept of living in alignment with your values and direct you to identify exactly what you want to achieve, providing a sense of motivation for your journey.

Of course, accomplishing a goal is never as simple as setting it. You'll likely be navigating the internal pressures of your parts, coupled with the external pressures of time, resources, and the balancing of valued living as a whole. For that reason, we'll look at some helpful ways to set goals that are actually achievable.

EXERCISE: Break It Down

This method may seem obvious, but it's also incredibly effective. Simply take any goal you have and break it down into the smallest possible step. You're more likely to meet your ultimate goal if you start with one half the size (or even smaller)—the success of meeting that little goal will give you momentum to tackle the rest.

For example, if your goal is to clean the house, you might set a series of smaller goals such as removing the items from one drawer and sorting them, gathering unwanted things into a bin, cleaning one section of one room at a time, and so on.

Give it a try—pick one task, maybe one that's been languishing on your to-do list for ages, and see if you can break it down until you have a goal that feels completely doable.

____

____

____

____

EXERCISE: SMART Goals

The SMART framework (Doran, 1981) is a popular method for goal setting. It has several variations but always involves asking yourself whether your goal meets five important criteria. For our purposes, these are:

- **Specific:** Is the target clearly defined?
- **Measurable:** What are the criteria to track your progress and success?
- **Achievable:** Is this goal realistic and attainable?
- **Relevant:** Is this goal aligned with your broader objectives and values?
- **Time-bound:** What is the specific time frame for completion?

If any of these criteria are not met, consider how you can revise that goal. For example, the goal to run a specific marathon that takes place in six months has a measurable outcome and time frame, and it may be aligned with the value of health, but depending on where you're currently at in your training, it may or may not be realistically attainable.

Does your own goal meet all five SMART criteria? If not, how can you revise it to meet them?

The Relationship of Habits and Goals

Goals and habits can be confusing, so let's take a moment to parse them out. While habits and goals are related concepts, they do differ in their nature, purpose, and implementation. Goals are specific targets, while habits are regular practice or routines established over time. Habits are about the process, while goals are about the outcome. For instance, running that marathon is a goal, while going for a daily run might become a habit.

What makes things complicated is that some of your goals may be around establishing habits that cultivate a healthy sense of self, build your discipline, and . . . support you in progressing toward other goals! For instance, you might create goals that will take you toward being a person who regularly exercises, journals, maintains an organized home, or connects with friends. These habits can then energize you to meet other goals, and ultimately, align with your North Star, so to speak.

EXERCISE: Values-Aligned Goals

We always want to make sure your big goals are underpinned by your values so that, even if you don't reach the big goal, the action you're taking is inherently meaningful.

First, consider where you would like to be in five years. Choose one value and consider what long-term goals could help take you to this vision.

From here, you are going to establish a series of smaller goals to take you to this final point. The final step will be to choose at least one action you can take within the next 24 hours. The

24-hour rule is vital—it ensures action toward your goal within a short time frame, which will motivate you to keep going.

- Choose a value you would like to work on: ______________________
- Long-term goal (within 1 to 5 years): ______________________
- Mid-term goal #2 (within 3 months to 1 year): ______________________
- Mid-term goal #1 (within 1 to 3 months): ______________________
- Short-term goal (within 1 to 4 weeks): ______________________
- Instant goal (within 24 hours): ______________________

Are there any daily habits that would take less than two minutes and would support you in achieving your goal? You might have already implemented them in the previous chapters; if not, take a moment now to consider how you might establish them.

____

____

____

____

Of course, an authentic life is not created by blindly sticking to your goals. In fact, this could be detrimental, even dangerous. Take the running goal example—if you're heading out the door but get a call from a dear friend who has just got some bad news, acting in alignment with your heart may mean not be going for that run and instead heading over to your friend's house.

I've heard folks say that these moments are "values conflicts." I happen to disagree. In my view, love is the one ultimate value. From learning and nature to creating and health, love—your capacity for compassion, connection, and self-actualization—underpins it all. Ultimately, love arises from our interconnectedness. So, when you feel stuck about what to do, tune into your interoceptive wisdom to clarify the choice most in alignment with love.

The Vitality Living Matrix

When unconscious patterns and survival reactions take hold, you may find yourself drawn to engage in behavior that doesn't align with your values. Before you engage in the behavior, you can access a moment of awareness to observe what is unfolding and choose how you will respond. This is why mindfulness and your window of tolerance are so important; they enhance your capacity to choose behavior that feels in integrity. This space can be called the *observation point.* It is a sacred place from which your interoceptive awareness provides you access to your felt sense of Self-energy, providing the clarity you need to take values-aligned action.

The matrix model for values-aligned living, shown in the following graphic, was developed by Dr. Kevin Polk (2014) as a way of simplifying how we relate the different experiences in our life. The model positions you in the center, at the observation point. Being present at the observation point gives you space to choose a response that will take you closer to growth and freedom.

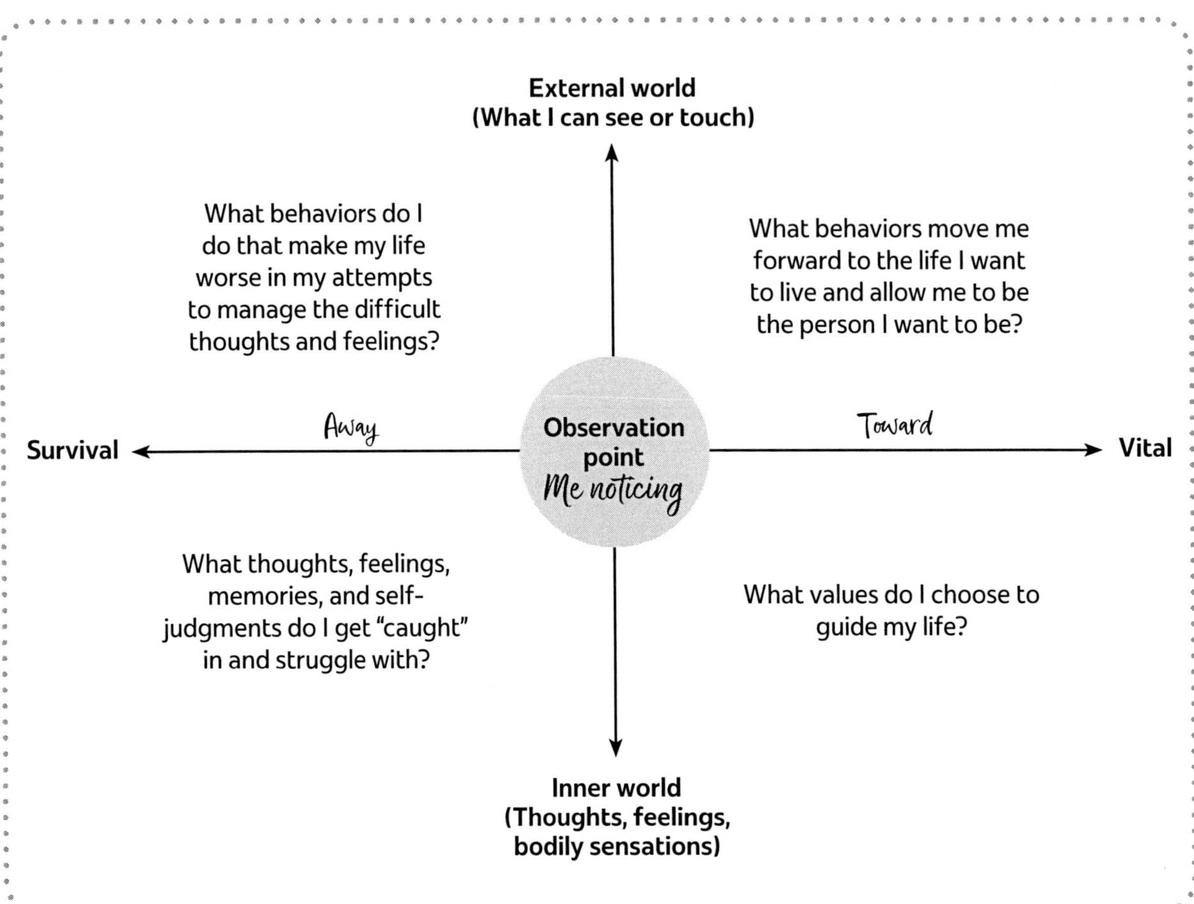

The horizontal line shows the continuum of lived experience from survival mode (fight, flight, freeze, or fawn) to vital mode (ventral vagal/Self-energy). The vertical line shows the continuum of information, from things that happen inside your own skin (inner world) to engaging with what you can see or touch (external world). Or, put another way, the external world captures all behaviors that people can see you doing, whereas your inner world is something that nobody but you will experience.

In the bottom left quadrant, you've got your inner survival mode experiences. This is where we find unhelpful thoughts, feelings, memories, and urges, as well as ancestral wounds, burdened parts, the inner critic, and other stories of your protective parts.

In the upper left quadrant are all the behaviors provoked by these survival stories. These could include canceling important plans, yelling at loved ones, drinking wine, taking pills, over- or undereating—any imbalanced behavior that is not aligned with your values (such as the behaviors you identified in chapter 10).

In the right lower quadrant are your values. This also includes your strengths, your ancestral wisdom, and of course your Self-energy. The upper right quadrant shows the external world experiences and behaviors that are aligned with your values, that keep you in integrity with your Self.

Knowing your own matrix will help you ascertain where you are on your journey and where you can make progress. This allows you to step out of autopilot and transform how you respond to pain and listen to the call of your heart. Use the template that follows to reflect on your parts, perceptions, inner experiences, values, and behaviors and get clearer about the behaviors that will take you to your unique vision of vitality.

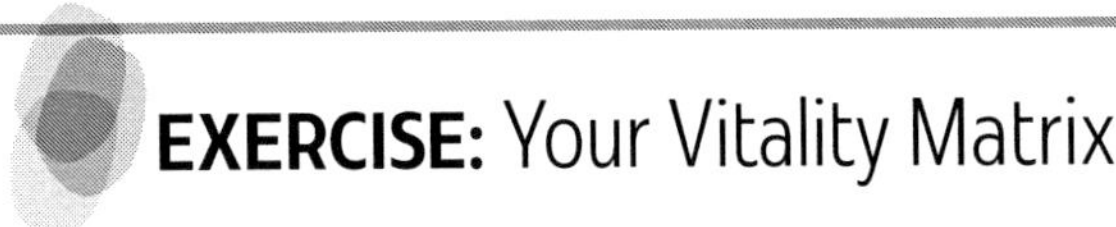

EXERCISE: Your Vitality Matrix

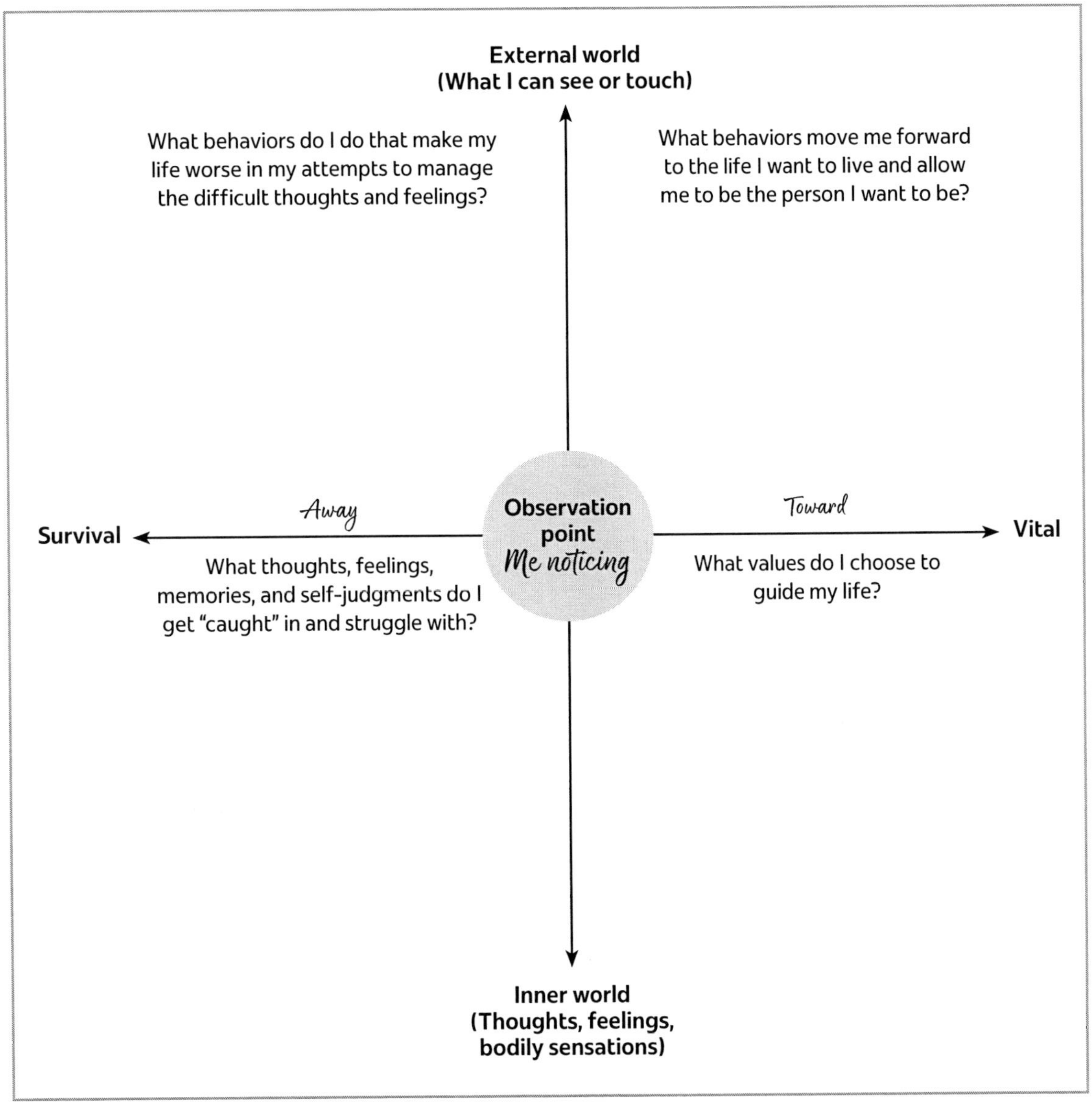

External world
(What I can see or touch)

What behaviors do I do that make my life worse in my attempts to manage the difficult thoughts and feelings?

What behaviors move me forward to the life I want to live and allow me to be the person I want to be?

Survival ← *Away*

Observation point
Me noticing

Toward → **Vital**

What thoughts, feelings, memories, and self-judgments do I get "caught" in and struggle with?

What values do I choose to guide my life?

Inner world
(Thoughts, feelings, bodily sensations)

Self-Energy Fueling

In doing this work with clients, I often encounter the assumption that being infused with Self-energy is synonymous with feeling uninterrupted joy all the time. This is not the case. Living in a state of Self-energy can certainly evoke joy, but it can also be present in feelings of anger, disgust, fear, or even sadness. Self-energy is a capacity to be with whatever you're feeling while maintaining a sense of clarity and calmness.

Remember that all emotions have valuable information for you. Sadness can clarify what you care about, anger ensures that things are fair, disgust and fear protect you from physical and social harm, and so forth. What makes these emotions complicated is processing them in survival mode—this makes your behavior likely to follow unconscious instinct, rather than clarity and wisdom. This is why you've learned different ways to clarify your inner experience. Looking at it through the lens of the many frameworks we've studied in this book—polyvagal states, the window of tolerance, the Self, inner parts, and the vitality matrix—will help you tune into your felt-sense experience, understand what it's telling you, and choose a values-aligned response. You'll likely find that different frameworks work for you at different times.

Responding to Mistakes

The journey to integrity doesn't mean you're always going to like everything about yourself or find a way to do everything right. Even with the best intentions, you'll mess up at times—there is really no way around that. You'll say the wrong thing or you won't say something when you should. You'll do the wrong thing or fail to act. You're not a saint, and your protective parts will take hold when you're tired, anxious, or overwhelmed. This is part of life.

Making mistakes can feel awful, and the shame spiral that can follow those moments when you behave against your values is particularly painful. This pain brings stronger pulls toward our survival strategies—we may quickly turn to directing anger toward ourselves or others. What we really need in these moments is to slow down, recognize that we're dysregulated in one way or another, and ask that wise Self to wrap its arms around us and to let us know we're okay. In other words, we need compassion for ourselves.

Without compassion, you will likely continue responding from survival mode, rather than taking wise action and reasonable accountability. Compassion allows you to say, "Yes, I made a mistake. I'm human." Not irreversibly flawed, worthless, unlovable, or any of the other painful stories our minds can run with. It empowers you to accept the opportunity to take action that ensures you keep evolving.

What do you do when you are not proud of your behavior, when something about your past actions does not feel integrated with how you choose to conduct yourself from this moment? If you believe an apology is warranted, how would this look? More importantly, what is your intention in this action? If your intention for apologizing is to feel better, this could backfire if the other person refuses your apology, or accepts it but doesn't want to restore the relationship. However, if your intention is to acknowledge your mistake and offer a repair, you'll be able to maintain integrity and access the humility to keep learning and growing regardless of their response.

You may also need to sit with grief. Sometimes things in your life just go wrong. You'll lose people you care deeply about, and you'll make mistakes that you have to live with. We all do. In these times, taking care of yourself, of your vulnerable inner child, will help you in healing, while aligning and directing your energy with your heart means you'll make mistakes less often in the future.

It can also be the case that others are responding to their own past patterning—you need to know this and recognize that it's not always about you. If you don't understand someone's response, your options are to accept it or to ask them to help you understand. Maybe you'll gain valuable information, maybe you won't. Because despite what your inner child desperately wants, not everyone will like you. Other folks have their own templates that trigger their protective parts, and something about you might trigger a painful pattern for them. You are not the person that can shift this; it's not your responsibility to change the inner landscape of another person if they don't want to let you in. What you can do is continue to nurture and soothe your own inner child while making an ongoing effort to live your life in integrity. You'll come to respect the person you're becoming, in the context of understanding where you've been. In this way, you challenge yourself every single moment to start anew and act lovingly, no matter what came in the moments before.

Equanimity

Like Sarah and Cole, your path forward is to cultivate a sense of spaciousness for whatever arises in your mind and body—be it positive or negative, helpful or unhelpful. *Equanimity* refers to that felt-sense experience of your connected ventral vagal state, your transcendent Self, your capacity to hold it all. It is a sense of groundedness that can anchor you in the pain of your inner experience without needing it to be different then what it is.

It points to an interesting paradox, one that has been hinted at throughout this book: The only way you can evolve into who you choose to be is by accepting yourself exactly as you are in this moment.

When you don't accept yourself or your inner experiences, your energy is spent thinking about how things "should" be different. This can quickly draw you into endless battle with your feelings of shame and suffering. Freedom from this pattern is found in the moment when you tune into your inner world with an understanding of the survival function of these patterns and an expanded sense of compassion and spaciousness to nurture what *is*. From this place of acceptance, you'll find capacity for steady attention to reality, energy for facilitating transformation, and clarity on your path forward.

Closing Reflections

Go back to the end of chapter 1 and see how you answered this question: "What are the things in your life that bring you the most suffering?" Consider what this means about what you care about.

____

____

____

____

Which values domains have you historically focused on in your life?

____

____

____

____

Which strategies will you use to ensure that you are aligning your life with your values?

____

____

____

____

Where do you think you'll struggle to stay on the vitality track—what tends to pull you into survival mode?

____

____

____

____

How do you plan to cultivate compassion and acceptance of yourself as you are now?

____

____

____

____

Takeaway Messages

- You hurt where you care: Often pain can give you an insight into what you care about.
- You have different values domains in your life, some of which you will be living more in alignment with and others less so. Reflecting on these domains can help you figure out where to invest your energy.
- Taking committed action to live life in alignment with your values is always possible, offering success on your journey (rather than just when a goal is accomplished).
- You can use the vitality matrix to clarify what pulls you toward survival mode and your motivation to take actions toward a values-aligned life.
- You cannot make change in your life without accepting yourself as you are now.

Conclusion: Connecting Your Journey Going Forward

You are inherently worthy of love, affection, wonder, and delight. May this be only the beginning of your journey to release the body armor and retire the protective parts of your past that have blocked you from accessing your true Self. As you engage in a vitality-generating lifestyle, ongoing memory integration and somatic release practices, coupled with present-moment awareness and skills to navigate moments of distress along the way, you'll find it easier to experience and embody clarity, compassion, curiosity, and connection.

Remember that healing will be an ongoing process. Courage and commitment will be required as you make space for pain, suffering, and the struggle of stepping back from unconscious patterns. Your capacity to hold painful experiences will increase over time, and you'll find yourself in a survival response less frequently.

In this journey of somatic psychology healing, you've worked through your body to transform your mind and through your mind to support your body. This bidirectional embodied healing process ensures you have access to a corrective experience for past wounds, enhances your felt-sense awareness and intuition, and aligns you with the life you want to live. Let's summarize the principles of this practice:

1. When you are depleted and disconnected, you're more likely to default to protective patterns that are not aligned with your heartfelt purpose.
2. Ensuring you are living a healthy lifestyle and that you have strategies to manage anxiety, overwhelm, and other distressing emotions builds your resilience and capacity to engage in healing and releasing practices.
3. Differentiating the felt sense of protective parts from your Self-energy-infused parts ensures you know when you are responding to instances of the remembered present, while present-moment awareness allows you to choose your heartfelt action based on your values.

We can simplify your action steps into:

1. Clarifying your felt-sense patterns (this can be in the form of parts or nervous system activation states—dorsal vagal, sympathetic, or ventral vagal—depending on what resonates with you)
2. Creating a resiliency routine that includes your established self-soothing and resourcing practices to enhance your vagal tone, body balance, and sense of Self
3. Ensuring you have a values-aligned vision for your life and are regularly acting in integrity with this

As we learned back in the beginning, your issues are in your tissues. But so is your path to healing. Throughout this book, you've cultivated an awareness of this inner wisdom, opened to it, and attuned to its guidance. In learning to listen to sensations, you access insights that can seem outside your conscious mind, that support deeper awareness of your emotional states, patterns, and needs. Your developing capacity to be open to your felt sense is what allows you the space to engage with your inner landscape in a way that is healing and empowering.

From this space of observation, vital actions can be actualized in your life. Sometimes they might be conscious and logical, but more and more you'll notice your felt sense is speaking to you. This is your intuition. As you listen to it, you'll find an enhanced connection between your body, mind, and emotional well-being that offers the anxiety relief you're seeking. Whenever you feel stuck, ask yourself, *Am I aware of what is unfolding inside my skin? Am I able to open to it? What steps do I need to take to engage in my life with integrity?*

I trust you on your journey to vitality, to love. You've already got the compass. So, take a yawn, relax your shoulders, unclench your jaw, open into your power pose, and feel into that deep sense of knowing that what you do matters right here and now.

References

Ahmadi, M. N., Clare, P. J., Katzmarzyk, P. T., del Pozo Cruz, B., Lee, I. M., & Stamatakis, E. (2022). Vigorous physical activity, incident heart disease, and cancer: How little is enough? *European Heart Journal, 43*(46), 4801–4814. https://doi.org/10.1093/eurheartj/ehac572

American Psychiatric Association. (2022). *Diagnostic and statistical manual of mental disorders* (5th ed., text rev.). https://doi.org/10.1176/appi.books.9780890425787

Badoud, D., & Tsakiris, M. (2017). From the body's viscera to the body's image: Is there a link between interoception and body image concerns? *Neuroscience & Biobehavioral Reviews, 77,* 237–246. https://doi.org/10.1016/j.neubiorev.2017.03.017

Bartholomew, K. (1990). Avoidance of intimacy: An attachment perspective. *Journal of Social and Personal Relationships, 7*(2), 147–178. https://doi.org/10.1177/0265407590072001

Bartholomew, K., & Horowitz, L. M. (1991). Attachment styles among young adults: A test of a four-category model. *Journal of Personality and Social Psychology, 61*(2). 226–244. https://doi.org/10.1037//0022-3514.61.2.226

Baumgartner, J. N., Quintana, D., Leija, L., Schuster, N. M., Bruno, K. A., Castellanos, J. P., & Case, L. K. (2022). Widespread pressure delivered by a weighted blanket reduces chronic pain: A randomized controlled trial. *The Journal of Pain, 23*(1), 156–174. https://doi.org/10.1016/j.jpain.2021.07.009

Bernstein, E. E., & McNally, R. J. (2017). Acute aerobic exercise helps overcome emotion regulation deficits. *Cognition and Emotion, 31*(4), 834–843. https://doi.org/10.1080/02699931.2016.1168284

Bond, F. W., Hayes, S. C., Baer, R. A., Carpenter, K. M., Guenole, N., Orcutt, H. K., Waltz, T., & Zettle, R. D. (2011). Preliminary psychometric properties of the Acceptance and Action Questionnaire – II: A revised measure of psychological inflexibility and experiential avoidance. *Behavior Therapy, 42*(4), 676–688. https://doi.org/10.1016/j.beth.2011.03.007

Bordoni, B., Purgol, S., Bizzarri, A., Modica, M., & Morabito, B. (2018). The Influence of breathing on the central nervous system. *Cureus, 10*(6), Article e2724. https://doi.org/10.7759/cureus.2724

Bratman, G. N., Anderson, C. B., Berman, M. G., Cochran, B., de Vries, S., Flanders, J., Folke, C., Frumkin, H., Gross, J. J., Hartig, T., Kahn, P. H., Kuo, M., Lawler, J. J., Levin, P. S., Lindahl, T., Meyer-Lindenberg, A., Mitchell, R., Ouyang, Z., Roe, J., . . . Daily, G. C. (2019). Nature and mental health: An ecosystem service perspective. *Science Advances, 5*(7), Article eaax0903. https://doi.org/10.1126/sciadv.aax0903

Broyd, S. J., Demanuele, C., Debener, S., Helps, S. K., James, C. J., & Sonuga-Barke, E. J. S. (2009). Default-mode brain dysfunction in mental disorders: A systematic review. *Neuroscience & Biobehavioral Reviews, 33*(3), 279–296. https://doi.org/10.1016/j.neubiorev.2008.09.002

Calderone, A., Latella, D., Impellizzeri, F., de Pasquale, P., Famà, F., Quartarone, A., & Calabrò, R. S. (2024). Neurobiological changes induced by mindfulness and meditation: A systematic review. *Biomedicines, 12*(11), Article 2613. https://doi.org/10.3390/biomedicines12112613

Chan, J. S. Y., Liu, G., Liang, D., Deng, K., Wu, J., & Yan, J. H. (2019). Therapeutic benefits of physical activity for mood: A systematic review on the effects of exercise intensity, duration, and modality. *The Journal of Psychology, 153*(1), 102–125. https://doi.org/10.1080/00223980.2018.1470487

Chapman, B. P., Fiscella, K., Kawachi, I., Duberstein, P., & Muennig, P. (2013). Emotion suppression and mortality risk over a 12-year follow-up. *Journal of Psychosomatic Research, 75*(4), 381–385. https://doi.org/10.1016/j.jpsychores.2013.07.014

Cooper, G., Hoffman, K., & Powell, B. (2009). *Circle of security: COS-P facilitator DVD manual 5.0* [DVD]. Marycliff Institute.

Cordero, L., Clark, D. L., & Schott, L. (1986). Effects of vestibular stimulation on sleep states in premature infants. *American Journal of Perinatology, 3*(4), 319–324. https://doi.org/10.1055/s-2007-999888

Corey, T. P., Shoup-Knox, M. L., Gordis, E. B., & Gallup, G. G. (2012). Changes in physiology before, during, and after yawning. *Frontiers in Evolutionary Neuroscience, 3,* Article 7. https://doi.org/10.3389/fnevo.2011.00007

Davis-Cheshire, R., Bennington, S., Hartsek, A., Kelly, T., Marinelli, J., & Perez, A. (2023). The impact of weighted blanket use on adults with sensory sensitivity and insomnia. *Occupational Therapy International, 2023*(1), Article 3109388. https://doi.org/10.1155/2023/3109388

Dello Iacono, A., Ashcroft, K., & Zubac, D. (2021). Ain't just imagination! Effects of motor imagery training on strength and power performance of athletes during detraining. *Medicine and Science in Sports and Exercise, 53*(11), 2324–2332. https://doi.org/10.1249/MSS.0000000000002706

Deng, L., & Deng, Q. (2018). The basic roles of indoor plants in human health and comfort. *Environmental Science and Pollution Research International, 25*(36), 36087–36101. https://doi.org/10.1007/s11356-018-3554-1

Dzedzickis, A., Kaklauskas, A., & Bucinskas, V. (2020). Human emotion recognition: Review of sensors and methods. *Sensors (Basel), 20*(3), 592. https://doi.org/10.3390/s20030592

Dias, B. G., & Ressler, K. J. (2014). Parental olfactory experience influences behavior and neural structure in subsequent generations. *Nature Neuroscience, 17*(1), 89–96. https://doi.org/10.1038/nn.3594

Doran, G. T. (1981). There's a S.M.A.R.T. way to write management's goals and objectives. *Management Review, 70*(11): 35–36.

Edelman, G. M. (1989). *The remembered present: A biological theory of consciousness.* Basic Books.

Feldman Barrett, L. (2017). *How emotions are made: The secret life of the brain.* Macmillan.

Freeman, M., Ayers, C., Peterson, C., & Kansagara, D. (2019). *Aromatherapy and essential oils: A map of the evidence.* Department of Veterans Affairs (US). http://www.ncbi.nlm.nih.gov/books/NBK551017

Gibson, J. E. (2024). Meditation and interoception: A conceptual framework for the narrative and experiential self. *Frontiers in Psychology, 15,* Article 1393969. https://doi.org/10.3389/fpsyg.2024.1393969

Gilbert, P. (2020). Compassion: From its evolution to a psychotherapy. *Frontiers in Psychology, 11,* Article 586161. https://doi.org/10.3389/fpsyg.2020.586161

Guggisberg, A. G., Mathis, J., Schnider, A., & Hess, C. W. (2010). Why do we yawn? *Neuroscience & Biobehavioral Reviews, 34*(8), 1267–1276. https://doi.org/10.1016/j.neubiorev.2010.03.008

Gupta, S., & Mittal, S. (2013). Yawning and its physiological significance. *International Journal of Applied and Basic Medical Research, 3*(1), 11–15. https://doi.org/10.4103/2229-516X.112230

Hamasaki, H. (2020). Effects of diaphragmatic breathing on health: A narrative review. *Medicines, 7*(10), 65. https://doi.org/10.3390/medicines7100065

Hara, M. (2007). Words for love in Sanskrit. *Rivista Degli Studi Orientali, 80*(1/4), 81–106.

Harris, R. (2009). *ACT with love: Stop struggling, reconcile differences, and strengthen your relationship with acceptance and commitment therapy.* New Harbinger Publications.

Hayes, S. C., Luoma, J. B., Bond, F. W., Masuda, A., & Lillis, J. (2006). Acceptance and commitment therapy: Model, processes and outcomes. *Behaviour Research and Therapy, 44*(1), 1–25. https://doi.org/10.1016/j.brat.2005.06.006

Hill, M. D. (2020). Adaptive information processing theory: Origins, principles, applications, and evidence. *Journal of Evidence-Based Social Work, 17*(3), 317–331. https://doi.org/10.1080/26408066.2020.1748155

Jeffries, F. W., & Davis, P. (2013). What is the role of eye movements in eye movement desensitization and reprocessing (EMDR) for post-traumatic stress disorder (PTSD)? A review. *Behavioural and Cognitive Psychotherapy, 41*(3), 290–300. https://doi.org/10.1017/S1352465812000793

Kabat-Zinn, J. (2013). *Full catastrophe living: Using the wisdom of your body and mind to face stress, pain, and illness (revised and updated edition).* Delta.

Kessler, R. C., Aguilar-Gaxiola, S., Alonso, J., Benjet, C., Bromet, E. J., Cardoso, G., Degenhardt, L., de Girolamo, G., Dinolova, R. V., Ferry, F., Florescu, S., Gureje, O., Haro, J. M., Huang, Y., Karam, E. G., Kawakami, N., Lee, S., Lepine, J.-P., Levinson, D., . . . Koenen, K. C. (2017.) Trauma and PTSD in the WHO World Mental Health Surveys. *European Journal of Psychotraumatology, 8*(Sup. 5), Article 1353383. https://doi.org/10.1080/20008198.2017.1353383

Killingsworth, M. A., & Gilbert, D. T. (2010). A wandering mind is an unhappy mind. *Science, 330*(6006), 932. https://doi.org/10.1126/science.1192439

Kim, H. J., Kim, J. W., Park, H. S., Moon, D. G., Lee, J. G., & Oh, M. M. (2019). The use of a heating pad to reduce anxiety, pain, and distress during cystoscopy in female patients. *International Urogynecology Journal, 30*(10), 1705–1710. https://doi.org/10.1007/s00192-018-3786-0

Knechtle, B., Waśkiewicz, Z., Sousa, C. V., Hill, L., & Nikolaidis, P. T. (2020). Cold water swimming—benefits and risks: A narrative review. *International Journal of Environmental Research and Public Health, 17*(23), 8984. https://doi.org/10.3390/ijerph17238984

Koenig, H. G. (2009). Research on religion, spirituality, and mental health: A review. *Canadian Journal of Psychiatry, 54*(5), 283–291. https://doi.org/10.1177/070674370905400502

Kumar Goothy, S. S., & McKeown, J. (2023). Anxiolytic effects of vestibular stimulation: An update. *Journal of Basic and Clinical Physiology and Pharmacology, 34*(4), 445–449. https://doi.org/10.1515/jbcpp-2023-0022

Le Noury, J., Nardo, J. M., Healy, D., Jureidini, J., Raven, M., Tufanaru, C., & Abi-Jaoude, E. (2015). Restoring Study 329: Efficacy and harms of paroxetine and imipramine in treatment of major depression in adolescence. *BMJ, 351,* Article h4320. https://doi.org/10.1136/bmj.h4320

Mahalakshmi, B., Maurya, N., Lee, S.-D., & Bharath Kumar, V. (2020). Possible neuroprotective mechanisms of physical exercise in neurodegeneration. *International Journal of Molecular Sciences, 21*(16), 5895. https://doi.org/10.3390/ijms21165895

Maslow, A. H. (1943). A theory of human motivation. *Psychological Review, 50*(4), 370–396. https://doi.org/10.1037/h0054346

Mehling, W. E., Acree, M., Stewart, A., Silas, J., & Jones, A. (2018). The Multidimensional Assessment of Interoceptive Awareness, Version 2 (MAIA-2). *PLoS ONE, 13*(12), Article e0208034. https://doi.org/10.1371/journal.pone.0208034

Moncrieff, J., Cooper, R. E., Stockmann, T., Amendola, S., Hengartner, M. P., & Horowitz, M. A. (2023). The serotonin theory of depression: A systematic umbrella review of the evidence. *Molecular Psychiatry, 28*(8), 3243–3256. https://doi.org/10.1038/s41380-022-01661-0

Nichol, B., Wilson, R., Rodrigues, A., & Haighton, C. (2023). Exploring the effects of volunteering on the social, mental, and physical health and well-being of volunteers: An umbrella review. *Voluntas, 35,* 1–32. https://doi.org/10.1007/s11266-023-00573-z

Nummenmaa, L., Glerean, E., Hari, R., & Hietanen, J. K. (2014). Bodily maps of emotions. *Proceedings of the National Academy of Sciences, 111*(2), 646–651. https://doi.org/10.1073/pnas.1321664111

Ouimet, A. J., Kane, L., & Tutino, J. S. (2016). Fear of anxiety or fear of emotions? Anxiety sensitivity is indirectly related to anxiety and depressive symptoms via emotion regulation. *Cogent Psychology, 3*(1), Article 1249132. https://doi.org/10.1080/23311908.2016.1249132

Payne, P., Levine, P. A., & Crane-Godreau, M. A. (2015). Somatic experiencing: Using interoception and proprioception as core elements of trauma therapy. *Frontiers in Psychology, 6,* Article 93. https://doi.org/10.3389/fpsyg.2015.00093

Peräsalo, J. (1988). Traditional use of the sauna for hygiene and health in Finland. *Annals of Clinical Research, 20*(4), 220–223.

Perrault, A. A., Khani, A., Quairiaux, C., Kompotis, K., Franken, P., Muhlethaler, M., Schwartz, S., & Bayer, L. (2019). Whole-night continuous rocking entrains spontaneous neural oscillations with benefits for sleep and memory. *Current Biology, 29*(3), 402–411.e3. https://doi.org/10.1016/j.cub.2018.12.028

Pfeiffer, J. R., Mutesa, L., & Uddin, M. (2018). Traumatic stress epigenetics. *Current Behavioral Neuroscience Reports, 5*(1), 81–93. https://doi.org/10.1007/s40473-018-0143-z

Polk, K. L. (2014). The psychological flexibility warm-up. In K. L. Polk and B. Schoendorff (Eds.), *The ACT matrix: A new approach to building psychological flexibility across settings and populations* (pp. 7–14). Context Press.

Porges, S. W. (1994). Orienting in a defensive world: Mammalian modifications of our evolutionary heritage. A polyvagal theory. *Psychophysiology 32*(4), 301–318. https://doi.org/10.1111/j.1469-8986.1995.tb01213.x

Porges, S. W. (2011). *The polyvagal theory: Neurophysiological foundations of emotions, attachment, communication, and self-regulation.* W. W. Norton & Co.

Post, S. G. (2005). Altruism, happiness, and health: It's good to be good. *International Journal of Behavioral Medicine, 12*(2), 66–77. https://doi.org/10.1207/s15327558ijbm1202_4

Quaedflieg, C. W. E. M., & Schwabe, L. (2018). Memory dynamics under stress. *Memory, 26*(3), 364–376. https://doi.org/10.1080/09658211.2017.1338299

Rebar, A. L., Stanton, R., Geard, D., Short, C., Duncan, M. J., & Vandelanotte, C. (2015). A meta-meta-analysis of the effect of physical activity on depression and anxiety in non-clinical adult populations. *Health Psychology Review, 9*(3), 366–378. https://doi.org/10.1080/17437199.2015.1022901

Roca, P., Vazquez, C., Diez, G., Brito-Pons, G., & McNally, R. J. (2021). Not all types of meditation are the same: Mediators of change in mindfulness and compassion meditation interventions. *Journal of Affective Disorders, 283,* 354–362. https://doi.org/10.1016/j.jad.2021.01.070

Russell, J. A. (1980). A circumplex model of affect. *Journal of Personality and Social Psychology, 39*(6), 1161–1178. https://doi.org/10.1037/h0077714

Saatcioglu, F. (2013). Regulation of gene expression by yoga, meditation and related practices: A review of recent studies. *Asian Journal of Psychiatry, 6*(1), 74–77. https://doi.org/10.1016/j.ajp.2012.10.002

Satpute, A. B., & Lindquist, K. A. (2021). At the neural intersection between language and emotion. *Affective Science, 2*(2), 207–220. https://doi.org/10.1007/s42761-021-00032-2

Spinhoven, P., van Hemert, A. M., & Penninx, B. W. J. H. (2017). Experiential avoidance and bordering psychological constructs as predictors of the onset, relapse and maintenance of anxiety disorders: One or many? *Cognitive Therapy and Research, 41*(6), 867–880. https://doi.org/10.1007/s10608-017-9856-7

Strauss, C., Lever Taylor, B., Gu, J., Kuyken, W., Baer, R., Jones, F., & Cavanagh, K. (2016). What is compassion and how can we measure it? A review of definitions and measures. *Clinical Psychology Review, 47,* 15–27. https://doi.org/10.1016/j.cpr.2016.05.004

Strosahl, K., & Robinson, P. (2024, January 31–February 1). *Focused ACT (FACT) for brief interventions: The basics and beyond* [Workshop]. ANZ ACBS 2024 Chapter Conference. Newcastle, NSW, Australia.

Tuck, I., & Anderson, L. (2014). Forgiveness, flourishing, and resilience: The influences of expressions of spirituality on mental health recovery. *Issues in Mental Health Nursing, 35*(4), 277–282. https://doi.org/10.3109/01612840.2014.885623

Veltkamp, G. M., Recio, G., Jacobs, A. M., & Conrad, M. (2013). Is personality modulated by language? *International Journal of Bilingualism, 17*(4), 496–504. https://doi.org/10.1177/1367006912438894

Venditti, S., Verdone, L., Reale, A., Vetriani, V., Caserta, M., & Zampieri, M. (2020). Molecules of silence: Effects of meditation on gene expression and epigenetics. *Frontiers in Psychology, 11,* Article 1767. https://doi.org/10.3389/fpsyg.2020.01767

Walsh, R. (2011). Lifestyle and mental health. *The American Psychologist, 66*(7), 579–592. https://doi.org/10.1037/a0021769

Wilson, K. G., & Murrell, A. R. (2004). Values work in acceptance and commitment therapy: Setting a course for behavioral treatment. In S. C. Hayes, V. M. Follette, and M. M. Linehan (Eds.), *Mindfulness and acceptance: Expanding the cognitive-behavioral tradition* (pp. 120–151). The Guilford Press.

World Health Organization. (2018). *Preventing suicide: A community engagement toolkit.* https://iris.who.int/handle/10665/272860

Yu, J., Yang, Z., Sun, S., Sun, K., Chen, W., Zhang, L., Xu, J., Xu, Q., Liu, Z., Ke, J., Zhang, L., & Zhu, Y. (2024). The effect of weighted blankets on sleep and related disorders: A brief review. *Frontiers in Psychiatry, 15,* Article 1333015. https://doi.org/10.3389/fpsyt.2024.1333015

Zhou, P., Critchley, H., Nagai, Y., & Wang, C. (2022). Divergent conceptualization of embodied emotions in the English and Chinese languages. *Brain Sciences, 12*(7), Article 7. https://doi.org/10.3390/brainsci12070911

Acknowledgments

Nothing in my life has been possible without the support, wisdom, and generosity of those around me and those who came before me; this book is no exception.

We are fortunate to live in a time when the connection between mind and body is becoming increasingly accepted and explored. I am enormously grateful to the psychologists and researchers whose work has shaped this field and these pages. To Dr. Steven Hayes—your work first ignited my passion for ACT, and your generosity and encouragement affirmed that I was stepping into a truly supportive community. Dr. Emily Sandoz, your supervision profoundly deepened my understanding of the healing value of attending to bodily experience. Dr. Kelly Wilson, your heartfelt focus on values and what I call "lifestyle medicine" continues to inspire me. Dr. Kirk Strosahl and Dr. Patricia Robinson, your pillars framework has made psychological flexibility so accessible. Dr. Jessica Borushok, your spark and encouragement helped bring this book to life. Dr. Stephen Porges, your work has illuminated the pathways to healing and understanding our nervous systems. Every researcher and clinician cited in these pages and upon whose work these frameworks have developed—thank you for your contributions to our understanding and healing.

Mum and Dad, thank you for empowering me to do hard things and for your unwavering belief in me. To my darling daughters, you made it delightfully difficult to pull myself away from your curiosity and cuddles to write. I am forever grateful for that tension and for every moment with you. Rob, I can't thank you enough for your love, encouragement, and endless feedback—this book would not exist without you. Dr. Kathleen Wright and Rachel Samson, thank you for reading parts of my early drafts; your insights and sound-boarding wisdom were invaluable (both on and off the pages).

To the PESI Publishing team, thank you for believing in this book. Kayla, your enthusiasm and support carried this project forward, and Chelsea, your thoughtful feedback helped refine these ideas.

My deepest gratitude goes to my clients—my greatest teachers. Thank you for entrusting me with your stories and courage in exploring the wisdom of both your minds and bodies. I am forever humbled.

And to you, the reader—thank you for being here. However you came to hold this book in your hands, I honor your openness, curiosity, and willingness to explore. It is a privilege to walk alongside you, and I hope this book is a helpful resource on your journey.

About the Author

KAITLIN N. HARKESS, PHD, is the host of the *Wisdom for Wellbeing* podcast and the founder of a holistic therapy practice of the same name. She is a clinical psychologist, Psychology Board Approved Supervisor, Registered Senior Yoga Instructor, and Registered Meditation Instructor. Kaitlin offers individual and group therapy sessions aimed at helping overwhelmed and burnt-out individuals develop the psychological skills necessary to improve their lives.

Kaitlin is passionate about integrative healing approaches and has taught body-based practices for nearly two decades in various settings, including yoga studios, community centers, and mental health treatment facilities. Her research on the psychoneuroimmunological effects of yoga for chronic stress and psychological distress was groundbreaking, as it was the first to explore the epigenetic impact of yoga practice. Remaining passionate about research, Kaitlin is a titleholder with the University of Adelaide's School of Psychology, convenes the Australian Psychological Society's Yoga and Psychology Interest Group, and trains mental health professionals on incorporating somatic psychology into their clinical practices.

Kaitlin lives on Kaurna Land in Adelaide, Australia, with her young family, where they enjoy the ocean, short winters, and a vibrant culture. However, she remains a mountain lover, having grown up in the Canadian Rockies. Hiking and outdoor adventures are as vital to her as her healing yoga practice.